WHICH? WAY T

WHICH? WAY TO
SAVE TAX
1992-3

Published by Consumers' Association
and Hodder & Stoughton

Which? Books are commissioned and researched by
The Association for Consumer Research and
published by Consumers' Association,
2 Marylebone Road, London NW1 4DF and
Hodder & Stoughton, 47 Bedford Square, London WC1B 3DP

Typographic design by Paul Saunders
Cover artwork by Larry Rostant
Index by Paul Nash

First edition August 1992

British Library Cataloguing in Publication Data

A catalogue record for this book is available from the
British Library.

ISBN 0-340-56659-0

Thanks for choosing this book . . .
If you find it useful, we'd like to hear from you. Even if it doesn't
live up to your expectations, we'd still like to know. Then we can
take your comments into account when preparing similar titles
or, indeed, the next edition of the book. Address your letter to
the Publishing Manager at Consumers' Association, FREEPOST,
2 Marylebone Road, London NW1 4DF.
We look forward to hearing from you.

Typeset by Litho Link Limited, Welshpool, Powys, Wales
Printed and bound in Great Britain by
Richard Clay Limited,
Bungay, Suffolk

Acknowledgements

Editor: Joanna Hanks

With thanks to the following for their help:

Anthony Bailey, Philip Cullum, Graeme Jacobs, John Kimmer, Joanna Langenhan, Pamela Nadash, Christopher Peers, Ewan Simpson, Virginia Wallis.

CONTENTS

1 *GETTING TO GRIPS WITH TAX*

Many different sorts of people will be using this book. Some will be having a first go at understanding the tax system; others will already know it quite well. And quite a number of our readers will be people who give tax advice to others. The first thing is to decide what you want the book to do for you. So where do you fit in?

Beginners

The best starting-place is Chapter 2, *How your tax bill is worked out*. This gives a step-by-step guide through the basics of the income tax system. Once you've mastered this chapter, the rest of the chapters on income tax should fall into place.

General readers

If you're reading for interest, or if you want to sharpen up your knowledge of tax, the whole book is your oyster. Each chapter looks at tax from a different angle. So if you're particularly interested in knowing how getting married (or divorced) can affect your tax bill, you could go straight to Chapter 4, *Tax and families*. Or if you are not sure how your investments are taxed, go to Chapter 12, *Investments*, which looks at investments in general, and includes details of schemes like personal equity plans (PEPs) and the business expansion scheme (BES), which have special tax perks.

Planning ahead

One of the major worries for many people is how to pass their money on to their children. Chapter 17, *Inheritance tax*, gives practical advice.

Checking a specific point

Start with the *Index*, which should give you quick guidance to the right place. Wherever there's space, we've given *examples* to illustrate what we say in the text. And we give *references* to Finance Acts – so that you can, if you want, give chapter and verse to your tax office, or your tax adviser. See opposite for the abbreviations we use.

Checking your tax bill over past years

If you're trying to adjust your tax bill from earlier years, Chapter 18, *Tax facts*, has a handy reference section with tax rates for the past six years.

Trouble with the Revenue?

Chapter 3 gives advice if you are in dispute with the Revenue, and gives details of the penalties you might face.

The taxes covered in this book

Income tax

Income tax takes up most of the book. It's by far the most important tax, not only for the government, for which it brings in more money than anything else, but also for ordinary people. Anyone with more than a very modest wage has to pay income tax. So do many people with no earnings but with money coming in from investments. The main aim of the book is to help you realise:

- what income tax is
- how it affects you
- how you can check your tax bill
- how you can make the most of the rules and pay less tax.

Capital gains tax

You may have to pay capital gains tax if you sell some of your possessions at a profit – or even if you give them away. The rules are complicated, and you're quite likely to find that there's no tax to pay. But it's as well to skim through our explanation in Chapter 14 to make sure that you're not at risk. And if you *are* at risk, we suggest ways of cutting down tax you have to pay.

Inheritance tax

With inheritance tax (which replaced capital transfer tax) there is no tax to pay on what you give away while you are still alive (with a few exceptions), as long as you live for at least seven years after making the gift. Even if you do die within seven years, there may be no tax to pay. Giving away possessions and money while you are alive won't save *you* tax, though it could mean less tax for your heirs: so don't threaten your own financial security in the rush to save tax.

Value added tax (VAT)

We don't go into detail, but there is a brief summary of VAT rules in Chapter 10, *Working for yourself*.

National Insurance

Although this is not called a tax, it is money that has to be paid to the government and what you have to pay varies with your income. We give some National Insurance details in Chapter 10, *Working for yourself*, and Chapter 16, *Building up a pension*.

References to statutes

Here's an explanation of what the letters and figures mean:

FA	Finance Act
ICTA	Income and Corporation Taxes Act 1988
TMA	Taxes Management Act 1970
TCGA	Taxation of Chargeable Gains Act 1992
CAA	Capital Allowances Act 1990
IHTA	Inheritance Tax Act 1984
s	Section
Sch	Schedule
IR	Inland Revenue leaflet
ESC	Extra-statutory concession
SI	Statutory Instrument
SP	Inland Revenue Statement of Practice

Schedules come at the end of Finance Acts. Lists of Inland Revenue leaflets and of extra-statutory concessions are in

Chapter 18 (p. 362). In addition, some *Tax cases* are mentioned – see below.

Here are some examples:

FA 1989 s8	Finance Act 1989, Section 8
ICTA 1988 s168 (8–20)	Income and Corporation Taxes Act 1988, Section 168, subsections 8–20
TCGA Sch 1 para 2	Taxation of Chargeable Gains Act 1992 Schedule 1, paragraph 2
SI 1975/610	Statutory Instrument number 610 of 1975
IR 6	Inland Revenue leaflet 6
SP 14/80	Inland Revenue Statement of Practice number 14 of 1980

Sometimes you'll see several references together. Where this happens, and the references are to different topics, we put the topic (in brackets) after the reference:

ESCA27 (interest relief); TCGA 1992 s223; ESC D3, D4 (capital gains)

Where to find the sources

Inland Revenue leaflets are free from tax offices or Tax Enquiry Centres (for exceptions, see p. 362). Tax cases and statutes should be in central reference libraries.

We give references to tax cases when the outcome of the case has an important effect on tax rules. Tax cases may be reported in more than one publication. References in this book are to *Tax cases* (TC) and to the *All England Law Reports* (All ER). So, for example, *1976 1 All ER p272* means that the case is found on page 272 of volume 1 of the 1976 All England Law Reports.

Note: A few of the measures proposed in the Budget had become law by the time the election took place on 9 April 1992. As a result there will be a second Finance Act for 1992. This had not been passed when we went to press.

Tax advice

There are three rules to follow if you want to keep your tax bill as low as possible:

- **keep in control** If you let your tax affairs get out of hand, you'll store up trouble and expense for the future.
- **make the right choices** In planning your life, the choices you make can drastically affect your tax bill. Of the 52 choices starting overleaf, any one might affect you.
- **act in time** Many of the choices you make have time limits attached to them (see pp. 20–2).

Keep in control

George Selwyn gets occasional bits of income from spare-time work. He keeps hardly any record of what he's been paid, or of who's paid him, or of what expenses (if any) he had to pay out of his own pocket. George hasn't told the Revenue about his spare-time income – he isn't dishonest, he just hasn't got round to it.

George is storing up trouble for the future. One day, the Revenue will catch on to the fact that George is making money on the side. And it won't know that George is honest. There's every chance that George will be summoned to a very unpleasant interview with a Tax Inspector, and asked to produce his accounts and receipts which he may not have. Eventually, he's likely to be faced with a tax demand which he can't really afford to pay. It may be quite a lot higher than he thinks it ought to be – but he has no records to prove that it's too high.

George's brother Jack hasn't got around to claiming higher-rate tax relief on a mortgage he took out three years ago. There's no real danger here – higher-rate relief is no longer available but, provided Jack claims tax relief within about six years of taking out the mortgage he'll still get it backdated. Meanwhile he's giving the Inland Revenue an interest-free loan.

These two examples are not unusual. They're ordinary, everyday examples of carelessness which can cost money.

So here are a few tips on keeping your tax affairs in order:

1 Keep clear records of income you get, and of any expenses you can set against your income. And keep your records up to date.

2 Keep the Revenue informed of what's going on. Tell

them if there's any change in your circumstances – for example:

- you get married
- you separate or get divorced
- you become unemployed, or retire
- you gain or lose a source of income
- you start or stop making a payment which qualifies for tax relief.

3 Check your tax. Whenever you get a tax bill, or a Notice of Coding, check to see that the figures are correct, and write to your tax office at once if you don't think they are.

Making the most of the rules

Here are 52 ways to pay less tax – one for every week of the year. See how many of them apply to you now, or might apply in the future. Making the right choice can reduce the amount of tax you have to pay.

Your family

1 Are you married? Make sure you get the married couple's allowance (p. 70).

2 Unmarried with children? You should claim the additional personal allowance (p. 88).

3 If you are married, does one of you own all the investments? Under independent taxation, there could be less tax to pay if you shared out the spoils differently. For instance, if only one of you is a higher-rate taxpayer (p. 76).

4 Paying maintenance under the old tax rules? You *might* save tax by opting for the new rules (p. 80).

5 Does your child use his or her tax allowance? Any child, no matter how young, can have an income of £3,445 without paying tax (p. 89).

6 Recently widowed? Make sure you claim all your allowances (p. 79).

7 Married this year? In this year only, the husband can choose not to take the married couple's allowance – it could save tax (p. 71).

In a job?

8 Can you get any fringe benefits? Many perks are taxed at much less than their value to you (p. 144).

9 Can you set any expenses against tax? See the table on p. 123 onwards.

10 Approaching retirement? It may be worthwhile making additional voluntary contributions to your pension scheme (p. 307).

11 Not in a pension scheme? You can get tax relief (at your top rate) on premiums contributed to a personal pension plan (p. 308).

12 A student? If you have vacation earnings, signing a form can save you the bother of paying tax now and claiming it back later (p. 91).

In business?

13 Self-employed? You may be able to save tax by employing your husband or wife (p. 193).

14 Loans for your business? See if they qualify for tax relief (p. 30).

15 Entitled to capital allowances? It may pay you to claim less than you're able to, and to roll on the balance to succeeding years (p. 184).

16 Business losses? You have three choices of how to deal with them – and the choice you make can affect your tax bill and your cash-in-hand (p. 189).

17 Losses in a new business? You can get tax relief by setting them against other income or capital gains (p. 192).

18 Should you register for VAT? See p. 195 for the answer.

19 Are you claiming all your expenses? See the table on p. 180.

On a low income?

20 Not a taxpayer? If you don't pay tax, and you've got money to invest, you should register as a non-taxpayer if you're putting it in a bank or building society account (p. 236).

21 Tax to claim back? Make your claim as soon as possible (p. 59). And if you'll be claiming tax back each year, arrange with the Revenue to get it paid in instalments (p. 99).

Elderly?

22 Approaching 65? You may be able to claim some allowances for the whole of the tax year in which you (or your wife) reaches 65: you don't have to wait for your 65th birthday (p. 93).

23 Not getting full age-related allowances? Consider switching to investments where the return is tax-free (p. 231). Beware of cashing in a life insurance policy where the return is taxable (p. 255).

24 Need more income? One solution might be to buy an annuity (p. 100). Or consider a home income plan (p. 104).

25 Can you make use of your husband's pension contributions? A married woman can get a state retirement pension based on her husband's contributions. It's worth doing so if this would be higher than the pension you would have got on your own contributions. And from 6 April 1990 (under independent taxation) even the extra has counted as the wife's income, so there could be less tax to pay if the wife hasn't fully used her personal allowance (p. 97).

26 Retiring from a business? You may be able to claim retirement relief from capital gains tax (p. 280).

27 Coming up to retirement – and with a personal pension plan? You may be able to get yourself a larger pension and cut your recent tax bills (p. 315). If you haven't got a personal pension plan, see whether you should take one out.

Investments and life insurance

28 Buying British Government stocks? If you buy them through the National Savings Stock register, income is paid to you without tax being deducted (p. 237) and the costs of the transaction are lower.

29 Have you made use of the annual capital gains tax exemption? Investing for capital gains, rather than income, may give you a better after-tax return (p. 272).

30 A large amount to invest, and worried about inheritance tax? Consider investing in certain types of property (p. 334).

31 Getting tax relief on a pre-March 1984 life insurance policy? Beware of extending the policy, or of altering it to increase the benefits. You may lose your tax relief (p. 260).

32 Self-employed, or in a job but not in an employer's pension scheme? You can get tax relief on a life insurance policy (p. 260).

33 Willing to take a risk? The Business Expansion Scheme (BES) gives you tax relief on your investments – though this is due to end after 1993 (p. 238).

34 Life insurance for your family? Cut your inheritance tax bill by making sure the proceeds aren't added to your estate (p. 261).

35 Made a loss when you sold some shares? Keep a record of any losses when you dispose of something. You may be able to use the loss to cut down any capital gains tax you have to pay (p. 273).

You and your home
36 Thinking of buying? There's tax relief available on your mortgage (p. 202).

37 A home to let? If you're borrowing to buy the home, see whether you can get tax relief on the interest you pay. For the expenses you can claim, see pp. 219 and 222.

38 Selling your house and garden separately? Sell the garden first (p. 211).

39 Working at home? See p. 213 for expenses you can claim.

40 More than one home? Be careful about which home you choose as your 'main home' for capital gains tax purposes (p. 207).

41 A home with your job and another which you own? Make sure that the home you own is free from capital gains tax (p. 215).

42 Moving house? You can get tax relief on two loans at once (p. 203).

43 Moving house when you marry? You may be able to get tax relief on three loans (p. 77).

44 Buying a home for around £30,000? Juggling with the price could save you more than £300 in stamp duty (as we went to press this was due to apply from 19 August 1992) (p. 296).

Passing your money on
45 Can 'estate freezing' save you tax? See p. 337.

46 Made a will yet? Make sure you word it correctly; otherwise, your spouse could be left short (p. 338).

47 Married with valuable property which one of you owns exclusively? Sharing some of it between you can cut down your inheritance tax bill (p. 336).

48 High income, and young children? Consider an accumulation and maintenance trust (p. 341).

49 Inheritance tax to be paid by your beneficiaries when you die? Making regular gifts out of income can get rid of a lot of the value of your estate. And you can give away at least £3,000 a year tax-free (p. 328).

50 A beneficiary under a will? You may be able to pay any inheritance tax by instalments (p. 346).

Charities
51 Giving to charity? Your gift could be worth a lot more if you make use of the tax breaks (pp. 32 and 33).

52 Can you have your charitable donations deducted straight from your pay? If not, you should ask your employer to set up a payroll giving scheme (p. 32).

Act in time

Tax rules are hedged round with time limits. They can be as short as 30 days and as long as six years or more. We start by explaining how far back you can go to claim personal allowances or tax relief that you've missed. After that, we give time limits for 15 tax choices.

The normal (six-year) rule

You may have forgotten to claim personal allowances in past years. Or, more likely, you may have forgotten to claim tax relief on, for example, a loan which qualifies for tax relief. Is it too late to make a claim? How far back can you go?

The answer is that you can go back six tax years into the past, i.e. you can claim tax relief, or allowances, for the six tax years before the current tax year.

Tax years run from 6 April in one year to 5 April in the next. So if you act *before* 6 April 1993, you can go back six tax years before the 1992–3 tax year – which takes you to the 1986–7 tax year. (See overleaf for later tax years.) This six-year time limit applies in a number of other cases – see pp. 20–22.

How much can you claim?

The *allowances* you can claim are the amounts which applied in the relevant tax year; the figures are on pp. 350 and 351.

Together with any extra tax relief you can claim, these will (in normal cases) reduce your taxable income for the relevant tax year. Your tax bill for that tax year will be recalculated, using the tax rates that applied at the time; the rates are on p. 352.

EXAMPLE

Charles Fox looks through his tax bills for previous years. In the 1986–7 tax year, his taxable income was £14,000, and his tax bill was £4,200.

Charles realises that he forgot to claim the additional personal allowance which he was entitled to for that year. In the 1986–7 tax year, this allowance was £1,320 (see p. 351). So Charles can subtract £1,320 from his taxable income, leaving him with a taxable income of £12,680. Tax (at 1986–7 rates) on that amount was £3,677. So Charles can claim back the difference between £3,677 and the £4,200 he paid – £523.

The six-year rule

Act before 6 April 1993
1992–3   1986–7
for the 1986–7 tax year

Act before 6 April 1994
1993–4   1987–8
for the 1987–8 tax year

Act before 6 April 1995
1994–5   1988–9
for the 1988–9 tax year

Act before 6 April 1996
1995–6   1989–90
for the 1989–90 tax year

Act before 6 April 1997
1996–7   1990–1
for the 1990–1 tax year

Act before 6 April 1998
1997–8   1991–2
for the 1991–2 tax year

Act before 6 April 1999
1998–9   1992–3
for the 1992–3 tax year

Time limits for 13 tax choices

1 Appealing against a *Notice of Assessment* (p. 44).
Time limit: 30 days from the date on the notice. You may also need to apply to postpone paying the tax asked for. Again, you have 30 days from the date on the notice.

2 In the tax year of marriage, choosing not to take the married couple's allowance (p. 71).
Time limit: the normal six-year rule applies.

3 Transferring the married couple's allowance, or part of it, to the wife (p. 72).
Time limit: the normal six-year rule applies.

4   Asking for business losses to be set against future profits from the same business (p. 189).
    Time limit: within six years of the end of the tax year in which the losses were made.

5   Asking for business losses to be set against other income of the year in which the losses were made (p. 190).
    Time limit: within two years of the end of the tax year in which the losses are to be set against income.

6   Asking for business losses to be set against other income of the following year (p. 190).
    Time limit: within three years of the end of the tax year in which the losses occurred.

7   Asking for losses in the closing year of a business to be carried back against past profits of the same business (p. 193).
    Time limit: within six years of the end of the tax year in which the business closes.

8   Asking for losses in a new business to be set against other income from previous years (p. 192).
    Time limit: within two years of the end of the tax year in which the losses were made.

9   Claiming retirement relief (p. 280). This can reduce your capital gains tax bill when you dispose of your business.
    Time limit: if retiring through ill-health, within two years of the end of the tax year in which you dispose of your business; if retiring over the age of 55, relief should be automatic.

10 If you own more than one home, choosing which one will be your 'main home' for capital gains tax purposes (p. 207).
    Time limit: within two years of the date on which you acquired the second home.

11 Choosing to pay an inheritance tax bill by instalments (p. 346).
    Time limit: within six months of the end of the month in which the gift was made. This time limit applies strictly for gifts on death, and it's advisable to stick to it for gifts during life, though for lifetime gifts made between 6 April and 30 September you could wait until 30 April of the following year.

12 Adding extra contributions to a personal pension plan (p. 315).
Time limit: see the detailed rules on p. 315.

13 Continuing a partnership when a partner joins or leaves (p. 198).
Time limit: within two years of the change.

Tax advice – where to find it

No one person – and no one book – can answer every tax problem. In the following paragraphs, we suggest sources of advice which, depending on your circumstances, you might find useful.

Start with this book
It's the obvious starting place. With nearly 400 pages of information and advice, it covers the great majority of tax situations.

Use Inland Revenue leaflets
These vary considerably in the amount of detail they give. Some are easy to read but quite sketchy. Others are labyrinthine. In between, they provide relatively straight-forward information, often with worked examples. Not all leaflets are up to date – though sometimes there are supplements, which should be given to you with the main leaflet. All leaflets are free, from tax offices and Tax Enquiry Centres. We list them on pp. 359–62.

Go to Tax Enquiry Centres
These Inland Revenue advice centres may be nearer (and more convenient) than your own tax office. They should be able to sort out most problems.

Use the **Which? Tax-Saving Guide**
This is the best short guide to the tax system, and takes you step by step through filling in your Tax Return. It's published in March each year.

Try **Simon's Taxes**
This is a nine-volume looseleaf tax encyclopaedia, certainly not worth buying unless you're a tax professional. But it's the best place to consult statutes. One of the problems for the ordinary person is that Finance Acts very often make changes to sections in earlier Acts, so you need to find a

version of the earlier Acts which contains all the changes. *Simon's Taxes* (Volumes G and H) do just that. Your local library might have a copy; otherwise, try a reference library or university library.

Get professional help
Only if your tax affairs are complicated, or you're making a will, may you need a professional to handle your tax affairs. If you're setting up a trust, or engaging in detailed inheritance tax planning, you'll need a professional adviser – a taxation consultant, accountant or solicitor. The level of competence and expertise varies enormously, and there's no easy way to find someone who's good. Try asking friends, or your employer.

2 HOW YOUR INCOME TAX BILL IS WORKED OUT

This chapter takes you through the stages involved in working out your income tax bill. Use it to get an overall picture of how all the elements of the tax system come together, and to find out where in the rest of the book you'll be able to check up on the particular details and difficulties that affect you.

What you pay income tax on

The good news is that you don't pay income tax on all the money you have coming in; instead, you pay it on only a part of that money, called *taxable income*. Much of this book is concerned with explaining how you reach this taxable income figure starting from the total of money you have coming in. In a nutshell, you:

- start with the money you have coming in during a *tax year* (explained on p. 35)
- subtract sums which don't count as income, or count as tax-free income (p. 26), to arrive at your income for tax purposes
- subtract items called *outgoings* (payments on which you get *tax relief*, p. 28) to arrive at your *total income* (p. 37)
- subtract items called *allowances* (slices of your income on which you don't have to pay tax, p. 34) to arrive at your *taxable income* (p. 37).

Finally, your tax bill is worked out by applying the *tax rates* (p. 35) for the current tax year to your taxable income.

EXAMPLE

Horace Walpole received £25,000 in the 1992–3 tax year. But he doesn't pay income tax on all of this. First, he takes away sums which aren't income: £300 he inherited and £1,550 of capital

24

gains from selling shares at a profit. Then he knocks off his tax-free income: £50 from a National Savings Ordinary account. The next things to go are his outgoings: £1,000 in contributions to his employer's pension scheme. Lastly he takes away his personal allowance of £3,445.

That leaves him £18,655 of taxable income, on which the first £2,000 is taxed at 20 per cent and the remainder at 25 per cent. So Horace's tax bill for the year is 20 per cent of £2,000 (£400) plus 25 per cent of £16,655, which is £4,163.75: £4,563.75.

Money	**£25,000**
subtract things which aren't income	
– inheritance	£300
– capital gains on shares	£1,550
Income	**£23,150**
subtract tax-free income	
– NSB Ordinary account interest	£50
Income for tax purposes	**£23,100**
subtract outgoings which qualify for tax relief	
– contributions to pension scheme	£1,000
Total income	**£22,100**
subtract allowances	
– personal allowance	£3,445
Taxable income	**£18,655**
Tax: 20% of £2,000	£400
25% of £16,655	£4,163.75
Total tax on £18,655	**£4,563.75**

Other taxes

The bad news is that you don't pay tax only on your taxable income – income tax isn't the only form of taxation. There are two other main taxes dealt with in this book: *capital gains* tax in Chapter 14 and *inheritance* tax in Chapter 17. So, in the example above, Horace Walpole will also have to work out if there is tax to pay on his inheritance and capital gains, which he subtracted right at the beginning of his calculation.

This chapter deals only with *income* tax.

What is income?

You may receive money from a number of different sources, such as from your job or pension, and perhaps some money from investment or savings. It's important to know how much of this money counts as income for tax purposes. If it's not income – or if it's tax-free income – there's no income tax to pay on it.

The main sources of income

- earnings from your job – see p. 121
- any spare-time earnings – see p. 140
- fees for work you do, and profits you make from running a business – see p. 176
- any other earnings from being self-employed – see p. 171
- pensions – see p. 97
- social security benefits – see p. 108
- rents from letting out property – see p. 217
- regular payments from someone else, like maintenance payments – see p. 84 – or covenant payments – see p. 32
- income from investments: e.g. interest from bank and building society accounts, dividends from shares, distributions from unit trusts – see p. 229.

Items which aren't income

- gifts and presents
- money you borrow
- money you inherit
- profits (gains) you make when you sell something for more than you bought it for, unless you did this as a business venture or as part of your business
- betting winnings – unless you bet (e.g. on horses) for a living
- lottery winnings
- premium bond prizes.

Tax-free income

Not surprisingly, there's no tax to pay on income which is tax-free. So you can forget about it when you're working out your tax bill.

Tax-free income from investments

- first £70 interest from a National Savings Ordinary account
- proceeds from National Savings Certificates (or, in most cases, from Ulster Savings Certificates if you live in Northern Ireland)
- interest from National Savings Children's Bonus Bonds
- part of the income from annuities except annuities you *have* to buy – see p. 100
- proceeds from Save-As-You-Earn contracts
- proceeds from a regular-premium investment-type life insurance policy (if held for 10 years or three-quarters of its term – whichever is shorter)
- most proceeds from a Personal Equity Plan see p. 242
- proceeds from a qualifying Tax Exempt Special Savings Account (TESSA) – see p. 244
- proceeds from some friendly society savings schemes – see p. 240.

Tax-free income from the state or local authorities

- many social security benefits – see p. 108
- a few special pensions (including the £10 Christmas bonus)
- community charge, housing benefit and rent rebates
- grants for improving or insulating your home
- most grants or scholarships for education.

Tax-free income from jobs

- some earnings from working abroad – see p. 163
- some fringe benefits – see p. 147
- in many cases, up to a total of £30,000 in redundancy pay, pay in lieu of notice, etc. when you leave a job – see p. 138
- gifts which are genuine personal gifts, i.e. not those given to you because you're an employee
- certain profit-related pay – see p. 121.

Miscellaneous tax-free income

- income from family income benefit life insurance policies

- the first year or so's income from a permanent health insurance policy
- interest from a delayed settlement of damages for personal injury or death
- strike and unemployment pay from a trade union
- interest on a tax rebate.

Outgoings and tax relief

Outgoings are things you spend your money on. Some outgoings qualify for tax relief, i.e. you can subtract them from your income before your tax bill is worked out, and so pay less tax.

EXAMPLE

Arnold Brown is self-employed, and in the 1992–3 tax year makes payments into a personal pension plan of £1,500. His spending is an outgoing which qualifies for tax relief, so he pays tax on £1,500 less of his income. As his income is well over the lower-rate band, he would have paid tax at the basic rate on the £1,500, i.e. at 25 per cent, which is £375, so he pays £375 less tax than he otherwise would.

The main items which qualify for tax relief

The main outgoings you can claim relief on are described briefly here; there are more details in the chapters and on the pages indicated.

The mechanics of getting the relief vary depending on the outgoings. You may have to claim money back from the Revenue (or you'll get a lower tax bill); get it back through your employer (by paying less PAYE tax each week or month); or give yourself tax relief by handing over less money in the first place. This section explains how relief is given.

Interest on loans for your home

Basic rules   You get tax relief on the interest you pay on the first £30,000 of loans to buy your only or main home. Since 6 April 1991 you have been able to get relief at the basic rate of tax only, and you'll get relief at the basic rate even if you pay tax on all your income at the lower rate of 20 per cent. If more than one of you shares a property, then you don't get relief on more than the first £30,000 of loans on the property as a whole, unless the loan was taken out before 1 August 1988, when each person (or each married couple) had their own £30,000 limit.

Loans taken out before 6 April 1988 to improve a main home, or to buy homes for dependent relatives or a former wife or husband, also qualify for basic-rate tax relief.

How to get it   In most cases, you make lower payments to the lender (the MIRAS system). Otherwise, write to your tax office and get the relief by paying less tax through PAYE, or by getting a tax rebate or a lower tax bill.

More details   See Chapter 11.

Interest on loans for property you let

Basic rules   Any amount of loans to buy or improve the property count for tax relief, provided it's actually let for at least half the year.

Some lettings (e.g. furnished holiday places) count as businesses, so the interest is an allowable business expense which reduces your *taxable profits* (see p. 176), rather than an outgoing which reduces your total income.

How to get it   Through a tax rebate or a lower tax bill.

More details   See p. 219.

Interest on a loan to buy an annuity

Basic rules   You get tax relief on the interest for up to £30,000 of loans to buy an annuity if you are 65 or over and the loan is secured against your only or main home. This is in addition to any tax relief you can get on mortgages to buy the home but again, the amount has been restricted to basic-rate tax relief from 6 April 1991.

How to get it   As for a loan to buy the home.

More details   See p. 104.

Interest on loans to pay inheritance tax

Basic rules   You get tax relief for up to 12 months on the interest you pay on a loan to pay inheritance tax when someone dies, provided you actually pay the tax before probate is granted or letters of administration are received.

How to get it   Through a tax rebate or a lower tax bill.

More details   See p. 345.

Interest on other loans

Basic rules   You can get tax relief on the interest you pay on loans for a variety of purposes connected with business:

- contributing capital to, or buying a stake in, a partnership (but not a limited one)
- buying a stake in, or lending to, a 'close' company (e.g. a family one)
- buying a stake in an employee-controlled company or industrial co-operative which employs you more or less full-time
- buying machinery or plant (e.g. a car or typewriter) for use in your job or in your partnership, provided capital allowances can be claimed for it. There's no relief on interest payable more than three years after the end of the tax year in which you took out the loan.

You must use the money borrowed for one of these purposes within a 'reasonable' time (usually six months) before or after taking out the loan. The loan must not have to be paid back within 12 months of being taken out, unless the interest is paid in the UK to a bank, stockbroker or discount house. And overdrafts and credit card debts don't qualify either.

These outgoings apply to individuals: *businesses* (including the self-employed and partnerships) can claim interest paid on loans, overdrafts and credit card debts for most business purposes as an allowable business expense.

How to get it   Through the PAYE system, or by getting a tax rebate or a lower tax bill.

More details   See p. 178 for allowable business expenses.

Expenses in your employment

Basic rules   You get tax relief on money you spend *wholly, exclusively and necessarily* in carrying out the duties of your employment. This is interpreted very strictly.

How to get it   Through the PAYE system in the following tax year, or by getting a tax rebate or a lower tax bill.

More details   See p. 123.

Maintenance payments

Basic rules   You get tax relief on maintenance payments you're legally obliged to make.
   For payments under an order applied for before 15 March 1988 (and in place by 30 June 1988), relief is limited to the amount you actually paid in the 1988–9 tax year and which qualified for relief. For orders applied for after 15 March 1988 (or not in place until after 30 June 1988) relief is limited to the level of the married couple's allowance (£1,720 in the 1992–3 tax year).

How to get it   Through the PAYE system, or by getting a tax rebate or a lower tax bill.

More details   See p. 80.

Pension payments

Basic rules   You get tax relief on contributions to employers' schemes or personal pension plans, and additional voluntary contributions (AVCs) either to an employer's scheme or a separate free-standing scheme.
   There are limits on the amounts of contributions that qualify for relief in any one year – between 15 per cent and 40 per cent of your earnings or profits depending on the type of scheme or plan you're in and, for personal plans, your age. But you may be able to claim tax relief on extra contributions if you didn't pay the maximum allowed in previous years.

How to get it   With employer's schemes (including AVCs) you get the relief automatically by paying less PAYE.
   With free-standing AVCs, or personal plans taken out by

employees after 1 July 1988, you give yourself basic-rate tax relief by subtracting an amount equivalent to the basic-rate tax on the payments before making them. If you pay higher-rate tax, you get the higher-rate tax relief through the PAYE system, or by getting a tax rebate or a lower tax bill.

With personal plans taken out by the self-employed, or by employees before 1 July 1988, you make gross payments (i.e. before-tax, see p. 36) and get both basic-rate and any higher-rate tax relief through the PAYE system (if you're employed) or by getting a tax rebate or a lower tax bill.

More details   See Chapter 16.

Covenant payments

Basic rules   You get tax relief on payments you make under deeds of covenant to charities. The covenant must be capable of lasting for more than three years.

Existing covenants to individuals on which you're already getting tax relief continue to be eligible for relief – provided you don't change them in any way. Covenants to individuals taken out after 15 March 1988 don't qualify for tax relief.

How to get it   You give yourself basic-rate tax relief by subtracting an amount equivalent to the basic-rate tax on the payments before making them. The charity can reclaim basic-rate tax from the Revenue. For example, if you want a charity to be £100 a year better off, you need give them only £100 less basic-rate tax at 25 per cent, i.e. £75. The charity will be able to claim a tax repayment of £25 (25 per cent of the gross equivalent – see p. 36 – of the £75 they get from you).

If you pay higher-rate tax, you get the higher-rate tax relief (not allowable for covenants to individuals) through the PAYE system, or by getting a tax rebate or a lower tax bill. The charity can't get the higher-rate tax relief.

Payroll giving

Basic rules   Payroll giving schemes are run by your employer. If your employer has such a scheme, you can get tax relief on payments through it to charities of up to £600.

How to get it   Your donations are taken from your pay before tax, so you get relief automatically.

Gift aid

Basic rules   You can get tax relief on single donations (i.e. other than covenants) made to charities after 1 October 1990. Each donation has to be for at least £400 to qualify from 7 May 1992, and there's no maximum. The relief applies only to genuine gifts (i.e. where you don't get any benefits in return) and only to gifts of money, not in kind. Gifts which have already qualified for tax relief (e.g. covenant payments or payroll-giving deductions) don't quality either, nor do bequests made on death.

How to get it   In the same way as for covenants to charities. But note that the lower limit of £400 is *net* of basic-rate tax (i.e. you can't give the charity £400 less 25 per cent tax).

Private medical insurance

Basic rules   You can get relief on some private medical insurance policies you take out for anyone (including yourself) who's 60 or over. There are restrictions on the types of policy that are acceptable, e.g. only conventional policies are covered, and any cash benefit for policyholders while they are in-patients must be limited to £5 a day.

How to get it   You get basic-rate relief by making lower payments to the insurer. If you pay tax at the higher rate, write to your tax office and get the higher-rate relief by paying less PAYE, or by getting a tax rebate or a lower tax bill.

More details   See p. 99.

Vocational training

Basic rules   Since 6 April 1992 you have been able to claim tax relief if you pay for your own 'qualifying' training. To qualify, the training must lead to National Vocational Qualifications or Scottish Vocational Qualifications up to level 4.

How to get it   You will get basic-rate relief by paying lower study and examination fees, so you will benefit even if you are not a taxpayer. Higher-rate taxpayers will be able to claim higher-rate relief from their tax office.

Allowances

Subtracting allowances from your income is the last step before tax on your income is worked out. Allowances work in the same way as outgoings: you subtract them from your income before your tax bill is worked out, and so pay less tax.

Everyone – whether single or married, male or female, employed, unemployed or a full-time student – automatically gets his or her own personal allowance. It can be set against all types of income, whether from earnings or investments. You get the allowance from the day you're born. However, you may qualify for extra allowances.

The main ones for the 1992–3 tax year are shown in the table starting below. But there were other allowances available in earlier tax years – see Chapter 18.

Allowances for 1992–3

Allowance	How much	More details
Personal	£3,445	see above
Personal (age 65-74)	£4,200	Chapter 5
Personal (75 or over)	£4,370	Chapter 5
The basic allowance that everyone gets; other allowances are in addition. 'Age-related' allowances for elderly reduced if income is above £14,200		
Married couple's	£1,720	Chapter 4
Married couple's (age 65–74)	£2,465	Chapter 5
Married couple's (75 or over)	£2,505	Chapter 5
Given to men, but may be transferable to the wife. 'Age-related' allowances for elderly reduced if income is above £14,200		
Special personal (wife age 65-74)	£3,400	p. 94
Special personal (wife 75 or over)	£3,540	p. 94
For married men previously entitled to an age allowance on wife's age only. Reduced if income is above £14,200		

Allowance	How much	More details
Additional personal For single and separated people, and some others, who have responsibility for a child	£1,720	p. 88
Widow's bereavement For a widow in the tax year her husband dies, and (unless she remarries) in the following tax year	£1,720	p. 79
Blind person's Anyone registered as blind with a local authority at any time during a tax year. You don't have to be completely blind to be able to register: the rule is that you have to be unable to perform any work for which eyesight is essential.	£1,080	If you are unable to use the full amount of this allowance, the unused portion can be transferred to your spouse whether or not he or she is blind. Each partner of a blind couple may have a blind person's allowance.
Death, superannuation benefits On pension, funeral, or life insurance part of trade union subscriptions and some friendly society policies	half what you pay for these benefits	p. 260
BES payments Investments in certain unquoted companies	what you invest up to £40,000	p. 238

Tax rates for the 1992–3 tax year

Lower-rate tax of 20 per cent is charged on the first £2,000 of your taxable income. *Basic-rate tax* of 25 per cent is charged on the next £21,700. Taxable income above £23,700 is taxed at the *higher rate* of 40 per cent.

Tax year

Income tax is an annual tax. In other words, there's a separate income tax bill for each year's income. Tax 'years' are not the same as ordinary years. Tax years run from 6 April in one year to 5 April in the next. So the tax year running from 6 April 1992 to 5 April 1993 is called the 1992–3 *tax year*.

Income for a tax year

Normally, your tax bill for a tax year is based on the income you actually receive during that tax year. But if you're self-employed, at present it's likely that your tax bill will be based on money you received in an earlier year. There are more details on p. 171. This can also apply to interest you get which is not taxed before it's paid to you – see p. 232.

Gross and net – what they mean

Throughout this book, you'll come across references to *gross payments* and *net payments*, and to *gross income* and *net income*. Here we tell you:

- the difference between gross and net
- how to get from gross to net (or from net to gross).

EXAMPLE

Spencer Percival has a mortgage of £23,000 under the MIRAS system (see p. 204). His mortgage is the type where he pays interest only – which amounts to £2,400 in the 1992–3 tax year. Like most people, Spencer makes his mortgage payments monthly, so each month's payment is £200. Because his mortgage is under the MIRAS system, he gets basic-rate tax relief by making lower payments to the lender. So instead of paying £200 a month, he gives himself a basic-rate tax relief of 25 per cent of £200 = £50. So he pays the lender £200 − £50 = £150.

- the £200 is the *gross payment*
- the £150 is the *net payment*
- the difference between the gross and net payments is the £50 *basic-rate tax relief*.

The same principle applies to *gross* and *net income*. If you receive income from which basic-rate tax has been deducted, the amount you get is the *net income*, and adding back the basic-rate tax brings you to the *gross income*.

How to find out the net amount

If you know the gross amount of a payment (or income), you find out the net amount by subtracting 25 per cent. If you've got a calculator, the quickest way is to *multiply* the gross amount by 0.75. So in the example opposite, £200 (gross) × 0.75 = £150 (net).

How to find out the gross amount

If you know the net amount of the payment (or income), you find out the gross amount by adding the basic-rate tax to the net amount. If you've got a calculator, the quickest way is to *divide* the net amount by 0.75. So in the example above, £150 (net) divided by 0.75 = £200 (gross).

Total income

In most cases, the important figure being worked towards in this chapter is *taxable income* – broadly speaking, the money you receive, less everything you can find that you don't have to pay tax on. For taxable income, it's irrelevant whether you're deducting an item because it's tax-free, an allowance or an outgoing.

But in a few cases, the important figure for tax purposes is *total income*. This is taxable income *plus* your allowances. In this case, it *does* matter whether a particular item is counted as an allowance or an outgoing: outgoings reduce your total income, allowances don't.

In this chapter, we've put all tax-deductible items into their correct places. But be warned that the Revenue sometimes confuses the issue:

- personal pension payments are an outgoing, as we've classed them. But on your Tax Return, you'll find them under 'Allowances'.
- Business Expansion Scheme payments, which are not covered on the Tax Return, effectively count as an allowance – they don't reduce your total income.

The total income figure is, most importantly, used in working out whether older people are entitled to the full age-related allowances or only reduced ones – see p. 95. But it's also the figure used when working out whether you are entitled to tax relief on life insurance policies taken out before 14 March 1984, or whether someone supporting you would have been entitled to the now-discontinued dependent relative allowance (see p. 350).

Tax Schedules

Tax Schedules go back to the earliest days of income tax. But although they sound off-putting, it can be useful to have a rough idea of what they mean. This knowledge can – in some cases – save you money.

What they are

They're a way of dividing income up into different types. For example, earnings from your job are taxed under Schedule E, whereas earnings from being self-employed are taxed under Schedule D. For a full list of what goes where, see below.

Why are Schedules important?

Dividing income into different bits may seem extremely unimportant. All income nowadays is taxed at the same rates, so why not lump it all together? But it's not quite that simple. Important differences still remain, and affect when you have to pay the tax on the income, and the *expenses* you can set against tax. Different Schedules have different rules. It can, therefore, be vitally important to ensure that income is taxed under a Schedule with generous (rather than stingy) rules about expenses, because the more expenses you can set against tax, the less tax you have to pay.

Cases

Some of the Schedules are divided up into Cases. So you can have a Schedule divided into Case 1, Case 2, Case 3 and so on. Traditionally, Cases are given Roman numerals – Case I, Case II, Case III, Case IV, Case V and Case VI.

Rules about expenses can differ from Case to Case. For example, Schedule D Case I income has fairly generous rules, whereas Schedule D Case III is the meanest.

Working through the Schedules

Schedule A

Schedule A income is investment income (unless it comes from carrying on a business).

What's taxed under Schedule A

Income from land – including income from unfurnished property. Income from furnished lettings is normally taxed under Schedule D Case VI or Schedule D Case I.

When the income is taxed

Schedule A income is taxed on a *current year basis* – i.e. your tax bill for the 1992–3 tax year is based on the income due to you in that tax year.

Expenses you can claim

- General expenses of managing the property, including maintenance, repairs, insurance (but not insurance of contents), fees of professional people, advertising costs, etc.
- Expenses connected with the land, including rent, rates (if you're liable to pay them), ground rent, easements, etc.

Costs of improving the property can't be set against tax, though you may get tax relief on interest on a loan taken out to improve the property – see p. 219. Capital expenditure may qualify for capital allowances – see p. 184.

If the repairs you make are because the previous owner let the property become dilapidated, you won't get tax relief on the cost of repair (unless the property passes to you on death, and the previous owner was your wife or husband).

Schedule B

Schedule B used to cover investment income from commercially managed woodlands in the UK. However, this schedule was abolished from 6 April 1988.

Schedule C

Schedule C income is investment income.

What's taxed under Schedule C
Interest paid in the UK on some government securities (UK government and foreign governments). Basic-rate tax is deducted before the interest is paid to you.

When the income is taxed
Schedule C income is taxed on a *current year basis* – i.e. your tax bill for the 1992–3 tax year is based on the income due to you in that tax year.

Expenses you can claim
None.

Schedule D Case I, Schedule D Case II

Case I and Case II income is earned income.

What's taxed under Case I and Case II
These two collect tax on the profits of being self-employed. If the profits are from a trade (e.g. window-cleaner, shopkeeper, manufacturer), you're taxed under Case I. If the profits are from a profession (e.g. barrister, architect, accountant), you're taxed under Case II. The tax rules in each case are virtually identical. Rent from lodgings in your own home may count as earnings from a trade.

When the income is taxed
At present, you're normally taxed on a *preceding year basis* – i.e. your tax bill for the 1992–3 tax year is based on the income due to you in your accounting period ending in the previous tax year. This is explained more fully on p. 232.

Expenses you can claim
Any expense incurred *wholly* and *exclusively* for your trade or business. This definition is more generous than for people who are employed – see p. 178.

Schedule D Case III

Case III income is investment income.

What's taxed under Schedule D Case III
The main items are interest (e.g. interest from National Savings accounts, interest from loans), income from

annuities and income from government securities (unless they're taxed under Schedule C). Other things taxed under this Case are annual payments (e.g. covenant or maintenance payments).

When the income is taxed

- *Interest* is normally taxed on a *preceding year basis* – i.e. your tax bill for the 1992–3 tax year is based on the income due to you in the 1991–2 tax year. More details on p. 232.
- **Covenant payments and maintenance payments** are (if taxable) normally taxed on a *current year basis* – i.e. your tax bill for the 1992–3 tax year is based on payments due to you in that tax year. Covenant payments are not liable to higher-rate tax.

Expenses you can claim

None. Case III income is often referred to as *pure profit income* – i.e. it's assumed that you don't have any expenses.

Schedule D Case IV, Schedule D Case V

Case IV and Case V income is investment income (unless it comes from carrying on a business).

What's taxed under Case IV and Case V

These two are both concerned with income from abroad. Case IV covers income from foreign securities, except for securities covered by Schedule C. Case V covers most other types of income from abroad – e.g. rents, dividends, pensions, trading profits, maintenance payments. Broadly speaking, if you're not domiciled in the UK, or (for UK or Irish citizens) you're not ordinarily resident in the UK, you're taxed only on money which comes to the UK. Otherwise, you're taxed on the lot – whether or not it reaches the UK. If the money comes from a pension, a tenth of the income normally escapes UK tax.

When the income is taxed

This income is normally taxed on a *preceding year basis* – i.e. your tax bill for the 1992–3 tax year is based on the income due to you in the previous tax year (or in your accounting year ending in the previous tax year, if the money comes from a trade or profession).

Expenses you can claim

If the money comes from a trade or profession, tax is charged on your taxable profits – so you can subtract the usual expenses in working these out. Otherwise, there are normally none.

Schedule D Case VI

Case VI income is investment income (and *post-cessation* receipts).

What's taxed under Case VI

Case VI is a rag-bag of odd bits of income which don't fit in anywhere else. Examples are income from furnished lettings (unless it counts as a trade – see p. 223); income from furnished holiday cottages; income from occasional freelance work; post-cessation receipts – i.e. after a business or partnership ends; income from investing in plays – unless you do this for a living.

When the income is taxed

This income is taxed on a *current year basis* – i.e. your tax bill for the 1992–3 tax year is based on the income due to you in that tax year.

Expenses you can claim

There's nothing in the tax acts about exactly what you can claim, but you have to pay tax on 'profits or gains'. So expenses necessarily incurred in making those profits are deducted when working out how much income is taxed. Losses can be set against other Case VI income for the same (or a following) tax year, but not against income from other Schedules or Cases.

Schedule E

Schedule E income is earned income.

What's taxed under Schedule E

- income from your employment – e.g. wages, expense allowances, tips, fringe benefits (if they're taxable)
- pensions from employers
- taxable social security benefits
- freelance earnings under a contract of employment.

This can be a grey area, but if, for example, you're a teacher, and receive some money for marking examination scripts the Revenue will normally tax this extra income under Schedule E.

When the income is taxed
On a *current year basis* – i.e. your tax bill for the 1992–3 tax year is based on the income due to you in that tax year.

Expenses you can claim
The rules are harsher than for self-employed people: you can claim only expenses which are *wholly, exclusively and necessarily* incurred in the performance of the duties of your employment. For example, you could spend money on something which was entirely for use in your job, but unless it was *necessary* you wouldn't be able to claim it against tax (see p. 122).

Schedule E is divided into three cases, of which Case I is by far the most important. Broadly, Case I catches income from employment if the employee is resident and ordinarily resident in the UK (see p. 163); Case II applies to people who normally live and work abroad, but who have some earnings arising in the UK; Case III applies to income remitted to the UK (by people resident in the UK) earned in employment abroad.

Schedule F

Schedule F income is investment income.

What's taxed under Schedule F
Dividends from companies resident in the UK, and distributions from unit trusts resident in the UK.

When the income is taxed
On a *current year basis* – i.e. your tax bill for the 1992–3 tax year is based on the income due to you in that tax year.

Expenses you can claim
None.

Notice of Assessment

The Revenue uses a Notice of Assessment to tell you your total tax bill for the year and to show how it has been worked out. As we went to press, there were plans to make cosmetic changes to the Notices of Assessment, and possibly to change the title. But the way the calculations work won't change. If you pay tax under PAYE and your affairs are straightforward, you may not be sent a Notice of Assessment – though you can ask for one if you wish. This isn't always a good idea, as you might then be asked to pay small amounts of tax unpaid because of roundings in the PAYE system. If you are refused a notice, it may be because this underpaid tax cancels out the overpayment you're claiming. If most of your income comes from earnings and pensions, you'll be sent a Schedule E Notice of Assessment like the one on pp. 50 and 51. Small amounts of investment income or freelance earnings taxed under Schedule D and property income taxed under Schedule A may also be shown on this notice. But if you have substantial amounts of these, you'll get a separate Schedule A and D Notice of Assessment like the one on pp. 46 and 47. If you have several sources of income and are liable to higher-rate tax, you may also get a higher-rate Notice of Assessment (form 900) showing how it's been worked out.

Appealing against a Notice of Assessment

If you get a Notice of Assessment, check it at once. If you think any of the figures on it are wrong, you must normally appeal within 30 days of the date on it. If it's a Schedule A or D assessment, you must still pay all the tax demanded, unless you also apply for a postponement of part or all of the tax. See p. 61 for details.

How to read a Schedule A or D Notice of Assessment

You'll get one of these assessments if you let property or work for yourself (full-time or spare-time), or have investment income not on your Schedule E Notice of Assessment. Here we describe Jenny Burns' Notice of Assessment for 1992–3, shown on pp. 46 and 47. The items in **bold** are all mentioned on the actual form.

In her accounting year which ended in the 1991–2 tax year, Jenny Burns made a profit of £17,200 from her shop, The Joke Shop, after deducting all her allowable business expenses. As well as this earned income she also gets money from investments which are not taxed before she receives them: the tax on these is handled in a different way, so the Notice of Assessment splits the figures into two columns, one for each type.

The **Source(s) of income** section shows her earned profit in the first column. In the second column are shown **Property rents** she gets from unfurnished lettings (after deducting allowable expenses these are expected to be £5,675 in the 1992–3 tax year), and untaxed **Investment income** of £1,740 that she received in the 1991–2 tax year.

In her business, Jenny claims **Capital Allowances** of £1,840, making the TOTAL CHARGEABLE for the business £15,360; and for unearned income, £7,415.

Jenny can claim a number of **Allowances**. She paid £1,700 into a **personal pension** plan, which she can set only against her earned income, i.e. business profits. But her other allowances can be set against either earned or unearned income. And, as she'll have to pay the tax on her unearned income in one lump at the beginning of 1993 (rather than in the two instalments she can pay her earned income tax bill), it makes sense for these all to be set off against her unearned income.

She has a PERSONAL allowance of £3,445; **Class 4 Nic relief** (see below) of £292; and interest of £520 on a home improvement **loan** she took out in 1987. The next row of figures in the assessment gives the TOTAL of these allowances; and these are subtracted from the TOTAL CHARGEABLE to give the **Net chargeable to tax** figures: for the business, £13,660; and for unearned income, £3,159.

These two figures are added together: £16,819 – not enough to pay higher-rate tax on. So the first £2,000 of unearned income is charged at the lower rate of 20 per cent with the balance of £14,818 charged at the basic rate of 25 per cent; and the tax payable on the two types of income is shown separately: for the business, £3,415; and for unearned income, £689.50. The **Net tax payable** row shows the totals of tax payable at basic and higher rates: for Jenny, these figures are the same as the previous row.

The next section works out CLASS 4 NATIONAL INSURANCE PAYABLE (see p. 194 for details). From Jenny's business **Profit** of £15,360 is subtracted the **Lower limit** of £6,120 to give the **Charged at 6.30% on** figure of £9,240, and an AMOUNT PAYABLE of £582.12. She gets tax relief on half of this amount: £291.06, or £292 rounded

**Inland Revenue
Income Tax**

District reference

000 000000 0

Income Tax (Schedule A or Schedule D) and
Class 4 National Insurance Contributions
YEAR ENDING 5 APRIL 1993

Date of issue
3 NOV 1992

Ms J BURNS
14 TWINTREES AVENUE
SWINSIDE SW30 0SF

Dear Madam,

This notice is addressed to you personally as required by
law but if you have a professional adviser or agent it is
desirable that you let him see this Notice of Assessment
IMMEDIATELY.
If you do not agree with the assessment you should appeal
in writing WITHIN 30 DAYS from the date of issue above.
If you also consider that the amount charged is excessive
you may apply to postpone some or all of the tax etc.
(see form 64D enclosed).

Yours faithfully
MR J. WILTSHIRE
HM INSPECTOR OF TAXES
BRIDGENORTH
WALKER HOUSE
CONISTON DRIVE
BRIDGENORTH
SHROPSHIRE   BR3 7TQ

Notice to pay:
Please pay the amount shown on the attached payslip, to
IR Accounts Office, Cumbernauld, Glasgow G70 5TR

How to pay: See back of payslip.

	1st INST	2nd INST
AMOUNT PAYABLE		
TAX	2379.00	1707.50
NATIONAL INSURANCE	291.06	291.06
TOTAL	2688.06	1998.56
PAYABLE 1 JAN 1993	2688.06	
PAYABLE 1 JUL 1993		1998.56

300 (CODA)

NOTICE OF ASSESSMENT 1992/93

Assessment number

Source(s) of income	£	Unearned Income
JENNY'S JOKE SHOP	17200	
Property rents		5675
Investment income		1740
TRADING DEDUCTIONS		
Capital Allowances	1840	
TOTAL CHARGEABLE	15360	7415
Allowances		
PERSONAL		3445
Class 4 NIC relief		292
Personal pension	1700	
Loan etc. interest		520
TOTAL	1700	4257
Net chargeable to tax	13660	3158

TAX CHARGEABLE

Lower rate @ 20% on £2,000	3415	400
Basic rate @ 25% on £14,818		289.50
Net tax payable	3415	689.50

CLASS 4 NATIONAL INSURANCE
PAYABLE

Profit	15360
Lower limit	6120
Charged at 6.30% on	9240
AMOUNT PAYABLE	582.12

Notes

47

up to the next £, as shown in the Allowances section of the notice. The bottom part of the form is the **Notice to pay**, together with a payslip. Jenny will have to pay in two instalments. In the **1st INST** is:

- all the unearned income tax of £689.50 plus half the earned income tax of £3,415, a total **TAX** of £2,397.00
- half the Class 4 due of £582.12: **NATIONAL INSURANCE** of £291.06 making a **TOTAL** of £2,688.06. This is **PAYABLE 1 JAN 1993**.

The **2nd INST** is made up of the other half of the earned income tax, plus remaining Class 4. This **TOTAL** of £1,998.56 is **PAYABLE 1 JUL 1993**. The payment form is for the first instalment; Jenny will receive a second one for the second instalment before the beginning of July.

How to read a Schedule E Notice of Assessment

Here we explain how a Schedule E Notice of Assessment is laid out, and how figures given in it are arrived at, using William Orange's notice for the 1992–3 tax year shown on pp. 50 and 51 as an example. The items in **bold** are ones that are actually mentioned on the Notice.

There are five sections in the Notice.

1 Income from employment, pensions, benefits, etc., and Deductions

This section has three columns:

- **Deductions** shows allowable expenses of employment – William paid £420 in expenses which the Revenue has accepted were 'wholly, exclusively, and necessarily' incurred in carrying out his duties.
- **Income** shows earned income such as wages, salary, perks, pensions and so on. William earned £29,580 from **ROYAL CITRUS FRUIT**, plus £2,000 in **BENEFITS IN KIND**.
- **Tax Deducted or Refunded** shows tax already paid on earned income, e.g. through PAYE, or (if there's an **R** in front of the figure) refunded.

TOTALS gives the sum so far of the three columns above. The **Amount of assessment** box shows the net income after subtracting the **Deductions** total: £31,160 for William.

2 Allowances, etc.

This section first deducts your allowances, and any outgoings you are entitled to for which you have not had tax relief, from your income calculated so far. William paid £520 in gross interest on a home improvement **LOAN** (taken out in 1987); has his own **PERSONAL ALLOWANCE** of £3,445; and (as he's married to Mary) claims the **MARRIED COUPLE'S** allowance of £1,720. **Total Allowances** shows the sum of these items.

The section then adds in income you have which is taxable but which hasn't been taxed yet. The **Less allowed elsewhere** figure of £1,850 shows that William has untaxed income of this amount (it is described in detail in section 4) which is counted in by reducing his total allowances from £5,535 to £3,685 – the **Allowed in this assessment** figure.

3 Amount chargeable to tax

This box shows the amount of your income on which you have to pay tax – £27,325 for William. It's arrived at by deducting **Allowed in this assessment** from **Amount of assessment**.

The next part of this section calculates how much tax is payable on this amount: the first part at the **Lower rate** of 20 per cent; the next £22,500 at the **Basic rate** of 25 per cent; the remainder, if any, at the **Higher rate** of 40 per cent. Note that the amount you pay basic-rate tax on could appear to be *more* than the limit for the basic-rate tax band – William's assessment shows him as paying basic-rate tax on £22,500 even though only the first £21,700 of taxable income is taxed at 25 per cent. All is explained in section 5. The total tax payable is shown in the **Tax Assessed for 1992–3** box.

Any tax over or underpaid from previous years is shown next (William doesn't have any) and is subtracted from or added to the Tax Assessed figure to give the **Net tax due** figure. **Less Tax deducted** is the amount of tax you've already paid – e.g. through PAYE – and is the same as the total **Tax Deducted** figure in Section 1 (£8,793 for William). It's taken away from **Net tax due** to leave, in William's case, **Net tax overpaid at 5 April 1993** of £1,478.00. There may be a cheque with the assessment, or it may come separately. If the figure showed **Net tax underpaid**, the extra tax would have been collected either by adjusting William's PAYE code or, especially if the amount was large, by requesting him to pay the Revenue within 30 days.

49

WHICH? WAY TO SAVE TAX 1992–3

Inland Revenue
Income Tax - Schedule E

YEAR ENDED 5 APRIL 1993
NOTICE OF ASSESSMENT AND STATEMENT OF TAX
UNPAID OR OVERPAID FOR 1992–93

Please use both lines of this reference if you write or call – it will help to avoid delay

246 / 1RCFI

| OR | 12 | 34 | 56 | A |

MR WILLIAM OF ORANGE
CLEMENTINE HOUSE
1 TANGERINE ST
LONDON

Date of issue

26 JUN 1993

Dear Sir,

This Notice of Assessment is addressed to you personally as required by law, but if you have a professional adviser or agent it is advisable that you let him see it IMMEDIATELY.

If you think the assessment is wrong you should appeal to me IN WRITING, WITHIN 30 DAYS from the date of issue of the Assessment Notice. You should say what you think is wrong with the assessment and, if necessary, let me have the correct details or state the date by which I may expect to receive them.

The enclosed notes give general guidance, and advice on appeals, and tell you how to check this Notice.

If you require any further information please do not hesitate to contact me.

Yours faithfully

MR J WILTSHIRE
HM INSPECTOR OF TAXES
BRIDGENORTH
WALKER HOUSE
CONISTON DRIVE
BRIDGENORTH
SHROPSHIRE   BR3 7TQ

5 Explanation

THE FIGURE FOR 'ADJUSTMENTS' IS MADE UP OF THE FOLLOWING:

MAXIMUM OF BASIC RATE	23700
LESS LOWER RATE BAND	2000
ADD FURTHER RELIEF DUE FOR:-	
1) PERSONAL PENSION CONTRIBUTION: PPR	1500
2) CHARITABLE PAYMENTS UNDER DEED OF COVENANT	400
TOTAL CHARGE AT 25%	23600

P70(T)

NOTICE OF ASSESSMENT 1992/93	

1 Income from employments, pensions, benefits, etc. and Deductions

	Deductions £	Income(R = Refund) £	Tax Deducted or Refunded £	See note
ROYAL CITRUS FRUIT		29580	8793.00	
BENEFITS IN KIND		2000		5
EXPENSES	420			7
TOTALS	420	31580	8793.00	
Less Total Deductions		420		
Amount of assessment		31160		

2 Allowances etc.

LOAN ETC INTEREST	520	16
PERSONAL	3445	19
MARRIED COUPLE'S	1720	20
Total Allowances	5685	
Less allowed elsewhere	1850	
Allowed in this assessment		3835

3 Amount chargeable to tax | 27329

Tax Chargeable

		£ p
Lower rate at 20.00% on	£2000	400.00
Basic rate at 25.00% on	£22500	5625.00
Higher rate(s) on	£2825	1130.00

Tax Assessed for 1992-3	7155

Net tax due	7155
Less Tax deducted	8793.00
Net tax overpaid at 5 April 1992	1638.00

4 Allocation of allowances and rates of tax

	Allowances	Rates of Tax 20%	25%	40%
Allowed elsewhere:				
UNTAXED INTEREST	350			
FURNISHED LETTINGS	1500			
DIVIDENDS	0		1000	
BSI RECEIVED	0		100	
Elsewhere total(s)	1850		1100	
This assessment	3835	2000	22500	2975
TOTALS	5685	2000	23600	2975

51

4 Allocation of allowances and rates of tax

This somewhat misleading section has more to do with calculating what extra tax you owe than with what allowances you are due.

The items listed in the **Allowed elsewhere** column are amounts of income which were not included in section 1. If the income hasn't yet been taxed, it's listed in the **Allowances** column; if it's an income you receive after basic-rate tax has been deducted, the 'grossed-up' (see p. 36) amount is listed in the **25%** column.

William has received **UNTAXED INTEREST** of £350 from his National Savings Investment account; and £1,500 from **FURNISHED LETTINGS** of a wing of Hampton Court. He received £750 in **DIVIDENDS** payments – but that's after tax, so the before-tax equivalent of £1,000 is shown in the **25%** column. Similarly, his building society interest of £75 is shown alongside **BSI RECEIVED** as the before-tax equivalent of £100.

The **Elsewhere total(s)** give the totals of the incomes on which William has paid no tax (£1,850) and on which he's already settled his basic-rate tax bill (£1,100 before tax).

The figures in the **This assessment** and in the **TOTALS** lines show you how much of your income is free of tax (i.e. your allowances) and how much will be taxed at 20, 25 and 40 per cent. However, neither of these last two figures is actually calculated in either section 3 or section 4: that's done in section 5.

5 Explanation

In the same way that section 4 slips in information on tax you owe under the heading of Allowances, section 5 covers giving you higher-rate tax relief under the heading of Explanation, and finally works out how much of your income is due to be taxed at 25 per cent.

The **MAXIMUM OF BASIC RATE** is the threshold at which basic-rate tax stops and higher-rate tax begins: £23,700 for the 1992–3 tax year. On some of your outgoings (e.g. personal pension plans taken out by employees after 1 July 1988) you're entitled to tax relief at your highest rate of tax, but you get relief automatically only at the basic rate. To allow for the extra relief due, the gross amount of these payments is added to the basic-rate band. This means that an equivalent amount of your income is taxed at the basic rate, rather than at the higher rate.

William pays £1,125 in personal pension plan contributions after basic-rate relief. These **PENSION CONTRIBUTIONS** gross up to £1,500. He has **CHARITABLE PAYMENTS UNDER DEED OF COVENANT** of £300 (£400 grossed up) as well. By adding these grossed-up sums to the basic-rate band, it reduces the amount of his income he has to pay higher-rate tax on by the same amount, and so automatically gives him the higher-rate relief to which he's entitled. The **TOTAL CHARGE AT 25%** shows how much of his total income he will have to pay basic-rate tax on – £22,500 (allowing for the £2,000 lower-rate band).

Now this final piece of the jigsaw is in place, William can look back through the puzzle to check how the other figures have slotted in. In section 4, the **TOTALS** figure at 25 per cent is the £23,600 calculated in section 5. In the same way that section 5 adjusts the basic-rate band upwards to give higher-rate tax relief on outgoings, section 4 adjusts it back downwards to collect higher-rate tax due on income that's had only basic-rate tax deducted: William's building society interest and dividends of £1,100. So the final **This assessment** figure for the amount of William's income that will be taxed at basic rate is £22,500. Section 3 gave the total **Amount chargeable to tax** as £27,325; so the final **This assessment** figure for the amount of William's income that will be taxed at the higher rate is £27,325 – £22,500 – £2,000 = £2,925. These two figures are transferred to section 3 so that William's final tax liability for the year can be calculated.

3 DEALING WITH THE REVENUE

In this chapter, we explain how to find your tax office, how the Inland Revenue will tell you how much tax you're paying, and what to do if you've paid too much or too little tax. We also go through what to do if you feel the Inland Revenue staff are treating you unreasonably.

The tax office which deals with your tax affairs is not necessarily the one closest to where you live. It depends on your circumstances:

- **Employees** As a general rule, your affairs will be dealt with by the tax office dealing with the area where you work, or, more particularly, the place from which you are paid. But there are exceptions. PAYE for all employees in Scotland is handled by one office in Scotland; if you work for a large national organisation, or in London or in another large city or town, your office may not be local. If you are a government employee – e.g. civil servant or member of HM forces – your affairs will be dealt with by one of the Public Departments offices in Cardiff. Your employer will be able to tell you which tax office deals with your affairs, and your reference number. Your reference number will be the one that applies to your employer: so all employees at the same workplace will have the same reference number. If you change your job, your reference number will change; your tax office may also change if your new employer is in a different area.
- **Self-employed** If you are in business on your own, or in partnership, your place of business, not your home address, will determine which tax office deals with your affairs.
- **Income mainly from pension or investments** If you are getting a pension from a former employer, your tax affairs may well be dealt with by the tax office dealing with the area in which the pension fund paying your

54

pension has its office. But if the pension from your former employer is fairly small, or your only pension is the state retirement pension or widow's pension, your affairs will be dealt with by the tax office dealing with the area in which you live.

- **Unemployed**   You stay with the tax office of your last employer.
- **Special cases**   If you have to fill in a Tax Return in your capacity as trustee, the tax office will be one of the limited number which deal with the affairs of trusts and settlements.

Your tax office is not concerned with the *collection* of tax – that is the responsibility of the Collector of Taxes. You'll deal with either a local Collection Office or one of the two Central Accounts Offices, depending on the address on your tax bill.

General enquiries

General tax enquiry problems can often be dealt with by telephoning any tax office – not necessarily the one which deals with your tax affairs – or a **Tax Enquiry Centre**, which is there specifically to deal with tax queries. Leaflet *IR52* has a full list of the addresses and telephone numbers of Tax Enquiry Centres (or try the telephone book under *Inland Revenue*).

If there isn't a tax office or Enquiry Centre near you, you could try your local Citizens Advice Bureau (address in the telephone book).

For enquiries specific to your particular tax affairs, it's always best to write to your own tax office – see opposite.

Over the past year, the Revenue has made a number of changes meant to improve its service to taxpayers. While you may not notice the behind-the-scenes administrative changes, others may be more obvious:
- most letters should receive a reply within 28 days
- trials of more flexible opening hours for tax offices
- more mobile tax enquiry centres are out and about
- leaflets and forms are being re-designed
- tax inspectors must now wear badges, and use their names in correspondence
- other improvements are being tested, such as the merging of Tax Inspectors and Tax Collectors.

In addition, the Taxpayer's Charter was re-launched. This states clearly that taxpayers are entitled to expect the Inland Revenue:

to be fair   The Revenue should treat everyone with equal fairness and impartiality – you should be expected to pay only what is due under the law.

to be helpful   It should be courteous, and assist you in getting your taxes right, by providing clear information to help you understand your rights and obligations.

to be efficient   It should be prompt, accurate, and keep your affairs confidential. Information obtained from you should be used only as allowed by the law. It should also strive to keep both your expenses and the expenses of the Tax Office down.

to be accountable   Standards, and how well the Revenue lives up to those standards, should be made public.

to be open to criticism   Taxpayers should be told how to complain, and be able to have their tax affairs looked at again. An appeal can be made either to an independent tribunal or your MP can refer you to the Parliamentary Commissioner for Administration.

In return, you the taxpayer have an obligation to be honest, to give the Revenue accurate information, and to pay your tax on time.

Copies of the Charter are available from local tax and VAT offices.

Tax forms

Tax Returns

There are several different types of Tax Return, designed for different types of taxpayer:

- **Form P1**   This blue form is the most straightforward Tax Return. If you are an employee, your affairs are not complicated, and you earn at a rate of less than £8,500 a year, this is the Tax Return you will probably be sent. It is also likely that you will *not* be asked to complete one each year (although this does not absolve you of the need to tell your tax office of any new source of income).
- **Form 11P**   This brown form goes to most employees.
- **Form 11**   This blue form is for people who are in business on their own, or in partnership, or whose main sources of income are chargeable to tax under Schedule D.

- **Form 1** This pink form is issued to partnerships for completion on behalf of the partnership and shows the partnership income for the tax year and how that income has been shared between the partners. It is sent out *in addition* to Form 11 which will be sent to the individual partners. Form 1 is also issued to the personal representatives of someone who has died, so that they can report the income arising during the period of administration of the estate. Form 1 goes to trustees of a settlement too. But Form 1 asks only for information about sources of income which have not had tax deducted before payment, so further forms are issued to trustees, which ask for information about income which has been paid after deduction of tax, including dividends from UK companies.

- **Form R40** This blue form is similar to Form 11, but is sent to people who claim a repayment of tax each year – e.g. people who have only investment income which is taxed before they receive it. Unlike all the previous Tax Returns, which are normally issued in April, Form 40 will be sent to you at the same time as the repayment for the previous year is dealt with and the cheque is sent to you.

- **Form R232** This mauve form is sent if you have to make a return on behalf of someone who cannot do so for him or herself – e.g. your child.

- **Forms 11W and 11WP** These mauve forms were sent out for the 1990–1 year only, for married women to claim their allowances on the changeover to a system of independent taxation for husbands and wives. 11WP is for those paying tax through PAYE, 11W for the self-employed.

- **Form 11PA** This turquoise form allows you to claim some special allowances (on the life insurance part of friendly society sickness policies, for instance) that aren't covered fully in Form 11P. If you think you're entitled to an allowance that Form 11P doesn't cover, ask your tax office to send you 11PA (there's a box on 11P you can tick to get 11PA).

Notice of Coding

Form P2(T) If you are an employee, you may be sent a Notice of Coding, usually Form P2(T), which shows the code number that your employer will use to calculate the tax to be deducted from your pay, and also explains how your code number has been arrived at – see p. 129.

Notice of Assessment

This form is used by the Revenue to show how much you owe and how the bill is worked out – see p. 44.

Correspondence and disputes

This section is about writing to – and talking to – the Revenue and solving problems that way. For the more formal procedures of an *appeal*, see p. 61.

Your move

There may well be times when it's your responsibility to write to your tax office. If you become entitled to a new allowance or, for example, get a taxable benefit such as a company car, you should write a brief letter giving all the relevant information. If a man gets married and wants to claim the extra allowance due, the tax office will need to know the wife's name and maiden name, date of marriage, and the name of her employer; her tax office and National Insurance Number would also be helpful.

When writing to your tax office quote your reference number. This will be shown on any Notice of Coding, Notice of Assessment or Tax Return which you have received. Your National Insurance number is important, as this is used for all employees as the tax reference.

Certain matters are given priority, e.g. repayments. So if you consider that you are entitled to a repayment, write *repayment claim* (preferably in red) at the top of your letter. Your claim is then more likely to get priority. In fact, as a general rule, it's helpful to head your letter with a brief reference to the subject of your letter.

. . . and theirs

After you have sent in your Tax Return, the tax office may write to you and ask for further information about the income shown or expenses claimed. All letters should now be signed by a Tax Inspector, so it will be clear to whom a reply should be sent.

Problem-solving

When replying to any letters from your tax office, give the information requested if this is possible (and try to see the request as reasonable).

If you are convinced that the Inspector is being *un*reasonable in a request for further information, a telephone conversation or meeting may succeed in sorting things out. A meeting should present no problem if your tax office is a local one. But if it's not, you can arrange with the local tax office for your file to be passed to them for a short period so that you can discuss your affairs with a local Inspector.

If (in your view) the person you are dealing with continues to be unreasonable, remind him or her of the requirements of the Taxpayer's Charter. If this step fails, you could write a personal letter to the District Inspector, whose name will appear at the head of any letter you receive, on your Tax Return and on any Notice of Assessment. Ask for a review of all the correspondence; you should summarise the main points in your argument again. The District Inspector should reply personally, and will either agree with you or set out fully the reasons why your argument is not accepted.

If you are still unable to get any satisfaction from your tax office, write to the Regional Controller who deals with your tax office (names and addresses of Regional Controllers can be got from any tax office). Mark your letter for his or her personal attention, set out concisely and clearly your grounds for complaint against your tax office and ask for an investigation. If you still have no joy, you could try your MP, who may refer your case to the Parliamentary Commissioner for Administration.

Claiming tax back

It's quite common for people to pay too much tax. For example, because:

- too much tax has been deducted under PAYE (see p. 127)
- you've paid too much tax on income you've received (see overleaf)
- you've paid too much tax in previous years – e.g. you've forgotten to claim an allowance or an outgoing. If this has happened in your case, you can claim back the tax overpaid in the six tax years before the tax year you're

now in. So if you claim before 6 April 1993, you can recover tax overpaid as far back as 6 April 1986.

What to do
- Write to your tax office, saying why you're making a claim, and (if you know) how much you're claiming.
- If you're sending back a Tax Return at the same time, write *repayment claim* at the top (preferably in red).

If your rebate is £25 or more, you may be entitled to some interest – called a *repayment supplement* and payable at 9.25 per cent in July 1992. But the rebate doesn't start to earn interest until 12 months after the end of the tax year for which it is due, or until the end of the tax year in which you actually paid too much tax, whichever is later. If the rebate due is less than £50, it won't be paid until the end of the tax year.

Mistakes by the Revenue

The staff in your tax office are not infallible, and mistakes do occur from time to time. It is therefore important to check all correspondence received from your tax office, such as a Notice of Assessment or Notice of Coding.

If the Revenue is after you for tax you owe due to a mistake on their part from tax years further back than the previous one, you may not have to pay all (or any) of the tax you owe. But this will apply only if you've taken reasonable care to keep your tax affairs in order and up to date, and if it was reasonable for you to believe you didn't owe any tax.

You may only have to pay a percentage of the tax owed (see below) depending on your gross income when you receive the *amended* assessment. The income limits go up by £3,300 if you're receiving a state retirement or widows's pension, or are 65 or over – so you'd pay nothing if your gross income was £15,300 or less.

£12,000 or less	none
£12,001–£14,50	25%
£14,501–£18,500	50%
£18,501–£22,000	75%
£22,001–£32,000	90%
£32,001 or more	all

The scale applies separately to the incomes of husband and wife.
ESC A19

Mistakes by you

You may discover that a mistake in past Tax Returns meant that you paid more tax than was actually due. If this has happened, it is possible to make a claim to have the appropriate assessment corrected and any tax you have overpaid repaid to you. The time limit for such a claim is six years from the end of the tax year in which the assessment giving rise to the overcharge was made. But you cannot get a repayment of tax overcharged as a result of an assessment determined by the Commissioners in the absence of the appropriate accounts or Tax Return (see *Appeals* opposite). Nor can you claim tax back if your Tax Return was completed on the basis of the law as it was then understood to be, which has since been changed following a decision in a case before the Courts.

TMA 1970 s33

Appeals

The Government is currently considering changes to the rules for hearing tax appeals. However, at present the procedure is as follows.

When you are sent any kind of tax assessment, it is important that you check it straight away. You are allowed 30 days from the date of the assessment in which to appeal against a Notice of Assessment if you consider it is incorrect. If you do not appeal within this period, the assessment becomes *final and conclusive* and cannot be altered unless you discover a mistake or omission in your return. The appeal, which must be in writing, is sent to the Inspector who issued the Notice of Assessment, and must state the grounds of the appeal. Your tax office will send you, with the Notice of Assessment, a pink appeal form which you can use to make your appeal. Although you could write your appeal in a letter, it helps your tax office if you use the appeal form provided, perhaps accompanied by a letter if appropriate.

If you are unable to appeal within the 30 days allowed – e.g. you are away on holiday or business or in hospital when the Notice of Assessment is issued – send in your appeal as soon as you can, with an explanation for the delay, and the Inspector will probably accept your appeal. If the Inspector is reluctant to accept a late appeal, you may request that your application for a late appeal be heard by the General Commissioners – see p. 62.

You also have to ask to be allowed to postpone payment of the tax you think excessive (you can do it on the same pink form). You have the same 30 days in which to do this, unless there's a genuine change in your circumstances which makes you think you've been overcharged (for instance, further work on your accounts reveals an error). If you do not apply for postponement, the whole of the tax charged on the assessment will be payable by the normal due date, and the Collector of Taxes will keep chasing you until it is paid.

If you make an application to postpone part of the tax charged and this is accepted by the Inspector, the tax not postponed becomes payable 30 days after the Inspector's agreement to your application if this is later than the normal due date.

If you do not pay the tax agreed as payable by the time it is due, the Collector of Taxes can charge you interest – in July 1992, at the rate of 9.25 per cent (8 per cent for inheritance tax) from the due date until the date of payment. If you are self-employed or run a business, note that the interest on overdue tax is not allowable as a business expense.

Settling the appeal

The vast majority of appeals against assessments are settled by agreement with the Inspector. It is quite likely, therefore, that after discussion or correspondence with your tax office you will reach an agreement on the correct amount of income chargeable, or the correct amount of relief or deduction due, and the Inspector will then revise the assessment in line with the figures agreed. Any further tax then due, as a result of the issue of that revised assessment, is due for payment 30 days after the issue of the revised assessment, or the normal due date if later.

Any further tax found to be due following the issue of a revised assessment may attract interest. The rules about the charging of interest are fairly complicated; but, broadly speaking, if the Notice of Assessment has been issued at the correct time, i.e. before the normal due dates for payment, interest will start no later than six months after the normal due date (for Schedule D Assessments, it will always be 1 July following the year of assessment). If the assessment is issued late, i.e. more than six months after the normal due date, interest will start from 30 days after the date of issue of the Notice of Assessment.

The Revenue has power not to charge interest if it comes to less than £30 (and normally does not do so).
TMA 1970 s31, s46, s49, s55, s86

Appeals before the Commissioners

If you are unable to reach agreement with the Inspector, two possible courses of action are open to you. You can give up, i.e. accept the Inspector's point of view and pay the tax due on the basis of his or her figures, or you can ask for your appeal to be heard before the Commissioners, who are independent of the Inland Revenue.

You appeal to the *General Commissioners* or the *Special Commissioners*. The Special Commissioners are tax experts. The General Commissioners are unpaid local people who hear appeals in your area; they aren't usually tax experts, but have a paid Clerk to advise them on legal matters.

In some cases you have no choice about whether to go to the General Commissioners or the Special Commissioners. For example, the Special Commissioners must consider your appeal in certain specified (and usually complex) circumstances, of if you're claiming because you made a mistake filling in the *Income* section of your Tax Return and the Inspector has refused your claim.

If, on the other hand, your appeal is about your PAYE code, or you're claiming tax back because you've failed to claim a personal allowance, the General Commissioners must deal with it.

Other appeals normally go automatically to the General Commissioners, too. But if your appeal depends on some fine point of law (as opposed to a matter of fact, or common sense) you can elect to have your appeal heard by the Special Commisioners. You must make this choice within 30 days of the date of the Notice of Assessment. The General Commissioners have the power to direct that your election be disregarded.
TMA 1970 s31, s33, s46

At the Commissioners

Taking an appeal before the Commissioners will certainly be time-consuming, and may be expensive if you engage someone to appear on your behalf. You can appear on your own behalf, and the Commissioners are required to hear any barrister, solicitor or qualified accountant who appears for you.

The preparation and presentation of your case before the Commissioners is extremely important. As appellant, it is up to you to prove your case – not for the Revenue to disprove it. Although the proceedings before the Commissioners are not as formal as in Court, the normal rules of evidence will apply. You, as appellant, will open the proceedings and put your case. The Inspector then responds by putting the view of the Inland Revenue; you then have a final opportunity to stress the important points in your own case and deal with any points raised by the Inspector which you had not previously covered. Any witnesses produced by either you or the Inspector may be cross-examined; and the Commissioners can summon anybody to appear before them.

When preparing your case, bear in mind that the Commissioners will know nothing about you or your affairs until the day of the appeal hearing. So introduce yourself, and the facts of the matter under dispute, as clearly and briefly as you can. If you want to show documents in support of your case, make sure you have enough copies for the Commissioners (there are usually three of them at a General Commissioners' hearing) and the Clerk. The Inspector will probably have copies already, but have extra copies just in case. You may want to refer to previously decided tax cases: the Clerk will almost certainly have copies of these available, but it would be as well to take copies of these, too.

It may be possible, before the hearing and in conjunction with the Inspector, to prepare an agreed statement of facts, supported by appropriate documents, which can be presented to the Commissioners. This will save time on the day of the hearing. However, it will still be necessary to explain the facts to the Commissioners and provide the Commissioners and Clerk with a copy of the agreed statement of facts and documents.

It is a good idea to have your own presentation typed out in full, with copies for the Commissioners and Clerk. Take the Commissioners carefully through the arguments, both for and against your case. Do not ignore the points you know the Inspector will make. If you deal with these points at the same time as you deal with your own, you are likely to strengthen your own case while at the same time reducing the impact of what the Inspector will say later.

You will also give the impression of being a reasonable person – there is almost certainly something in the Inspector's argument, and it is just as well if you are seen to recognise this.

If, in spite of all your efforts, the Commissioners decide in favour of the Inspector, and you don't agree, you must immediately register your dissatisfaction with the decision. If you don't do this immediately, you lose the right to take the case further. Do this verbally at the end of the hearing, or (if the decision is communicated by letter) by an immediate written reply. You may then, by giving notice in writing to the Clerk within 30 days, require the Commissioners to state and sign a case for the opinion of the High Court (see below). You must also pay the fee of £25.

TMA 1970 s50, s56, FA 1984 Sch 22

. . . and after

The tax payable as a result of the decision of the Commissioners must be paid, regardless of any request for the opinion of the High Court.

The decision of the Commissioners on a question of fact (for instance, what your business takings were) is final and can be overturned only if the decision was one that no reasonable body of Commissioners could have reached on hearing the evidence.

Otherwise, an appeal against the decision of the Commissioners can be made only on a point of law. The appeal is normally to the High Court, then to the Court of Appeal and ultimately to the House of Lords. But certain appeals against the decision of the Special Commissioners may be referred direct to the Court of Appeal, missing out the High Court. Some appeals may skip the Court of Appeal and go straight to the House of Lords. In Scotland, the equivalent of the High Court is the Court of Session, and an appeal from the Court of Session is direct to the House of Lords.

The taking of an appeal through the procedure outlined above can be very expensive. At the Commissioners' hearing each party pays its own costs. However, if you or the Inland Revenue are found to have behaved unreasonably in pursuing your case, costs can be awarded. In the later stages of appeal it is usual for the costs of both sides to be awarded against the unsuccessful litigant. You could be faced with a bill running to many thousands of pounds, so

think very carefully before you start on this road. If you feel that your case has been mishandled – that you've suffered maladministration, bias, or delay, for example – your MP can refer your case to the Parliamentary Commissioner for Administration, also known as the Parliamentary Ombudsman.
TMA 1970 s50, s56

Investigations

The Inland Revenue may start an investigation, or enquiry, into your affairs. These fall broadly into three categories:

- an enquiry into an omission of a source, or sources, of income from your Tax Return, or an understatement of the income declared
- an enquiry into your business accounts
- a more serious investigation into your affairs when the Inland Revenue suspects fraud or wilful default.

An investigation into the last category may well be conducted by one of the Inland Revenue Enquiry Branch Offices and not your local tax office. If you find that the Enquiry Branch is investigating your affairs, you would be well advised to seek professional advice.

The Inland Revenue receives information from a variety of sources. For example, banks are required to make a return of interest credited to their customers of more than £500 in one year (for building societies, the figure is £1,400). Information such as this is compared with the taxpayer's return, and if the income is not shown, the Inspector will write to the taxpayer suggesting that the Tax Return submitted is incomplete and ask him or her to reconsider the entries made. If you receive such a letter, go over your Tax Return carefully (you should always keep a copy of what you fill in). If you find that you have omitted something from your Tax Return, make a full report of all income omitted for all years concerned as soon as possible.

If the amount of tax is not substantial, it should be possible to agree a settlement fairly quickly. But be prepared to pay, in addition to the amount of tax which is due on the income or capital gain previously omitted from your Tax Return:

- an amount of interest at the appropriate rate, calculated from the date the tax ought to have been paid, assuming it had been declared at the proper time

- a penalty – see below.
  TMA 1970 s88, s95

Penalties

If you have underpaid tax, you can be liable for a penalty of up to 100 per cent of the tax due. In practice, it would be this great only in the worst cases of fraud, followed by obstruction in the investigation.

The Inspector uses a rough 'tariff' scale to reduce the 100 per cent figure, according to the circumstances of the case. This could be:

- up to 30 per cent for making a full disclosure of your true situation
- up to 40 per cent for full co-operation in the investigation: answering questions honestly; attending interviews; supplying information fully; paying tax on account as soon as it's possible to estimate what you owe
- up to 40 per cent for gravity. If your failure to pay the correct tax is due to a mistake rather than a deliberate attempt to hide income, you'll get a bigger discount for gravity.

How many 'Brownie points' you'll earn for each of these factors depends on the Inspector's assessment. It's up to you to persuade the Inspector that you're worthy of bigger discounts.

The offer in settlement

At the end of the enquiry the Inspector will ask you to sign a *Certificate of full disclosure*. The declarations previously signed on your Tax Return have been proved to be incorrect, and this new Certificate confirms that, taking into account the income disclosed in the enquiry, you have now made a full return of all your income for the years covered by the enquiry. The Inspector will also ask you to make a formal offer in settlement of the tax lost, interest and penalties, and will normally suggest the amount of the offer which he or she considers the Board of Inland Revenue will accept. By deducting the tax and interest from the amount of the offer suggested by the Inspector, you can calculate the amount of penalty suggested. If you feel this is unreasonable, it is open to you to make a reduced offer in settlement. This will be considered by the Inland

Revenue Head Office, in the light of the recommendation of the local Inspector, and may well be accepted if reasonable. Once the offer has been accepted, the tax is payable direct to the Collector, within a period agreed in advance with the Inspector, and no formal assessments will be made.

Offers in settlement can include provisions for the charging of interest if the amount due under the settlement is not paid by the agreed date. Previously, it was not possible for the Inland Revenue to charge interest if the amount due was paid late.
SP6/86

Enquiry into your business accounts

Business accounts are sometimes selected for detailed investigation, but only if the Inspector suspects the figures are not correct. Inspectors look for inconsistencies: profits lower than for similar businesses; expenses higher than seems justifiable; savings larger than the business profits could generate; or information from other sources (for instance your bank, on interest paid to you) that's different from what you've told the Revenue.

The first you'll know about it may be when the Inspector writes and asks some detailed questions about your accounts. If you have an accountant acting on your behalf, and in particular in the preparation of your accounts, the Inspector will probably first direct these questions to your accountant. It is possible that the enquiry will be settled by correspondence, but it is more usual for the Inspector to request an interview with you, and your accountant if you have one.

The interview with the Inspector

This can be a daunting experience, particularly for first-timers. The Inspector will want to establish why the pattern of your business is different from others of the same type (there may be perfectly good reasons for this, of course), and will also want to ensure that any adjustments made for tax purposes – e.g. private use of a car – have been worked out correctly. So you'll be asked a lot of searching questions about your business: how you run it, how frequently you make up your books, how purchases and sales are recorded, how frequently you bank your takings, whether you bank all your takings and pay for all purchases by cheque, or whether you keep cash to pay for purchases or wages. It is usual to try to establish an approximate total for your living expenses, including such items as the cost of clothes, holidays, entertainment, general household expenses, and so on, to see if the money you have drawn from your bank is adequate. From this information, the Inspector will form a view about the accuracy of your accounts and the need to continue the enquiry. If your explanations are satisfactory, and if your business accounts reflect all your takings and only business expenses, this will probably be the end of the enquiry. The Inspector may suggest some adjustments to the private proportion of any expenses, but these are likely to be minor.

If, however, the Inspector is not satisfied with your explanations, or the money you have drawn out does not reflect accurately your total living expenses, he or she will seek to increase your profit for tax purposes to reflect the adjustments considered necessary. If the adjustment is of a fairly minor amount, the Inspector may not suggest any adjustments to previous years' accounts. But if the adjustment for the current year is more substantial, the Inspector may well seek to adjust the profits for previous years, too.

The Inspector will make full notes of the interview, and will forward copies to you or your accountant for approval. It is important to review these notes carefully and report any inaccuracies you find to the Inspector immediately, so that corrections can be made and the revised notes agreed between you. This can be important if you fail to reach agreement with the Inspector and the matter has to be taken before the Commissioners, when the notes of the meeting will probably be introduced as evidence.

Settling the enquiry

If you are able to agree with the Inspector the amount of any adjustment to your business profits for tax purposes, the enquiry can be settled. If the adjustments are fairly minor, the Inspector will probably simply revise the assessments and you will be asked to pay the tax to the Collector in the usual way. If, however, the adjustments are more substantial and cover a number of years, the Inspector will probably seek a settlement on the lines described above, to include interest and penalties.

4 TAX AND FAMILIES

Everyone, however young (or old), is potentially a taxpayer. In this chapter we explain the income tax rules that affect various members of the family – married couples (both during and after the marriage), couples living together, children and students. If you're approaching 65, you'll find more information in Chapter 5, *When you are older*.

Tax and marriage

From the 1990–1 tax year, independent taxation of married couples replaced the system whereby a married couple was treated as one person, with a wife's income regarded as that of her husband. This means that a husband and wife are each:

- taxed on their own income, both earned and investment income
- given their own tax-free allowances
- given their own tax bands – in 1992–3 this means that a husband and wife can each have £2,000 of taxable income taxed at the lower rate and £21,700 taxed at the basic rate of 25 per cent
- responsible for their own tax affairs – dealing with the Revenue, paying their own tax and receiving any tax rebate due.

When you get married

After marriage you continue to get your own personal allowances but the husband can also claim the *married couple's allowance* (£1,720 in the 1992–3 tax year). You may get a higher married couple's allowance if either partner is 65 or older during the tax year – see p. 93.

In the year in which you get married, you can claim the full married couple's allowance if the marriage takes place before 6 May. If the wedding is on or after that date, your married couple's allowance for that year will be reduced by one-twelfth for each complete month after 6 April that you remain single – see the chart below.

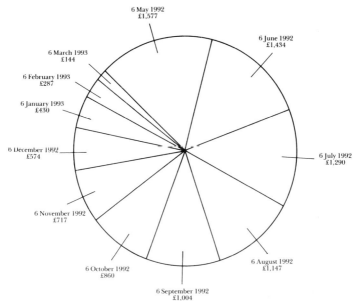

So if, for example, you get married on 10 September 1992, you have been single for five complete months of the tax year and so get seven-twelfths of the married couple's allowance for the 1992–3 tax year, that is £1,004.
ICTA 1988 s257 s257A

Additional personal allowance when you marry
This is paid to single people who have a dependent child, and is equal to the married couple's allowance (£1,720 in the 1992–3 tax year). So either the man or the woman (or both) could be claiming it when they get married.

If a man is claiming an additional personal allowance before he gets married he can choose to keep it for the tax year in which he gets married instead of claiming the married couple's allowance. It is worth doing this as you will get the whole allowance no matter what the date of the wedding, whereas if you claimed the married couple's allowance this could be reduced, depending on the date of the marriage.
ICTA 1988 s259, s261

71

A woman who is claiming the additional personal allowance before getting married can continue to claim it for the remainder of the tax year in which she marries.

After the year of the marriage neither husband nor wife can claim this allowance unless the wife is totally incapacitated for the whole of the tax year and there is a dependent child. In this case the husband can claim the allowance in addition to the married couple's allowance. For full details of this allowance, see p. 89.

How to claim the married couple's allowance
Tell your Tax Office that you want to claim the married couple's allowance as soon as possible after the wedding. If you pay tax under PAYE, use **form 11PA**, which you can get from any tax office.

Can allowances be transferred?

The personal allowance is non-transferable. So no matter how low your income is, you will not be able to transfer your unused allowance to your husband or wife. (Special arrangements can exist for couples where the husband is unable to use his personal allowance in 1992–3 – see p. 74.) The married couple's allowance *is* transferable.

In the first instance, the married couple's allowance will be given to the husband. But if his income is less than the total of his personal allowance plus the married couple's allowance he can transfer unused allowances up to the amount of the married couple's allowance to his wife. But for 1992–3 you can't transfer the allowance from husband to wife in any other circumstances – e.g. if she pays tax at a higher rate than her husband. This will change from 6 April 1993, when the married couple's allowance will be completely transferable and married women will be able to claim 50 per cent of the allowance in their own right. Note that you need to elect to reallocate the allowance in the tax year prior to the year in which you want to reallocate it. So you need to notify your tax office by 5 April 1993 if you want to share the allowance for 1993–4, or the wife is to have all of it. A form should be available from your tax office.

When working out how much of the married couple's allowance you can transfer in 1992–3, you have to work out your total income for tax purposes (including taxable social security benefits, earnings, income from savings and investments, and income from property). This includes the grossed-up amount of bank or building society interest you receive – see p. 236.

EXAMPLE 1

Jeremy gave up work in July 1992 to prepare for college in October; his wife, Katie, works but doesn't earn enough for it to affect Jeremy's grant, so he'll get a full grant from his Local Education Authority. This does not count as income for tax purposes, and so is not included in the calculations.

Before giving up work, Jeremy had earned £4,000 in the 1992–3 tax year. He also has some money in a building society account from which he got £160 in interest; knowing that he was going to college Jeremy had registered as a non-taxpayer to have his interest paid gross – see p. 236.

Jeremy's income – earned	£4,000
– investment	160
	£4,160
less allowances – personal	£3,445
– married couple's	£1,720
	£5,165
Allowances exceed income by	**£1,005**

So £1,005 of the married couple's allowance can be given to Katie to set against her income.

You can also transfer the blind person's allowance between husband and wife (and *vice versa*) if the person who gets the allowance is unable to make use of some (or all) of it (see p. 35 for details of who can claim this allowance).

How to transfer allowances
If you know (or suspect) that you will want to transfer part of the married couple's allowance, the husband can indicate this on his Tax Return.

The Revenue will send you **form 575** to complete and will then estimate the amount of allowance to be transferred. This will then be given to the wife on a provisional basis, either through her PAYE code (if she is employed or receiving an occupational pension) or on her tax assessment (if she is self-employed).

After the end of the tax year, the Revenue will check its estimate. If it was too low, a rebate of tax already paid will be sent to the wife. If the estimate was too high, she will owe some tax which will be collected the following year by adjusting her PAYE code or by altering the tax assessment.

A blind person's allowance is transferred in a similar way.

Transitional allowance

As already mentioned, husbands and wives can't normally transfer any unused portion of their personal allowance to their spouse. But this rule could mean that the total allowances given to a married couple drop simply as a result of the change to independent taxation in 1990–1. To avoid this special rules can be applied where a husband's income was lower than his personal allowance in 1990–1, and they can continue to be applied in 1992–3 and later years, too. These rules mean that a husband can transfer some of his unused personal allowance to his wife – the amount transferred is known as the *transitional allowance*.

To benefit from the transitional allowance rules in the 1992–3 tax year you need to have been eligible for transitional allowance in 1990–1 and 1991–2 as well.

Working out transitional allowance for 1990–1
Slightly different rules apply depending on whether you were married before or during the 1989–90 tax year and what other allowances you were getting before the wedding. But the principle is similar in all cases and the end result is that the total allowances given to a couple in 1990–1 are the same as those in 1989–90.

To claim transitional allowance in 1990–1 all the following must apply:

- the husband's income for 1990–1 must be below his personal allowance, i.e. less than £3,005
- you must have been married and living together since the 1989–90 tax year

- you must not have elected to have the wife's earned income taxed separately from her husband's income in 1989–90.

To work out the transitional allowance for 1990–1:

Step 1 Add up the couple's allowance for 1989–90.

Step 2 Deduct the wife's personal allowance and the married couple's allowance given to her for 1990–1.

Step 3 Deduct the husband's taxable income (or an estimate of it) for 1990–1.

The answer gives the amount of transitional allowance given to the wife in 1990–1. If the husband had no earnings the maximum transitional allowance for a couple not eligible for the higher age related personal allowances was £2,435 in 1990–1.

EXAMPLE 2

Janice and Ian Edwards have three young children and they have decided that Ian should run the house and look after the children while Janice works full time. Ian works in the local pub a couple of nights a week earning about £22 a week.

Step 1 In 1989–90 Ian and Janice's total allowances were the married man's allowance (£4,375) and the wife's earned income allowance (£2,785). The total is **£7,160**.

Step 2 Janice's allowances in 1990–1 are her personal allowance (£3,005) and the married couple's allowance (£1,720), a total of £4,725. Deducting this from the total in Step 1 gives **£2,435**.

Step 3 Ian's earnings in 1990–1 were £1,056. Deducting this amount from the figure in Step 2 gives **£1,379**. This is the amount of Ian's personal allowance that is transferred to Janice as a transitional allowance.

In later years
The amount of allowance that can be transferred in later years is the smaller of:

- the amount of the husband's personal allowance which he can't use himself, *or*
- the amount of allowance transferred from husband to wife the previous year *less* any increase in her personal allowance and the married couple's allowance.

Each tax year a husband can continue to give the unused part of his allowance until it is reduced to nil by the increases in allowance or earnings, or until the marriage ends. The maximum amount of transitional allowance for a couple not eligible for the higher age-related personal allowances in 1991–2 was £2,145 and for 1992–3 is £1,995.

EXAMPLE 3

Janice and Ian's circumstances were virtually unchanged in 1991–2 except that he earned £24 per week (see Example 2 on p. 75). The transitional allowance given for 1992–3 was the lesser of:

- Ian's unused allowance (£3,295 – £1,248 = £2,047), *or*
- the amount of allowance transferred in 1990–1 (£1,379) *less* the increase in Janice's personal allowance (£290) and married couple's allowance (which stayed the same), i.e. £1,379 – £290 = £1,089.
  Janice's transitional allowance is therefore £1,089.

In 1992–3 Ian's earnings totalled £1,600. The transitional allowance available for 1992–3 will be the lesser of:
- Ian's unused allowance (£3,445 – £1,600 = £1,845), *or*
- the amount of allowance transferred in 1991–2 (£1,089) *less* the increase in Janice's personal allowance (£150) – again there was no change in the married couple's allowance – i.e. £1,089 – £150 = £939.

Janice's transitional allowance for 1992–3 is therefore £939.

ICTA 1988 s257, s257B, s257D, s259, s261, s265

Joint investments

If you have investments or savings in joint names, any income you get will be treated automatically as if it were paid to you in equal shares, and each of you will be responsible for paying tax due on your share.

But if you own the investments in unequal shares, the income can be taxed accordingly. For the Revenue to do this you have to make a joint written declaration setting out in what proportions the investment, and consequently the income, are shared between you. This declaration will take effect from the date it is received by the Revenue.

A note of warning: you can't simply choose the proportions that are most convenient for you. You can make a declaration only according to your actual shares of the property and income. Of course, if you decide to split the investments into separate accounts in sole names and the other partner has no control or interest in either the investment or the income, then the income will belong to the partner whose account it is in, and will be taxed accordingly.

ICTA 1988 s282, s282A, s282B

What happens to your mortgage(s) when you marry?

If you and your husband or wife each had a mortgage which qualified for tax relief before you married and you were not living together, and you intend to sell both homes, you can:

- continue to get the tax relief on the old homes for up to twelve months *and*
- jointly get tax relief on up to £30,000 of loans to buy your new home.

Alternatively, if you decide to live in one of your existing homes you can:

- continue to get tax relief on the home you're selling for up to 12 months *and*
- continue to get tax relief, as before, on the home in which you live.

If you were living together before you married and qualified for mortgage interest relief on up to £60,000 on a joint mortgage (because you exchanged contracts before 1 August 1988), you will not get any tax relief on the amount of loan over £30,000 from the date you get married.

Who gets the tax relief on a mortgage?
Normally, the tax relief will be split evenly between you if

you have a joint mortgage, or given to the person in whose name the mortgage is, if it is not a joint one. But you can choose the proportions in which you get the interest relief. Unlike the declaration you have to make about joint assets (see pp. 76–7), you can choose the proportion which is most beneficial to you and your husband or wife. For example, a wife can *elect* to have all the tax relief even though the loan is in her husband's name.

Situations in which it may be worth making an *allocation of interest election* include:

- where one partner is not a taxpayer, or pays only a small amount of tax, and tax relief is not given at source, i.e. the loan is not under the MIRAS scheme (see p. 206)
- where you or your husband or wife is aged 65 or more (see p. 93).
- where the couple have a bridging loan which was taken out (or applied for) before 6 April 1991 and qualifies for tax relief, and either husband or wife pays tax at the higher rate
  SP10/1980; ESCA A35, ICTA 1988; s354, s355, s356A

How to make an allocation of interest election
You need to complete **form 15** which has to be signed by both of you and sent to the Revenue no later than 12 months after the end of the tax year to which you want it to apply.

Once you have made an election it will continue until you choose to change it by completing another form 15, or withdraw it by completing **form 15.1**.

Covenants to charity

Money given to a charity under covenant qualifies for tax relief at your highest rate of tax as long as the covenant is designed to last for more than three years. If you pay tax at basic rate and agree to give a charity £75, you pay only £75, and the charity can claim £25 basic-rate tax relief from the Revenue so the charity gets £100 in total.

Under the old rules for taxation of married couples a wife could make a covenant, but the tax relief would have been claimed by the husband on his Tax Return. However, from the 1990–1 tax year a covenant made by a married woman counts as an outgoing from her own income. If she doesn't pay as much tax as the tax relief due on the covenant she has to pay the balance to the Inland Revenue. If she pays no tax, she has to pay over the whole amount of the tax relief – £25 if she had covenanted £75.

If you find yourself in this situation and if both your husband and the charity agree, you could stop your covenant and start a new one in your husband's name. There is no tax advantage for a non-taxpayer to give money to charity under a covenant.

If you have a joint covenant, then each of you can claim tax relief on half the sum covenanted.

Death of a spouse

In the tax year in which your husband or wife dies, these rules apply:

- **After the death of the wife**, the husband continues, for the rest of the tax year, to get the married couple's allowance in addition to his personal allowance to set against his own income. He can't, for that year, get the additional personal allowance unless his wife was totally incapacitated and he has a dependent child. In the following years, until he remarries, he gets the personal allowance, and any other allowances to which he's entitled. For example, if he has a 'qualifying' child living with him he can claim the additional personal allowance (see p. 88). If the husband remarries within the same tax year, he *doesn't* get the reduced married couple's allowance (see p. 70) – he continues to get the full amount.
- **After the death of the husband**, the wife gets any of the married couple's allowance which her husband had not used against his income up to the date of his death plus the widow's bereavement allowance (see below) plus the additional personal allowance if she has a dependent child living with her after her husband's death – and, of course, her personal allowance. In subsequent years, she gets the personal allowance and any other allowances to which she is entitled.

Widow's bereavement allowance

This can be claimed by a widow in the tax year of her husband's death, and in the following tax year, unless she remarries before that year begins. The allowance is £1,720

in the 1992–3 tax year, no matter when in the year her husband dies.
ICTA1988 s262; IR91

> **If your spouse leaves any money** when he or she dies, see *Inheritance tax*, p. 318, for the tax rules.

Separation and divorce

After separation or divorce, the same income may have to support two households instead of one, so it's vital that you plan your finances carefully. This section shows you how to keep as much money as possible for yourself, your spouse (or ex-spouse) and your children, and how to keep the Revenue's share to a minimum.

Typically, separation or divorce will involve one or both of these:

- the payment of maintenance
- two homes instead of one.

It's important that husband and wife decide *together* the most tax-efficient way of paying maintenance, and the best solution to the housing problem.

The end of the marriage

Your marriage can end by *divorce*, or (for tax purposes) by *separation*. Almost the same tax rules apply in each case. The Revenue treats you as separated if:

- there's a *deed of separation*, or
- there's a *decree of judicial separation*, or
- maintenance is payable under a *court order*, or
- the separation is likely to be *permanent*.
  ICTA1988 s257, s259, s266, s282

If you separate, tell your tax office straight away. Even if you weren't paying tax before, still get in touch with the local tax office – you may have dealings with them later. You can find the address in the telephone book under *Inland Revenue*.

Maintenance – if you pay it

Maintenance payments are regular payments made out of your income to maintain your divorced or separated spouse, or your children, or both. There are two types of maintenance payments:

- **enforceable payments** – if you're legally obliged to make them, e.g. under a deed of separation, or a court order
- **voluntary payments** – if you can't be made to pay up.

You don't get tax relief on any voluntary payments you make.

If you make enforceable maintenance payments, the rules on tax relief vary depending on whom the maintenance is paid to and when the legally binding agreement was made. But even if you pay under a court order certain payments won't qualify for tax relief:

- payments for which you already get tax relief in some other way, e.g. mortgage payments
- payments made under a foreign court order or agreement
- capital payments or lump sums, even if they are paid in instalments.

Agreements made after 15 March 1988
Maintenance paid to your ex-husband or ex-wife You can get tax relief on enforceable payments up to the *maintenance deduction* limit of £1,720 in 1992–3 (i.e. on an amount equal to the married couple's allowance). All periodical payments and any bills you pay on behalf of your spouse count towards this, if they are covered by a court order or other legally binding agreement. But tax relief stops if your ex-husband or ex-wife remarries.

Maintenance paid to children You can't get tax relief for these if payments are made direct to a child and count as a child's own income. (If the wording of the court order says that the money is paid to your ex-spouse for the children, then tax relief is available within the limit shown above.)

Agreements made before 15 March 1988 (in place by 30 June 1988)
Maintenance paid to your ex-husband or ex-wife The tax relief you can get on enforceable payments is limited to the amount of maintenance payments you paid which qualified for tax relief in the 1988–9 tax year. For example, if you paid £2,000 maintenance in the 1988–9 tax year, you'll get tax relief on no more than £2,000 of maintenance payments in future tax years, no matter how much you increase payments. The only exception to this rule is where

the court order provided for automatic increases in payments, e.g. where the maintenance you pay is linked to the rate of inflation. In such circumstances you can get full tax relief on the payments you make.

Maintenance paid to children   The tax relief you get is limited to the amount of maintenance you paid which qualified for tax relief in 1988–9.

Should you switch to the new rules?

If you are getting tax relief under the old rules where the amount of relief is limited to the amount you received in the 1988–9 tax year, in some circumstances you could be better off if you elect to get relief under the new rules.

If you pay maintenance only to an ex-husband or ex-wife and have increased the amount since April 1989, your tax relief will not have been increased to take this extra into account. So if you are still paying less than the maximum maintenance deduction (£1,720 in 1992–3) you would get more relief by switching to the new rules. But if you are also getting tax relief on payments made direct to a child, don't switch to the new rules, as you will lose all the tax relief on these payments.

If the amount of maintenance you pay to an ex-spouse is above the tax relief limit under the new rules (£1,720 in 1992–3) you should not elect to receive the maintenance deduction as it will have the effect of reducing your tax relief.

EXAMPLE 4

Harriet and Charles have been divorced since 1987. When they divorced, Charles was ordered to pay £20 a week maintenance to . Harriet and £10 a week to each of their two children who live with her. In 1988–9 he paid £1,040 to Harriet and £520 to each of the children.

Harriet and Charles have now agreed that she should receive an extra £520 a year maintenance and a new court order is being drawn up. Charles wonders what the situation regarding tax relief is.

As the initial court order was made before the rules changed in 1988, the amount of tax relief that Charles can claim in 1992–3 is limited to the amount he received in the three previous tax years, i.e. £1,040 for the payments to Harriet and another £1,040 for the payments to the children. He won't be able to claim extra tax relief just because he has increased payments.

If Charles elected to get tax relief under the new rules when he increased the maintenance he pays, he would get an extra £520 tax relief for the increase in payments to Harriet; but he will lose the £1,040 relief he gets for payments made to the children.

Charles decides to stick to the old arrangements for tax relief as the total relief he gets will be higher than if he switched.

EXAMPLE 5

Marion and Eric divorced in 1985 when their children had grown up. Eric is unable to work through illness and Marion pays him maintenance under a court order. . She's been paying £25 a week for the last few years, but has increased it to £35 since the start of the 1992–3 tax year.

In the 1988–9 tax year Marion paid £1,300 in maintenance and received this much tax relief. In 1990–1 and 1992–3 she paid the same amount and received tax relief on the same amount. In the 1992–3 tax year she will get the same amount of tax relief even though the total of payments made will be increased to £1,820.

But if Marion elects to get tax relief under the new rules, she can claim a maintenance deduction of £1,720. The amount of tax relief being claimed increases by £420, a tax saving of £105 a year for Marion, who is a basic-rate taxpayer.

How to switch to the new rules
You need to complete **form 142** and return it to the Revenue within 12 months of the end of the tax year to which you want the new rules to apply. So if you want the new rules to apply for the 1992–3 tax year you have until 5 April 1994 to decide. You also have to write to the person to whom you make the payments to let him or her know that you have asked to switch to the new rules.

Once you have made an election, you cannot withdraw it, so make sure that you will be better off by doing so.

How to make the payments
Most enforceable maintenance payments should be paid in full, without deducting any tax. You will get tax relief

through an adjustment to your PAYE code (see p. 131) or it will be shown on your tax assessment (see p. 44) so that you get a lower tax bill.

The exception to this rule is payments made to children once they reach 21 (as long as the court order or agreement has not been changed since 15 March 1988). With these, you get basic-rate tax relief by deducting tax and handing over the net amount. (Any higher-rate tax relief will be given through an adjustment to your PAYE code or your tax assessment.)

Maintenance – if you receive it

Whether you have to pay tax on any maintenance you get depends on whether it's voluntary or enforceable and when the agreement was made.

If you receive *voluntary* maintenance, i.e. the person making payments can't be made to pay up, you don't have to pay tax on what you get.

If you receive *enforceable* maintenance, i.e. it's paid under a court order or other legally binding agreement:

- if the agreement was made after 15 March 1988 (or if it was applied for before then but wasn't in place by 30 June 1988), what you receive is treated as tax-free income
- if the agreement was made before 15 March 1988 (or it was applied for before that date and was in place by 30 June 1988) and you're a divorced or separated spouse, you won't pay tax on the first £1,720 of maintenance you receive in the 1992–3 tax year. Anything over this amount will count as taxable income. But the taxable amount of maintenance is 'pegged' to the amount on which you paid tax in 1988–9. This means that if the amount of maintenance you get increased after 5 April 1989 you won't have to pay tax on the extra you receive. If the person paying maintenance changes to the new rules (see opposite) you won't be taxed on any maintenance you get.
- If the agreement was made before 15 March 1988 and you're a child receiving maintenance from a parent or step-parent the amount that counts for tax is 'pegged' to the amount that was taxable in 1988–9. Any increases since then are not taxable. However, you will only pay tax once your taxable income exceeds your personal allowance. If you are 21 or over the maintenance you

receive will already have had basic-rate tax deducted from it. If you don't have enough income (including the gross amount of maintenance) to pay tax or the amount of tax deducted is higher than your tax bill for the year, you can claim a refund from your tax office.
ICTA 1988 s347A, s347B; FA 1988, s38, s39

Maintenance to a partner you weren't married to
You can end up paying maintenance to a former partner even if you were never married to him or her. If you separate after living together, no tax relief will be available on any maintenance payments whether they are enforceable or voluntary. But the income received from such payments will be tax-free to the recipient.

Claiming social security benefits?

Any payments received by you or your children – whether they're voluntary or enforceable – may be taken into account if you claim means-tested benefits, including income support, family credit, housing or community charge benefit. Check with your local social security office or Citizens Advice Bureau.

Allowances

In the tax year in which you part, you'll get the following allowances:

- a husband will get his own personal allowance plus the full married couple's allowance
- a wife will get her own personal allowance plus the additional personal allowance if she has at least one child living with her.

In following tax years, both ex-partners will get their own personal allowance plus any other allowances they are entitled to, e.g. additional personal allowance (see p. 88) or blind person's allowance (see p. 35). A husband can continue to claim the married couple's allowance if all the following apply:

- he is still married, i.e. is separated but not divorced
- since the separation he has wholly maintained his wife by making voluntary maintenance payments
- he is not claiming an additional personal allowance.

ICTA 1988 s257F

Inheritance tax

Gifts between husband and wife don't count for inheritance tax purposes – and this applies even after separation *right up to the moment of divorce* (i.e. when the decree absolute is granted).

After divorce, the following gifts are normally tax-free:

- maintenance for your ex-spouse or children
- transfers made under the divorce settlement
- in some cases, money given to you following a change to an agreement you made on or before your divorce – get professional advice
- gifts which would, in any case, be tax-free, e.g. those made out of your income as part of your normal spending. See *Inheritance Tax*, p. 318, for more details.

What happens to your home?

After separation or divorce, you and your ex-spouse will probably need *two* homes instead of one, which may mean two mortgages. Below, we explain the rules about tax relief on mortgage interest, and show you how to keep your tax bill to a minimum.

The general rules
You get basic-rate tax relief on the interest you pay on up to £30,000 (in total) of loans to buy your only or main home. Until 6 April 1988 you could also get tax relief on loans for home improvements and for buying a home for a dependent relative or for a former husband or wife, though these all counted towards the overall limit of £30,000. If you took out a loan for one of these purposes before that date you can continue to get tax relief.

From the date of separation or divorce (whichever comes first) each of you can get tax relief on interest you pay on a mortgage of up to £30,000. So you can each get tax relief if you each take out a mortgage for your own home.

Maximising tax relief
If one of you is faced with having to pay two mortgages, you need to arrange your affairs so that you get two lots of mortgage relief:

- **If you sell the old home and each buy a new home** you will each get tax relief on up to £30,000 of your mortgage, provided you pay the interest yourself.

- **If one of you stays in the old home** he or she can get tax relief on any increase in the mortgage (up to the limit of £30,000) needed to buy out the other person's share or interest in the home.

If your ex-spouse can't afford it

If you are not paying maintenance up to the amount on which you can get tax relief (see p. 82) you could increase payments (remembering that they have to be enforceable in order to claim tax relief). Your tax bill will decrease and your ex-spouse will find it easier to make mortgage payments. His or her income will rise, but the tax bill stays the same as maintenance isn't taxable.

Raising a lump sum

You might need to raise a lump sum for your ex-spouse – to enable him or her to buy a new home while you stay on in the old one. But if you have to borrow to raise the lump sum, make sure you get tax relief on the interest you pay.

You could raise a lump sum by taking out a mortgage (or a second mortgage) on the old home, and the interest on this loan would qualify for tax relief *provided* it's used to buy out the other person's share. So if, for example, the old home is owned jointly by you and your ex-spouse, you can specify that the lump sum is being used to buy out their share.

Even if the house is in your name only, your ex-spouse may still have an interest in it which you cannot buy out. For example, the interest could be the right to occupy the home. Make sure that the separation or divorce agreement says that you're buying out this interest – then you'll still get tax relief.

ICTA 1988 s354, s355, s356A

Transferring the home

You don't normally have to pay *capital gains tax* if you sell or give away your only or main home – see p. 207. But if you transfer the home to your ex-spouse, things are more complicated.

If you move out and transfer the home to your ex-spouse, you won't have to pay CGT, provided the transfer takes place within three years of the separation. But after three years, part of the gain you make on the transfer *is* a chargeable gain, unless:

- your ex-spouse has lived in the home ever since you moved out, *and*
- you haven't yet chosen another home as your main residence for CGT purposes.

If you stay in the old home and your ex-spouse moves out, you can later transfer it to him or her without having to pay CGT, provided you haven't chosen another home as your main residence.
ICTA1988 s354–s357, s369; TCGA 1992 s222–3

Capital gains tax

A husband and wife are each allowed to make net taxable gains of £5,800 in the 1992–3 tax year before having to pay CGT. Gifts between husband and wife don't count for CGT purposes – but this doesn't apply if you're divorced or (except in the tax year of separation) if you're separated.
TCGA 1992 s3, s58

Tax if you have children

If you've got children, it may make a difference to *your* tax bill. Here, we deal with things you may need to watch out for.

Additional personal allowance

The additional personal allowance is equal to the basic married couple's allowance – £1,720 in the 1992–3 tax year. You can claim it (in addition to your personal allowance) if you have a dependent child and:

- you are a single person (whether or not you are living with someone as man and wife)
- you are a married woman separated from your husband
- you are a woman who married after the start of the tax year and who had a child living with you before you got married
- you are a married man who doesn't get the married couple's allowance because you are separated from your wife
- you are a married man whose wife will be totally incapacitated throughout the tax year.

In order to claim additional personal allowance, you must have one or more 'qualifying' children living with you for all or part of the tax year. A qualifying child is one who is under 16 at the start of the tax year, *or* who is in full-time education, *or* who is undergoing full-time training (lasting at least two years) for a trade, profession or vocation.

The child must be either:

- your legitimate (or legitimated) child, step-child or legally adopted child, or
- any other child who is under 18 at the start of the tax year, and whom you maintain at your own expense (a younger brother or sister, say).

If two people can claim the additional personal allowance for the same child (i.e. if the child lives with each of them for part of the year), the allowance is divided between them in agreed proportions. If they can't agree, the allowance is divided in proportion to the time the child spends with each of them during the year.

Note that the amount you can claim doesn't depend on the number of children you're bringing up: the most you can get is £1,720 whether you have one child or ten. And if you're not married but living with someone as man and wife, you can get only one additional personal allowance between you.

Your children's income

This section describes how children's income is taxed, and how to make the most of your child's tax-free allowances.

Income

No matter how young your children are, they will be taxed on their earned income just as if they were adults. They will also be taxed on their investment income, unless the investment was given to them by their parents, in which case it will usually be taxed as the parent's income (see opposite).

Grants or scholarships to pay for children's education don't count as their income, and so don't affect their tax bill. But if the scholarship is paid by the parent's employer as a perk of the job, the parent may be taxed on it – see the table on p. 151 for details.

Allowances

Children can also claim allowances in the same way as adults. All children are entitled to the basic personal allowance (£3,445 in the 1992–3 tax year), which means that they can have income of £3,445 before they have to pay any tax. And if they qualify for any other allowances, this figure will be even higher. For example, a 17-year-old bringing up a younger brother or sister at his or her own expense could claim the additional personal allowance – £1,720 in the 1992–3 tax year – on top of the basic personal allowance.

Children's investment income

Remember that children can have income of at least £3,445 before they have to pay tax. But investment income is often paid after basic-rate tax has been deducted. So if your child gets investment income, and this income (including the gross amounts) is £3,445 or less, any tax deducted can be claimed back from the Revenue. For how to claim tax back, see p. 91. If the income comes from a building society or bank (other than the National Savings Bank) account, you should complete **form R85** and hand it in to the institution, in which case tax won't be deducted at source – see p. 236. Tax won't be deducted from the income from National Savings Children's Bonus Bonds.

If *parents* give a child something which produces investment income – e.g. if they open up a National Savings Investment account for their child – the income is usually taxed as the parents' income, unless the child is 18 or over, or married.

There are two exceptions to this rule:

- if the income which comes from investments given by the parents is less than £100, or
- if the parents set up an *accumulation trust* for the child and the interest is 'accumulated' (i.e. not spent) until the child reaches 18, or marries.

  ICTA 1988 s64, s234, s468 (investment income); s343 (building society interest); s165, s331 (scholarships); s663–s670 (settlements on children)

How to check your child's tax bill

Write down all the sources of your child's income, the *gross* (i.e. before deduction of tax) amounts and how much tax (if any) has already been deducted. It might help if you fill in a

Tax Return for your child (you can ask your tax office to send you one).

Then write down all your child's outgoings and allowances, to work out the tax-free income he or she is entitled to receive. If the gross income is less than or equal to tax-free income, then your child shouldn't be paying tax, and you can claim back any that has already been deducted.

If the child's gross income is *more* than his or her tax-free income, work out how much tax is due on the difference. If this is less than the amount already deducted, you can claim back the difference.

If you find that your child is due a rebate you can reclaim it using the special Tax Claim **form R232** – obtainable from your tax office. And the child can make his or her own claims if the tax was deducted from income 'within his or her control' – e.g. if tax was deducted from the child's earnings from a holiday job.

Check your children's tax bills every year, and make sure you reclaim any tax overpaid. Don't forget that you can also reclaim any tax owing from the previous six years – see p. 19 for more information.

But note that if your child *owes* any tax, then you, as the parent or guardian, are responsible for paying it out of your own income, if the tax isn't paid from the child's income.

Tax and students

As a student, you may have to pay tax, just like anyone else. But certain things don't normally count as income for tax purposes:

- student grants from a local education authority (LEA)
- parental contributions – unless paid under a deed of covenant (see p. 32)
- certain non-LEA discretionary grants – e.g. from the DSS
- post-graduate grants from one of the research councils
- most other awards or scholarships – but always check with your tax office.

If you are being sponsored through college (e.g. by a company or by one of the armed forces), or if you are on a sandwich course, the money paid to you to cover the time spent *at college* is usually tax-free – but, again, check with your tax office. The money paid to cover the time you spend *at work*, however, does count as your income for tax purposes.

Any income which isn't tax-free is added together and, if it comes to more than your outgoings and allowances, you'll have to pay tax on the excess.
ICTA 1988 s331; SP4/86; IR 60

Vacation jobs

Earnings from vacation jobs count as income. But you and your employer can fill in a form to say that your total earnings, plus all your other income for the year, won't exceed the personal allowance – and then tax won't be deducted under PAYE. You can get the form (called **P38S**) from tax offices.

---

5 WHEN YOU ARE OLDER

Older people are liable to tax on their income in the same way as anyone else. But many people over 64 pay less tax than a younger person receiving the same income. In this chapter we look at special age-related allowances. We also look at other aspects of income tax which are likely to be of special concern to older or retired people.

Higher personal and married couple's allowances

If you were 64 or over before the start of the tax year, i.e. you will be 65 at some time during the tax year, you qualify for an increased personal allowance (depending on your 'total income' – see overleaf). This higher personal allowance is up to £4,200 for the 1992–3 tax year, compared with the basic personal allowance of £3,445. So if you pay basic-rate tax on up to £755 less of your income, you can make a saving of up to £188.75 (25 per cent of £755). If you were 74 or over before the start of the tax year, the maximum allowance goes up to £4,370 – a further saving of up to £42.50.

Similarly, the married couple's allowance can go up to £2,465 if either partner was 64 before the start of the tax year, and £2,505 if either became 74 before the start of the tax year.

You won't get the full amount of the extra allowances if your total income is above a certain amount – £14,200 in the 1992–3 tax year. The extra allowance will be reduced by £1 for every £2 by which your total income exceeds this limit. Husband and wife each have a total income limit of £14,200.

The amount of married couple's allowance is always based on the husband's total income:

- even if he qualifies for the extra allowance because of his wife's age, i.e. she is 64 (or 74) before the start of the tax year but he isn't

- even if he has transferred part or all of the married couple's allowance to his wife (see p. 72) and her total income exceeds £14,200.

When a married man starts to lose the extra allowances, it is his personal allowance which is reduced first. When it has been reduced to the level of the basic personal allowance, he may then start to lose the extra married couple's allowance.

Your allowances will never be reduced to below the basic personal or married couple's allowances.

Younger husbands and independent taxation

If you qualified for the married man's age allowance in the 1989–90 year because of your wife's age, under the independent taxation of husband and wife which started on 6 April 1990, you could be worse off. However, you can claim a special allowance instead of your basic personal allowance if your married couple's allowance added to your basic personal allowance is less than you received in 1989–90. The special allowance is equal to the single age allowance for your wife's age group in 1989–90. You carry on getting the special allowance in future tax years until your basic personal allowance is more than the special allowance, or until your marriage ends. Of course, the special allowance will be reduced if you exceed the total income limit.
ICTA 1988 s257

Total income

Your 'total income' is, basically, your gross income less your outgoings. It doesn't include any tax-free income, but *does* include the gross amount of any building society or bank interest – see pp. 36 and 236. Add up your gross (before-tax) income for the tax year, then deduct your tax-allowable outgoings (but *not* your allowances).

Adding up your income Don't forget to include the gross amount of any interest from which basic-rate tax has been deducted before you get it, e.g. building society or bank interest and the whole of any taxable gain on a life insurance policy. Ignore any tax-free income, e.g. from National Savings Certificates.

Deducting your outgoings Remember to deduct all income on which you don't pay tax, including:

- interest you pay which qualifies for tax relief. If you have a mortgage and pay the interest net of tax under MIRAS deduct the gross amount of interest – get this figure from the lender
- pension contributions you pay and payments you make to a personal pension
- half of any Class 4 National Insurance that you pay if you're self-employed
- the gross amount of covenant payments to charity and other covenants drawn up before 15 March 1988
- donations under the payroll giving scheme
- the gross amount of maintenance payments on which you can get tax relief
- tax-free profit-related pay
- any other outgoings.

'Total income' over £14,200 – beware!

If your 'total income' for the tax year looks as though it will be above £14,200 but below the point at which you lose the benefit of age-related allowances altogether, you should select your investments carefully. If you have investments which produce income which is included in your 'total income', you would almost certainly benefit by exchanging them for investments which are tax-free (like National Savings Certificates). This applies equally to interest from building societies and banks (which is 'tax-paid', *not* tax-free) and to gains on certain life insurance policies – see Example 2 on p. 106.

The sliding scale

If your total income is more than £14,200, your extra allowances are reduced by half the excess. For example, if you're aged 73, your personal allowance could be £4,200. But if your total income is £14,500, this is £300 more than £14,200, and your allowance would be reduced by ½ of £300 = £150. Your personal allowance would be £4,200 − £150 = £4,050.

The table overleaf shows what your age-related allowances would be for different example levels of 'total income'.

total income £	personal allowance 65–74 [1] £	married couple's allowance 65–74 [1] £	personal allowance 75+ [1] £	married couple's allowance 75+ [1] £
14,200	4,200	2,465	4,370	2,505
14,300	4,150	2,465	4,320	2,505
14,400	4,100	2,465	4,270	2,505
14,500	4,050	2,465	4,220	2,505
14,600	4,000	2,465	4,170	2,505
14,700	3,950	2,465	4,170	2,505
14,800	3,900	2,465	4,070	2,505
14,900	3,850	2,465	4,020	2,505
15,000	3,800	2,465	3,970	2,505
15,100	3,750	2,465	3,920	2,505
15,200	3,700	2,465	3,870	2,505
15,300	3,650	2,465	3,820	2,505
15,400	3,600	2,465	3,770	2,505
15,500	3,550	2,465	3,720	2,505
15,600	3,500	2,465	3,670	2,505
15,700	3,450	2,465	3,620	2,505
15,710	3,445	2,465	3,615	2,505
15,800	3,445	2,420	3,570	2,505
15,900	3,445	2,370	3,520	2,505
16,000	3,445	2,320	3,470	2,505
16,050	3,445	2,295	3,445	2,505
16,100	3,445	2,270	3,445	2,480
16,200	3,445	2,220	3,445	2,430
16,300	3,445	2,170	3,445	2,380
16,400	3,445	2,120	3,445	2,330
16,500	3,445	2,070	3,445	2,280
16,600	3,445	2,020	3,445	2,230
16,700	3,445	1,970	3,445	2,180
16,800	3,445	1,920	3,445	2,130
16,900	3,445	1,870	3,445	2,080
17,000	3,445	1,820	3,445	2,030
17,100	3,445	1,770	3,445	1,980
17,200	3,445	1,720	3,445	1,930
17,300	3,445	1,720	3,445	1,880
17,400	3,445	1,720	3,445	1,830
17,500	3,445	1,720	3,445	1,780
17,600	3,445	1,720	3,445	1,730
17,620	3,445	1,720	3,445	1,720

[1] Age at any time during the tax year

Using the table
Find your 'total income' and then read off your personal allowance. If you are married, you each have a personal allowance and together you can get the married couple's allowance. Read across to find the amount you are entitled to.

How pensions are taxed

Some pensions are tax-free. But others are taxable. The following pensions are taxable and normally count as earned income:

- **state retirement pension** including any graduated pension, additional pension (i.e. SERPS) or invalidity addition you receive
- **non-contributory retirement pension** for people of 80 or over who are getting less than the normal state retirement pension
- **pension from a former employer** paid to a former employee or his/her widow/widower and/or dependants
- **personal (or self-employed) pension**, but if you weren't eligible for tax relief on all the payments you made into the plan, part of the pension counts as investment income
- **partnership retirement annuity**, but part may count as investment income if certain conditions are not met.

Married woman's state retirement pension

A married woman's state retirement pension counts as her income if based on her own National Insurance contributions. And since 6 April 1990, a pension based on her husband's contributions counts as her income, too. But any *adult dependency addition* her husband gets with his pension while she is under 60 will count, for income tax purposes, as his income.

Tax on state retirement pensions

Although the state retirement pension is taxable, tax isn't deducted from it before it is paid. If you get an age-related allowance, and the basic state pension is your only income, you won't have to pay any tax because the pension comes to less than the allowance. But there may be some tax to pay if your state pension, added to any other taxable income you get (e.g. a pension from your former employer or investment income), comes to more than your total outgoings and allowances.

The amount of pension which will be included in your income is the total of the weekly amounts payable over the tax year. This applies even if your pension is paid monthly or quarterly.

97

Annuities from pension schemes and plans

An annuity you've bought voluntarily is taxed differently from an annuity which comes from an employer's or personal pension scheme – see p. 100.

If the annuity was provided by a pension scheme you've belonged to, the *full* amount of what you get is taxable but treated as earned income. Many insurance companies will deduct tax from each payment under PAYE, so the correct amount of tax should be deducted. Other companies will deduct tax at the basic rate, but if your income is too low for you to pay tax, ask the company for a form to send to your tax office to advise it of your income. The company can then make each payment in full, without deducting tax.

ICTA 1988 s656, s657 (annuities); s597 (pensions)

Pensions from abroad

You are normally liable for tax on nine-tenths of any pension from abroad, whether or not it is brought into the UK. With certain pensions, only half the amount is taxable, and certain war widows' pensions are tax-free. Pensions from abroad are generally taxed on a *preceding year* basis, so your 1992–3 tax bill will be based on nine-tenths of any pension you got from abroad during 1991–2. Note that pensions paid to the victims of Nazi persecution by the governments of West Germany and Austria are tax-free.

ICTA 1988 s196, s330

How tax is collected on pensions

If you get a pension from your former employer, the tax due on the whole of your income will, as far as possible, have been collected under PAYE from your employer's pension. You may find on your Notice of Coding that the amounts of state pension and any untaxed investment income the Revenue expected you to receive over the tax year have been subtracted from your allowances. This can make it look as though your employer's pension is being taxed at a higher rate than your earnings were before you retired.

If you don't get a pension from a former employer, and your state pension plus any other income comes to more than your total outgoings and allowances, you will be sent a special Notice of Assessment, unless the tax on the excess comes to £70 or less, in which case the tax is not normally collected.

If you've paid too much tax on your investments

With many types of investments, such as certain British Government stocks, income is paid after tax, at the basic rate, has been deducted. The same applies to income you get from a covenant taken out before 15 March 1988 (and from certain types of trusts), and to some alimony or maintenance payments (see p. 84). With dividends and most unit trust distributions, you will get tax credits. If you don't pay tax – or if your tax bill comes to less than the total of tax deducted plus tax credits received – you will have paid too much tax. So you should claim a rebate.

If you are in a situation like this you may well be sent a special Tax Claim **form R40** instead of the normal kind of Tax Return. You should fill it in and send it back to your tax office with your tax vouchers (which give details of tax deducted and tax credits). You don't need to wait until the end of the tax year to do this: claim as soon as you have received all your relevant investment income for the year (i.e. income paid with a tax credit or after tax has been deducted). Note that the Revenue will pay claims part way through the tax year only if they are for more than £50. If you reclaim less than £50, you won't be paid until the end of the tax year.

The Revenue will work out how much tax you are owed (if any) and send you a rebate. Arrangements can be made for repayment of tax by instalments during the year – ask your tax office for details.

If you have to claim tax back regularly but aren't sent form R40, ask your tax office for it. If you claim only occasionally, write to your tax office, giving details of why you are claiming and how much you are claiming (if you know).

Private medical insurance

Since 6 April 1990, tax relief has been available on certain private medical insurance policies for people aged 60 and over. Broadly speaking, policies which qualify are the typical policies which pay for conventional medical treatment, but with one exception: they should not pay a cash benefit if you opt to be treated under the National Health Service instead of going privately. There should be no need to work out whether your policy qualifies – your insurer will be able to tell you (and will be able to advise on switching to a policy which does qualify, if necessary).

Even non-taxpayers can benefit from this relief, as basic-rate tax relief is paid directly by the government to the insurer; your insurer should charge you the net premium. If you pay tax at the new 20 per cent rate, you will still get the benefit of tax relief at the higher basic rate. Higher-rate taxpayers will have to claim the extra relief from their tax office and will get it either through their PAYE code or by getting a lower tax bill.

The tax-relief is available to *anyone* who pays eligible private medical insurance premiums on behalf of someone who is 60 or over (as well as to people who pay the premiums themselves). This means that if someone who pays your premiums is a higher-rate taxpayer, he or she will be able to claim higher-rate relief.

The relief is available on joint policies which a husband and wife have, even if only one is 60 or over.
FA 1989 s54–s57

Annuities

An annuity offers an income for life, and favourable tax treatment. But it's an offer you should refuse if you're under 75 (if a woman) or under 70 (if a man).

What is an annuity?

With an annuity, you hand over your money to an insurance company in return for a guaranteed income for the rest of your life. The older you are at the time you buy the annuity, the higher the income you can get; and a man gets a higher income than a woman of the same age (on average, men don't live as long). To give an example: in return for handing over £10,000, a 75-year-old woman who paid tax at the basic rate could (in April 1992) have got an income before tax of about £1,500 for life, however long she lived. But what you get depends on interest rates at the time you buy the annuity – five years earlier, for example, the income would have been only £1,300 a year. Note, however, that once you have handed over your money, you cannot ask for it back.

Type of annuity

This section deals with *immediate annuities*. With these, the company starts paying you the income 'immediately' – which is insurance language for six months after you buy the annuity (although it can be sooner, at a price). There are also *deferred annuities*, where you pay a lump sum now and arrange for the income to start much further in the future; deferred annuities form the basis of some personal pension plans (see p. 308). The most common type of immediate annuity is a *level annuity* where the income is the same each year. For a given outlay, this type gives you the largest income to start with – though, of course, inflation is likely to erode its buying-power over the years. Another type is an *increasing annuity*, where your income increases regularly by an amount you decide on when you buy.

A *single life* annuity stops when the person buying it dies. A *joint life and survivor* annuity carries on until both the person buying the annuity and someone else, usually a wife or husband, are dead.

Should you buy?

Whether or not an annuity proves to be a good buy in the long run depends on three imponderables:

- how long you will live; obviously an annuity will be a better buy if you live for years and years after buying it
- what happens to interest rates (and therefore annuity rates) after you have bought your annuity. If they go up, you'll be left with a relatively poor-value annuity – if they go down, you have a bargain
- the longer-term effect of inflation on the buying-power of your income.

So weighing up these uncertainties with the one certainty that you lose control of your capital, we conclude that annuities are not a good buy for women under 75 or men under 70. Only for people over these ages does the extra income offered by an annuity – as compared with conventional investments – become a compelling argument. And even then think carefully before buying, be quite sure that you are willing to part with the capital you use, and shop around for the best company.

Tax treatment

If you have bought the annuity with your own money, part of the income from it is treated for tax purposes as your initial outlay being returned to you, and is tax-free. The remainder of the annuity income counts as interest (i.e. as investment income) and is taxable.

The insurance company normally deducts tax at the basic rate from the taxable part of your income before paying you. If you are liable for less tax than the insurance company deducts, for example, you pay tax at the 20 per cent rate, you can claim tax back from the Revenue. If your taxable income from all sources – including income from the *taxable* part of the annuity – is equal to or less than your age-related allowances (see p. 93), you can apply to have your annuity income paid without deduction of tax by completing **form R89**.

The amount of the tax-free part of the income – called the capital element – is worked out according to Inland Revenue rules. It is a proportion of the income from the annuity. For each type of annuity the tax-free amount is based on your age when you buy the annuity, the amount you pay for it, how often the income is paid and whether payments are guaranteed for a period even if you die.

A man gets a larger tax-free amount than a woman (corresponding to his shorter life expectancy).

With increasing annuities, the tax-free amount increases at the same rate as the income from the annuity increases. For example, for a 75-year-old woman buying an annuity that increases by five per cent a year, the tax-free amount in the first year would be £66.40 for each £1,000 spent on the annuity (much less than the £94.16 for a level annuity) but increasing by five per cent each year.

An annuity is treated in this special way only if you buy it voluntarily with your own money, not if it's bought for you by, say, a pension scheme (when the whole of the income from the annuity is taxable and counts as earned income).
ICTA 1988 s18(2)–(4) (taxed as interest); s656, s657, s658 (tax-free element)

Tax warning: annuities and age-related allowances

By and large, if you buy an annuity out of your savings or investments which had been giving you a taxable income, you don't have to worry about the possible effect on age-related allowances (see p. 93). The chances are, in a case like this, that the *taxable* part of your annuity income will be less – or in any event not much higher – than the taxable income you were getting from your savings (a large part of the income from an annuity, remember, is tax-free).

But if you buy the annuity with savings or investments that were *not* earning you a taxable income, and if you are at present getting the benefit of age-related allowances, you might find that your allowance is reduced. The same could apply if, for example, the annuity is bought for you by your pension scheme (in which case the whole of the annuity income is taxable).

EXAMPLE 1

Shirley Alpine, 75, lives alone on a state retirement pension of £2,815 for the full 1992–3 tax year. She also receives alimony from her former husband totalling £11,665 gross, before deduction of tax; of this £9,945 is taxable (see p. 84). She has no outgoings. Her 'total income' (see p. 95) works out as follows:

state retirement pension	£2,815
taxable part of alimony	£9,945
'total income'	£12,760

Since her 'total income' is under £14,200, she qualifies for an age-related allowance of £4,370. The amount of income on which she will pay tax is £12,760 − £4,370 = £8,390.

To boost her income, she decided to cash in her National Savings Certificates and Premium Bonds (which she's had no luck with) and is thinking of spending the full £25,000 proceeds on an annuity, which will bring in £4,550 a year before tax. The tax-free capital element of the annuity is £2,354, so the remaining £2,196 would be taxable. Her new 'total income' works out as:

state retirement pension	£2,815
taxable part of alimony	£9,945
taxable part of annuity	£2,196
'total income'	£14,956

Shirley's 'total income' is £756 over the £14,200 limit. Her age-related allowance would therefore be reduced by half of £756, i.e. £378.

Because Shirley's taxable income is well over the £2,000 band for tax at 20 per cent (see p. 00), she would be paying tax at 25 per cent not only on the £2,196 taxable part of the annuity income,

103

but also on an additional £378 of income, which is the amount by which her allowance is reduced. The effect of the reduction in her allowances is to increase Shirley's expected tax bill for the annuity by £94.50 to £643.50. So she thinks again and decides to buy a smaller annuity while hanging on to some of her investments.

Home income schemes

If you're elderly and own your own home, you may be able to boost your income with a home income scheme. Some of these schemes, which we describe here, have tax advantages. A 75-year-old woman, for example, with a home worth £40,000, could increase her income after basic-rate tax by about £1,600 a year. A man of 75 would get about £700 more.

The basics

Whoever is running the scheme – a building society or insurance company – arranges a loan for you based on the security of your home. Provided you are 65 or over and the money from the loan is used to buy an annuity for you, you'll qualify for basic-rate tax relief on up to £30,000 of the loan. While you live, you get the income from the annuity – after deduction of loan interest and basic-rate tax (see overleaf). When you die, the loan is repaid out of your estate (possibly, but not necessarily, from the sale of your home).

Basic-rate tax relief is given to you under the MIRAS scheme – which means that the building society or insurance company will allow for tax relief at 25 per cent on the loan interest when working out how much income to hand over to you. You get the benefit of this 'tax relief' in full, even if you pay little or no tax.

The schemes are available for freehold houses, and for leasehold property with a substantial part of the lease still to run (50 to 80 years, depending on the company). The most you can borrow is a percentage (e.g. 65 or 80 per cent) of the market value of your home. There's usually a minimum and maximum loan (and normally not more than £30,000, which is the maximum on which you can get tax relief). You may be able to take part of the loan in cash in return for a rather lower income.

Inflation will reduce the buying power of your fixed income from these schemes, but it correspondingly reduces the value of your debt – so rising prices don't work wholly against you. And provided that the value of your home goes up, you may be able to use the increase in value to get a further loan which could be used to buy another annuity. *ICTA 1988 s365*

How a home income scheme works

Step 1   You mortgage your home to the tune of £25,000 and get in return an annuity of, say, £3,160.

Step 2   Before you receive the annuity income, basic-rate tax is deducted from the taxable part of the annuity, say, £200.

Step 3   The mortgage interest you owe is also deducted (after first deducting basic-rate tax relief), say, £1,550.

Step 4   So the extra income you are left with is £3,160 – £200 – £1,550, which equals £1,410.

Should you buy?

It makes very good sense for an elderly person to be able to continue to live in his or her own home, while spending some of the accumulated value of that home. But the financial arguments may be less favourable. It would be realistic to assume that the elderly person concerned may not always be able to cope alone and may sell up and move in with relatives. In this situation, someone who has taken out a home income scheme could lose out (particularly if left with a rather poor-value annuity).

Some types of scheme may land your heirs with a debt when you die, particularly if property prices are falling. Others are linked to investment bonds, rather than an annuity. The value of the bonds can decrease as well as rise, so there may not be enough money to pay both the mortgage and your income.

All in all, a home income scheme is a useful last resort – but try other ways of increasing your income first.

Age-related allowances

If, before taking out a home income scheme, you were

getting the benefit of age-related allowances (see p. 93), the chances are that you will continue to benefit. And if age-related allowance was in your case restricted (because your 'total income' was over £14,200) you may well find that your allowance will be *increased*. This welcome, but rather unexpected, state of affairs comes about because the gross mortgage interest is deducted from your gross income in working out your 'total income'.

EXAMPLE 2

Before taking out a home income scheme, Mrs Anna Smythe, a 75-year-old widow, who has no outgoings, had a 'total income' of:

state retirement pension	£2,815
pension from former employer	£13,259
'total income'	£16,074

Mrs Smythe's total income was therefore £1,874 over the £14,200 limit. Her age-related allowance was cut by half of £1,874, i.e. £937 was deducted from the allowance of £4,370. But the age allowance will never be reduced to below the level of the basic personal allowance of £3,445, which is what Mrs Smythe will get.

However, Mrs Smythe's tax situation looked very different after taking out a home income plan with a loan of £15,000. Her 'total income' then worked out as:

state retirement pension	£2,815
pension from former employer	£13,259
taxable part of annuity	£468
gross income	£16,542
less outgoings: gross mortgage interest	£1,350
'total income'	£15,192

Her total income is now only £992 over the £14,200 limit. Her age-related allowance will therefore be reduced by half of £992, i.e. £496. This leaves Mrs Smythe with £3,874 of age-related allowance, which is £429 *more* than she had before taking out the home income scheme. Her after-tax income goes up by not just the money from the home income scheme (about £810 a year), but by a further 25 per cent of £429, i.e. £107.25, because of her increased age-related allowance.

If you don't pay tax

You still get the benefit of the basic-rate 'tax relief' on the mortgage. And you should claim back from the Revenue the basic-rate tax deducted from the interest element of the annuity. You may be able to arrange for this tax not to be deducted in the first place – see p. 102.

6 *SOCIAL SECURITY*

If you're getting social security benefits, you may think you don't have to worry about tax at all. For many people this will be true, as the majority of benefits are not taxable. But pensioners, widows, sick and unemployed people could all find themselves in the tax net. This chapter explains the rules.

Tax and benefits

	tax-free	taxable
Unemployed or on strike	Part (or all) of income support.	Unemployment benefit. Sometimes part (or all) of income support.
Families with children	Maternity allowance. Maternity payments from social fund. Child benefit. One-parent benefit. Child's special allowance. Guardian's allowance. Family credit.	Statutory maternity pay.
Elderly people	Income support.	Retirement pensions (except additions for children). Old person's or over-80s pension.
Widows	Widow's payment. Additions paid for children. War widow's pension (including allowances for children and rent).	Widowed mother's allowance. Widow's pension.
Disabled or sick	Sickness benefit. Invalidity benefit. Severe disablement allowance. Attendance allowance. Disability working allowance. Disability living allowance. Disablement benefits paid because of injury	Statutory sick pay. Invalid care allowance (except additions paid for children). Invalidity allowance paid with retirement pension.

Disabled or sick (cont.)	at work or an industrial disease. Disablement pensions paid as a result of service in the forces or the merchant navy or to civilians for war injuries. Extra pension paid to police and fire staff injured on duty, beyond what they'd have got if retired through ill-health.	
Other benefits	Income support (if not unemployed, on short-time work or on strike). £10 Christmas bonus. Housing benefit (i.e. rent rebate). Community charge benefit. Funeral payments from social fund. Some annuities and pension additions for gallantry awards such as the George Cross. Benefits paid by foreign governments similar to tax-free UK benefits. YT (Youth Training) allowance. Special pensions paid by the governments of West Germany and Austria to UK victims of Nazi persecution.	Enterprise allowance.

ICTA 1988 s617, s638

How are benefits taxed?

Taxable benefits are paid gross – i.e. before any tax is deducted – and are taxed as the earned income of the person claiming benefit. If you're claiming extra benefit for your spouse (or someone living with you as your spouse), it is taxed as your income. The one exception to this rule is where a man is claiming an increase in his state pension for his wife, when the extra will be taxed as if it were her income. Tax-free benefits shouldn't be entered on your Tax Return, but you do need to give very basic details of any taxable benefit you've received during the tax year.

At current rates of benefits and tax-free allowances, if your only taxable income is state benefits, you probably won't owe any tax. But if you have other income that puts your taxable income above your total outgoings and allowances, there'll be tax to pay. Special rules apply if you're off sick (see p. 113) or claiming unemployment benefit or income support because you're unemployed – see overleaf.

109

For other benefits, if you are working (or getting an employer's pension), any tax due will be collected through PAYE. It will look as if you are paying much more tax than others earning the same amount. But this is because *all* the tax due on your benefits is being collected at the same time as tax on your pay. See example on p. 112.

Special codes

If your taxable state benefits are greater than your tax-free allowances and you're taxed under PAYE, your earnings (or employer's pension) will have to be taxed at a higher-than-normal rate, e.g. at 30 per cent rather than 25 per cent, to collect the tax on your state benefits. Your tax code will then include the letter F (F will be replaced by K from 5 April 1993).

If you're not taxed under PAYE

You will be sent a Notice of Assessment telling you how much tax you owe on your benefits. But the Inland Revenue does not want to be bothered with collecting small amounts of tax, so won't normally send you an assessment if your total tax bill (*including* the tax on your benefits) would be less than £70. Above £70, you pay tax on the lot.

In the past, this *assessing tolerance* was quite important to some people (particularly widows and single women aged 60 to 64) receiving taxable state benefits, because the total amount of benefit they had in a year was a little bit higher than their personal allowance. They would technically have had to pay tax on their benefits, even if these were their only source of income. But because the tax due was less than the assessing tolerance, they didn't have to pay the tax.

Tax if you're unemployed

If you are unemployed and have to be available for work to be able to get benefits, some or all of the benefit you get will be taxable. The same applies if you're claiming benefits because you've been laid off or are on short-time work. To find out how much of what you get is taxable, have a look at the table overleaf. If you're in any doubt, check with your local social security office.

Note that if you are on strike or involved in a strike you

won't get benefits for yourself. But you can claim income support (IS) for your partner (whether you're married or not) and for any dependent children. The taxable part is either the weekly amount paid to you, or half the income support personal allowance, i.e. half of £66.60 (half of £50.60 if you're both under 18).

How much of your benefit is taxable?

Standard weekly rates of benefits 1992–3 Unemployment benefit	Under state pension age	Over state pension age
Basic benefit	£43.10	£54.15
Addition for dependent adult	£26.60	£32.55
Addition for each dependent child	–	£10.85

If you get only unemployment benefit (UB):

	taxable	tax-free
	What you get for yourself and your husband or wife (or someone who looks after your child)	Any increase for children (but there is no extra benefit for children unless you are over pension age)

If you get income support (IS), whether or not you also get UB:

	taxable	tax-free
For a couple	What you get in IS (or in IS plus UB) *or* the standard weekly rate of UB for a couple, whichever is smaller	The rest of your benefit
For the single person	What you get in IS (or in IS plus UB) *or* the standard weekly rate of UB for a single person, whichever is smaller	The rest of your benefit

How much tax?

If you are unemployed and living on benefits for a full year with no other taxable income, your total taxable benefit will be below your allowances – see p. 34. So there'll be no tax to pay.

Because of the way the PAYE system works, if you become unemployed at some point in the tax year, you may have paid more tax on your earnings than you need to have done (see example opposite). But if you're claiming benefits, you won't get your tax rebate at once. Instead, you'll get it when you start work again or (unless you're on strike or involved in a strike) at the end of the tax year, whichever comes first. In most cases, the rebate will be paid to you by your unemployment benefit office and you'll also get a statement showing how much taxable benefit you have been paid. If you think the figure is wrong ask the benefit office to explain it. If you're still unhappy, you should write to the benefit office within 60 days of the date on which the statement was issued. Your tax office will then send you a Notice of Assessment after the end of the tax year, which you can appeal against in the normal way (see p. 61), but *only* if you've made a written objection to your statement.

If you are unemployed and not claiming any taxable benefit, you can claim a tax rebate after being unemployed for four weeks. You'll have to claim on **form P50** – get this from your tax office.

ICTA 1988 s152

EXAMPLE

Joe Doyle becomes unemployed on 5 October 1992 at which point he has earned £6,000 in the 1992–3 tax year and paid £873 tax under the PAYE system. He claims unemployment benefit and income support for himself and his wife, of which £69.70 a week is taxable. He is still unemployed at the end of the tax year and is owed a tax rebate. His tax position is shown below.

Earnings	£6,000
Taxable benefit	£1,777
	£7,777
less personal and married couple's allowances	£5,165
Taxable income	£2,612
Tax at 20 per cent on £2,000	£400
Tax at 25 per cent on £612	£153
Total tax	£553
Tax paid under PAYE	£873
Rebate due	£320

If you owe tax after being on strike or unemployed

If you start work again before the end of the tax year, your benefit office will give you a new **form P45** showing how much taxable income you've had and how much tax you've already paid. Your new employer will then deduct the right amount of tax, including that due on your benefit, from your earnings for the rest of that tax year. You will also be sent a statement of how much taxable benefit you've had.

When you return to work after a strike or if you are still unemployed at the end of the tax year, your benefit office will send you a **form P60U** which includes details of how much taxable benefit you've had in that tax year.

Although you won't get a tax demand from the Inland Revenue straight away, once you're working your PAYE code will be adjusted so that the tax you owe on benefits will be collected from your earnings.
ICTA 1988 s152, s204

Tax if you're off sick

Employers usually have to pay their employees statutory sick pay (SSP) for their first 28 weeks of a spell of illness. SSP is treated just like your regular earnings, so tax is deducted from it under PAYE. If the amount of sick pay you get is lower than the amount you can earn each week (or month) before paying tax, your employer will give you a refund of some of the tax you've already paid in each pay packet.

If you can't get SSP, you might be entitled to claim sickness benefit. It's not taxable, but you need to have paid enough National Insurance to get it.

After you've been off sick for 28 weeks, you'll start getting invalidity benefit instead (providing you've paid enough in National Insurance). This benefit is not taxable. If you get any further sick pay from your employer, it will continue to be taxed in the same way as your normal earnings. But if you don't, you will have paid too much tax on your earnings since the start of the tax year and you'll get a refund on your usual pay-days.

Tax if you're having a baby

Employers have to pay statutory maternity pay (SMP) for up to 18 weeks to women who leave work or take time off work to have a baby providing they have worked for the employer for long enough. SMP is taxed in the same way as regular earnings – so tax is deducted under PAYE. If the amount of maternity pay you get is lower than the amount you can earn each week (or month) before paying tax, in each pay packet you will get a refund of some of the tax you have already paid.

If you don't meet all the SMP conditions, you might be able to get maternity allowance for up to 18 weeks. You need to have paid enough in National Insurance to get the allowance, but it's not taxable. You might be able to get sickness benefit if you can't get either SMP or maternity allowance – it's not taxable, but it does depend on how much you've paid in National Insurance.

7 WORKING FOR AN EMPLOYER AND SPARE-TIME INCOME

Most of us work for an employer, and tax on our wages or salaries is collected under the Pay-As-You-Earn system (PAYE). Your earnings are taxed in the way described in this chapter if you are employed under a *contract of service* and are paid a wage or salary on a regular basis. If you are employed under a *contract* (or contracts) *for services*, and are paid when you send in a bill or invoice, you are likely to count as self-employed. Details of how self-employed people are taxed are given in Chapter 10.

Earnings from employment are taxed under the rules of Schedule E, earnings from self-employment under Schedule D (see pp. 40 and 43). See Chapter 8 for detailed rules about fringe benefits, and Chapter 9 if your job involves working abroad for some or all of the time.

One basic tax rule to start off with: if you work for an employer, your earnings from your job are taxed on what's known as a *current year basis* – i.e. in the 1992–3 tax year you pay tax on the pay you receive in that tax year.

It is worth knowing that the PAYE system collects tax not only on earnings but also on pensions from a job, sometimes on regular freelance earnings and, often, on pensions from the state. There's not much you can do about that. But PAYE is also used, quite often, to collect tax on investment income. If this happens to you, you may be paying tax on the investment income sooner than you need to. You can ask for a separate, and later, bill instead.
ICTA 1988 s19, s617; IR56

> ## Sub-contractors in the building industry
> Even though you may regard yourself as self-employed, basic-rate tax will be deducted from all your earnings unless you hold a subcontractor's tax certificate. See Inland Revenue leaflet *IR40* for more details.

Understanding your payslip

When you look at your payslip, you'll see that there's a large gap between your earnings before any deductions – *gross pay* – and your take-home pay – *net pay*. To help you understand your payslip, we've given an example below. Your payslip may well be laid out rather differently, but the same type of information should appear.

Not all the deductions on your payslip are to do with income tax. For example, National Insurance (NI) contributions you pay should also be shown – more details on p. 136. Other deductions could be for pension contributions, season ticket loans, trade union subscriptions or gifts to charity under a payroll giving scheme.

	a		*b*	*c*	*d*		
EMPLOYEE NAME				EMPLOYEE NO		DEPT	
GEORGE WATKINS		BAILEY DELCO LTD		676		51	
BASIC	OVERTIME ETC	HOLIDAYS	BONUS/OTHER PAY	ADJUSTMENT	TAX-FREE ALLOWANCE	PERIOD	DATE
2000.00						3	30/6/92
E/E NI	E/E NI TO DATE	DED 1	DED 2	TAX CODE	GROSS TO DATE	TAX TO DATE	TAX THIS PERIOD
141.57	424.71	49.50		510H	6000	1108.75	369.67
E/R NI	GROSS PAY	CUMULATIVE PENSION	PENSION DEDN	PRE-TAX B	PRE-TAX C	TOTAL DEDUCTIONS	NET PAY
208.00	2000.00	210.00	70.00			630.74	1369.26

e f g h i j k l m n o p q r

How the figures match up
On the payslip above, there's a large difference between £2,000.00 (the figure for gross pay) and £1,369.26 (the figure for net pay). Here's how you get from one to the other. (We've left blank spaces for you to fill in your own figures.)

1. Gross pay	£2,000.00	£
Deductions		
2. Pension contributions [1]	£70.00	£
3. Tax	£369.67	£
4. National Insurance [1]	£141.57	£
5. Other deductions (in this case, for season ticket loan)	£49.50	£
6. Total deductions	£630.74	£
1 − 6	= £1,369.26	£

[1] What you pay (not your employer's contributions)

A quick check on tax

If you're a basic-rate taxpayer, you can use this to check that the tax deduction on your payslip is broadly correct for 1992–3.

Gross pay	A
Pension contributions, plus payroll giving, plus tax-free profit-related pay [1]	B
Free-of-tax pay	C

(Take your current PAYE Tax Code, add the figure 9 to the end [2] and divide by 12 if paid monthly or 52 if paid weekly.)

Add B to C and subtract the total from A	D
Multiply D by 0.25	E

Then, to take account of the new lower rate band, deduct £8.34 for every month in the tax year, or £1.93 for every week (shown as 'Period' on the pay slip on p. 116).

	F

F should be roughly equivalent to the tax deducted for the month or week.

[1] Don't include if your employer's scheme is not an 'approved' or 'statutory' one
[2] For example, if your PAYE code is 329 (ignoring any letters), make this 3299; if it's 510, make it 5109

Key to payslip entries

a **Basic** Pay before additions for things like overtime or bonus.

b **Holidays** Depends on company policy. May include your pay while you're on holiday, or only exceptional payments (e.g. pay in lieu of holiday).

c **Adjustment** On this payslip, statutory sick pay and pay from company's own sick pay scheme (less any amount attributable to contributions you've made to the scheme) or statutory maternity pay are entered here.

d **Tax-free allowance** Depends on company policy. Non-taxable payments (e.g. evening meal or travelling allowance) paid with salary may be entered here.

e **E/E NI** Employee's National Insurance contributions for the month.

f **E/R NI** Employer's National Insurance contributions for the employee.

g **E/E NI to date** Employee's National Insurance contributions since the beginning of the tax year.

h **Gross pay** This is the month's salary before deductions. Would include overtime and bonus if these were paid.

i **Ded.1/Ded.2** Deductions – such as repayment of company loan, an advance on salary, your contributions to your employer's medical bills insurance scheme, a payment under a payroll giving scheme – would be entered in these boxes. In this example, Ded.1 is the monthly repayment of a season ticket loan.

j **Cumulative pension** Employee's contributions to company pension scheme since the beginning of the tax year.

k **Pension dedn** Employee's contributions to the company pension scheme for the period covered by the payslip. If it is a 'statutory' or 'approved' scheme you get tax relief on contributions you pay (within certain limits – see p. 301) so they will be deducted before tax is worked out on the rest of your pay. 'Statutory' schemes are for civil servants, employees of nationalised industries, etc.; other schemes have to be approved by the Revenue.

l **Tax code**   PAYE code number. For how this worked out see p. 128.

m **Pre-tax B/Pre-tax C**   Depends on company policy. Boxes like these could be used to show things like additional voluntary contributions to the company pension scheme or profit-related pay (which are non-taxable and deducted from your pay before calculating tax due) and certain expenses or benefits (e.g. lunch allowance paid in cash) which have to be included in pay for the period and taxed under PAYE. On this payslip, amounts in these boxes will be included in pay to be taxed if marked by a plus sign.

n **Gross to date**   Total pay (before deductions) since the beginning of the tax year.

o **Tax to date**   Total tax deducted since the beginning of the tax year.

p **Total deductions**   Total of all deductions from gross pay for the period covered by the payslip.

q **Tax this period**   Tax deducted for the period covered by the payslip (a month in this case).

r **Net pay**   Take-home pay – i.e. what's left of gross pay after the figure for total deductions has been subtracted.

Form P60

At the end of each tax year, your employer will give you **form P60** (or an equivalent form). This is a record of your total pay (including overtime, etc.) for the tax year – and of how much tax you've paid. Note that some P60 forms don't include the contributions to an 'approved' or 'statutory' pension scheme under the figure for pay (i.e. what's shown is pay *less* pension contributions).

What counts as earnings

The basic rule is that any money you get from your employer is taxable, unless: it's a genuine personal gift; or it's spent on an *allowable expense* (see p. 121); or it is genuinely not in any way a payment for the job you do (except for any 'profit-related' pay – see overleaf). So all the following count as pay:

- normal wages or salary; commission; tips; bonuses; holiday pay; overtime; cost-of-living allowance; London weighting; arrears and advances of pay
- fees and other expenses you get for being a company director
- any expense allowance from your employer (though you won't be taxed on anything spent on *allowable expenses* – see p. 122)
- money your employer pays to cover expenses in your job. If you've paid the expenses out of your pocket and your employer pays you back, you're taxed only on any profit you make from the difference. If the expenses are *allowable* – see p. 122 – you're not taxed on what your employer pays
- the taxable value of certain fringe benefits your employer gives you – see Chapter 8
- sick pay from your employer (including *statutory sick pay*); sickness benefits payable from an insurance scheme your employer arranges – see p. 137
- maternity pay (including *statutory maternity pay*)
- pay in lieu of notice and redundancy or leaving payments in excess of £30,000 (though see p. 138)
- most lump sum payments on taking up a job, including payments made by your new employer before you leave your old job
- taxable unemployment benefit if it is paid to you by your employer under arrangements with the Department of Employment
- earnings (including all the things above) from any additional jobs.

Other things that count as earnings are pensions from former employers, state retirement pension, and other taxable social security benefits.
ICTA 1988 s131

Profit-related pay

If part of your pay is linked to the profits made by the company you work for, you can get tax relief on your profit-related pay if the scheme meets certain Inland Revenue conditions. It must:

- be set up by a profit-making private sector employer
- run for at least one year and be open to at least 80 per cent of the workforce or a section of the workforce (a PRP scheme may be set up for a department, say). Part-timers and employees who have been with the firm for less than three years can be excluded
- be registered with the Inland Revenue before it starts.

If these conditions are met, you can get tax relief on any profit-related pay you get up to the point where your PRP is £4,000 or 20 per cent of your total pay (whichever is less) – a maximum saving of £500 for a basic-rate taxpayer. You get the tax relief through the PAYE system. National Insurance contributions have to be paid on profit-related pay.
ICTA 1988 s171

Expenses in your job

Two questions you might ask are:

- if I pay expenses out of my own pocket, can I get tax relief on what I pay?
- if my employer pays expenses for me, will I escape being taxed on what my employer pays?

The answer to both questions depends on whether the expenses are *allowable expenses* for tax purposes. The table on pp. 123–6 shows the main items which are, and aren't, allowable. If an expense is allowable, the answer to both questions is yes. If it's not allowable:

- you get no tax relief on what you pay yourself
- you're taxed on what your employer pays, *less* anything you pay towards the cost.

For an expense to be allowable, the money must be spent *'wholly, exclusively and necessarily in the performance of the duties of your employment'*. So if you get a fixed expense allowance and don't spend all of it on allowable expenses, you are taxed on the difference. Note that *'necessarily'* means

121

necessary within the context of your job, and not simply necessary to you. So if working late means that you'll have to stay in a hotel overnight because your home is a long distance away, the hotel bill won't be allowable if the job could be done by someone else living closer to your workplace. However, small differences in individual circumstances (or in a Tax Inspector's assessment of them) may mean that an expense disallowed for one person is allowable for someone else. Allowable expenses can be set off only against earnings from your job, not, for example, against investment income.

Expenses paid out of your own pocket

In trades where it's customary to provide your own tools or clothing (e.g. plumbing) many trade unions have agreed a *fixed deduction* for upkeep and replacement of these things. For example, there may be a fixed amount of £70. You can claim the whole fixed deduction as an allowable expense even if you don't spend it all. And if you spend more, you can claim more.

Expenses your employer pays for

If an expense *isn't* allowable, it counts as part of your pay and you're taxed on it – either under PAYE or by getting a separate tax bill. If an expense *is* allowable, how it's dealt with varies:

- has your employer got a *dispensation* for the expense? In broad terms, a dispensation means that your employer doesn't have to give the Revenue details of expenses paid to you and you don't have to declare them in your tax return. A dispensation won't be given unless the Revenue is satisfied that it's for allowable expenses (and nothing else), and that your employer keeps proper control over expenses
- if there isn't a dispensation, and you count as earning at a rate of £8,500 a year or more (see p. 145), your employer has to tell the Revenue at the end of the tax year about all expenses paid to you (or for you) for which there isn't a dispensation. This is done at the end of the tax year on **form P11D**. You'll have to enter all these expenses in your tax return, and be taxed on any which aren't allowable. Allowable expenses have to be

entered twice – as income and as outgoings. Entering them as outgoings means that you don't pay tax on them

- if you don't count as earning at a rate of £8,500 or more a year, expenses for which there's a dispensation are ignored, as are other allowable expenses, including 'scale payments' (e.g. a mileage allowance) which have been agreed between your employer and the Revenue. Other expenses, if they're not allowable, haven't been taxed as part of your pay and total more than £25 a year, are declared by your employer on **form P9D**, and any tax due is normally collected under PAYE in a later tax year.
TA 1988 s198, s201, s577

Expenses in your job

	Expenses normally allowed	Not allowed
To get a job	Cost of retraining provided by employer to acquire new work skills, if you have left or are about to leave your job. This includes fees, books, travelling and extra living costs for the course.	Agency fees. Expenses of interview.
Training	Cost of fees and essential books you buy for a full-time external training course lasting for four weeks or more. Your employer must either require you or at least encourage you to attend the course, and must go on paying your wages while you are on it. Possibly, extra cost of living away from home and extra travelling expenses, if away for under a year.	Fees and book purchases for other courses or evening classes – even if required to take course by employer. Examination fees. Re-sit courses or examinations.
Fees and subscriptions to professional bodies	Subscriptions to professional bodies provided membership is relevant to your job. Fee for keeping your name on a professional register approved by the Inland Revenue – but only if this is a condition of your employment.	

	Expenses normally allowed	Not allowed
Clothes	Cost of replacing, cleaning and repairing protective clothing (e.g. overalls, boots) and functional clothing (e.g. uniform) necessary for your job and which you are required to provide. Cost of cleaning protective clothing or functional clothing provided by your employer, if cleaning facilities are not provided.	Ordinary clothes you wear for work (e.g. a pinstripe suit) which you could wear outside work – even if you'd never choose to.
Tools, instruments	Cost of maintaining and repairing factory or workshop tools and musical instruments you are required to provide. Cost of replacing instruments and tools, less any amount from sale of old, provided new ones not inherently better than old. Often, fixed amounts agreed with trade unions (see p. 122).	Initial cost of tools and instruments, but may be able to claim *capital allowances* (see p. 182).
Books and stationery	Cost of reference books necessary for your job which you have to provide (e.g. actuarial tables, government regulations). If the book's useful life is more than two years you may have to claim *capital allowances* instead (see p. 184). Cost of stationery used strictly for your job (e.g. business notepaper if you are a sales rep). Possibly, cost of books essential for a full-time training course (see opposite).	Cost of other books. Subscriptions to journals to keep up with developments. General stationery (e.g. pens, notepaper, etc.).
Use of home for work	Proportion of heating and lighting costs, and, possibly, proportion of telephone, cleaning and insurance costs. If part of home is used *exclusively* for business, you may be able to claim a proportion of rent. But these expenses are allowed only if it is necessary that you carry out some of your duties at or from home (i.e. if it is an express or implied condition of your employment). Exclusive business use of part of your home may mean you have to pay business rates and some capital gains tax if you sell your home (see p. 213).	Personal community charge.

	Expenses normally allowed	Not allowed
Interest	Interest on loans to buy equipment (e.g. car, typewriter) necessary for your job.	Interest on overdraft or credit card.
Travelling	Expenses incurred strictly in the course of carrying out job. *Running costs of own car*: whole of cost if used wholly and necessarily in carrying out your job, proportion of cost if used privately as well. Work out what proportion your business mileage bears to your total mileage, and claim corresponding proportion of cost. If your employer requires you to use your car for business purposes, and you're paid less for doing so than it costs you, work out the full cost to you and claim the extra. *Company car*: if you pay for running costs (e.g. petrol, repairs, maintenance), claim proportion of cost of business mileage. Occasional late-night journeys home or extra travel costs if public transport disrupted by industrial action.	Travel to and from work (but if you travel to or from a job abroad, see p. 167). Cost of buying a car and depreciation – may be able to claim a *capital allowance* (see p. 184) but only if the car is necessary for you to carry on your job and it is necessary for you to provide one.
Spouses travelling together	Allowed only if cost paid by (or for) employer, and if wife or husband has, and uses, practical qualifications directly associated with trip, or if their presence is necessary for essential business entertaining of overseas trade customers, or if your health is so poor that it is unreasonable to travel alone. Often only a proportion of cost is allowed.	
Entertaining	Expenses of entertaining customers (but only if you can claim these expenses back from your employer, or pay them out of an expense allowance given specifically for entertaining). Employees of non-trading organisations like schools, local authorities and trade unions can claim all entertaining expenses, but only if spent *wholly, exclusively and necessarily in the performance of your job* (see p. 121 for what this means).	Any other entertaining expenses.

	Expenses normally allowed	Not allowed
Hotel and meal expenses	If you keep a permanent home, reasonable hotel and meal expenses when travelling in the course of your job. But if, say, you're a single person living in a hostel, and give up your room when travelling, you can claim only extra cost of reasonable hotel and meal expenses over your normal board and lodging.	Meals, unless you wouldn't normally have had one at that time.

Pay as you earn (PAYE)

Principles

PAYE is a way of collecting tax bit by bit over the tax year. The Revenue gives you a PAYE code which indicates an estimate of the amount of free-of-tax pay you're entitled to over the tax year. Any excess over this free-of-tax amount will be taxed. For how the free-of-tax amount is worked out, see the illustrated Notice of Coding on pp. 132 and 133. Each pay-day, you'll be allowed one fifty-second or one-twelfth (depending on whether you're paid weekly or monthly) of the free-of-tax amount.

Mechanics

Your *Notice of Coding* will show you how your PAYE code is calculated; your employer is just told what your code is. Your employer then uses your code, and the *Tax Tables* supplied by the Revenue, to deduct the right amount of tax from your pay.

The *Free Pay Tables* allow your employer to work out how much of each month's or week's pay is free of tax. For example, if your code is 501H, this gives you up to £5,019 free-of-tax pay for the tax year. Because of roundings in the tables, code 501H actually works out at £5,019.04 over the year if you're paid weekly. On monthly pay, you'll get one-twelfth of £5,019.00 (= £418.25) of your pay free of tax each month. If you're paid weekly, you'll get one fifty-second of £5,019.04 (= £96.52) of your pay free of tax each week. Any excess, after deducting pension contributions to 'statutory' or 'approved' schemes, payments to charity under a payroll giving scheme and the tax-free part of profit-related pay under an approved scheme (see p. 122), is taxable. The *Taxable Pay Tables* tell your employer how much tax to deduct.

As the Tax Tables work on a cumulative basis, this makes dealing with a change to your PAYE code part-way through a tax year comparatively simple – see below.

PAYE code changes during the tax year

If your code goes up (i.e. you get a higher number) you get more free-of-tax pay and so pay less tax. Because the PAYE system works cumulatively, you will have been given too little free-of-tax pay since the start of the tax year so that the first time your new code is used you'll pay less tax than usual to make up for the time you were paying too much; you may even pay no tax and get a rebate. For the rest of the tax year you'll pay less tax each pay-day.

EXAMPLE

Boris's code for the 1992–3 tax year was 344L. This meant that he could earn £287.42 a month free of tax.

On 4 June, Boris got married and became entitled to the married couple's allowance – a reduced amount of £1,577 for the year of marriage (see p. 70). In August, Boris told the Revenue he'd got married, and was sent a revised Notice of Coding showing his new code, 502H. This meant that he was entitled to £419.84 free-of-tax pay for every month of the tax year (including April and May before his marriage), i.e. £132.42 a month more than before.

The Tax Tables (which calculate tax on whole £s only) give a reduction in his tax bill of £33 a month (at the basic rate of 25 per cent).

In addition to this regular monthly saving of £33, Boris got an extra £165 in his pay when his employer first used the new code in September. This was a rebate of tax for the first five months of the tax year when he paid too much tax. So Boris's total extra pay in his September pay packet was £198.

If your code goes down (i.e. you get a lower number) you will have been given too much free-of-tax pay since the start of the tax year and so paid too little tax. If the amount of underpaid tax is large and would mean a sharp drop in your take-home pay the first time the code is used, the Revenue will tell your employer to apply your new code on a *Week 1* or *Month 1* basis. For the rest of the tax year you'll get one fifty-second or one-twelfth of your new tax-free pay (depending on whether you're paid weekly or monthly) each pay-day. So on each pay-day, you pay the amount of tax you would have paid if your tax code had been correct at the beginning of the tax year. But you will still owe the underpaid tax from the pay-days before your code was changed. This will be shown as a deduction on your next year's Notice of Coding so that the unpaid tax will be collected over the whole of the following year. If, however, you receive an assessment for the year showing a substantial amount of underpaid tax, you'll be sent a bill for the tax due.

Notice of Coding

Not everyone gets a Notice of Coding each tax year. You're likely to get one if, for example, you're a higher-rate taxpayer or if certain of your outgoings this year look like being more (or less) than last year. Most Notices of Coding are sent out in January or February each year and apply for the tax year starting on the following 6 April. To work out your PAYE code for the 1992–3 tax year, say, the Revenue initially used the allowances for the 1991–2 tax year and estimated your outgoings. When allowances changed in the Budget, your PAYE code – in most cases – changed automatically, and you probably didn't get a new Notice of Coding. For other changes, you may get a new Notice of Coding part-way through the tax year.

You get a separate PAYE code for each job in which your earnings are taxed under PAYE – and, normally, a separate Notice of Coding giving your code for each job. If possible, all your outgoings and allowances are included in the code for your main job.

Whenever you get a Notice of Coding, you should check that it's correct. If you think there's a mistake tell the Revenue at once. The same applies if your circumstances change during the tax year (e.g. if you become entitled to a new allowance or incur a new outgoing). If your PAYE code is not correct at the end of the tax year you'll have paid the wrong amount of tax under PAYE, and either have to claim

a rebate, or be faced with more tax to pay in a later year. To get your code changed, write and tell the Revenue why your code is wrong and send your most recent Notice of Coding if you've still got it. If not, quote the tax reference number which is on all forms and letters the Revenue sends you.
ICTA 1988 s203 Regulations 6(2), 7(b)(d), 8

Not sent back your Tax Return?

If you've received a Tax Return but haven't returned it, you may get a Notice of Coding showing a special deduction which reduces your PAYE code, possibly to zero, and, as a result, the amount of free-of-tax pay you can have. This is because the Revenue thinks you have income you haven't declared and has decided to estimate the amount of tax you might owe. To get this sorted out — and, if necessary, your code changed — you'll have to send back your completed Tax Return.

How to read a Notice of Coding
On pp. 132 and 133 we show you what a Notice of Coding might look like and explain the main headings which might appear, though your Notice will include only things which apply to you. Some Notices of Coding are still hand-written and look different from the computer-printed version shown here but they contain exactly the same information.

Allowances
Here you'll find details of the personal allowances you are entitled to and the Revenue's estimate of any outgoings you have on which tax relief isn't given automatically.

Outgoings
Expenses   An estimate of any allowable expenses in your job which qualifies for tax relief (see p. 122). If you're counted as earning at a rate of £8,500 a year or more (see p. 146), for example, it will include expenses for which your employer does not have a *dispensation*.

Professional subs   Subscriptions to professional bodies which qualify for tax relief.

Ret annuity relief   Payments into personal pension plans taken out before 1 July 1988.

Personal pension   Payments to a personal pension scheme taken out since 1 July 1988 or into a free-standing AVC scheme (see p. 307) if made by a higher-rate taxpayer. If you pay tax at basic rate only, there'll be no entry here as you get the tax relief by making net payments to the pension provider.

Bldg socy int/loan etc int   For loans or mortgages where you don't get tax relief under MIRAS there will be an estimate of the interest you'll pay in the 1992–3 tax year.

Maintenance payments   The amount of maintenance you pay which qualifies for tax relief (see p. 81).

Taxed payment   Extra tax relief for higher-rate taxpayers on covenant payments will be shown here.

Personal
Details of the allowances you're entitled to will be included here. If you are entitled to one of the higher levels of allowance because of your age, this may be reduced if your income is above a certain amount (see p. 95). An estimate of your total income for the tax year will be shown under the heading **Age est income**.

Deductions
In this section you'll find details of income you get which is taxable but is paid without any tax being deducted, e.g. taxable perks from your job, etc. The tax owed on this income will be collected through the PAYE scheme by deducting the total from your total allowance.

State pens'n/benefit/pension   Includes state pensions and benefits, or employers' pensions not taxed before you get them.

Benefits in kind/(Car)/Car fuel   Perks from your job which count as taxable income (see Chapter 8).

Taxable expenses pyt   Payments from your employer to cover expenses in your job (see p. 123).

Part-time earnings/tips/commission/other earned income
Extra income from your main job and freelance or part-time earnings on which you don't pay tax under PAYE.

Adjust unemp benefit   Includes taxable benefits you have

130

claimed because of unemployment (see Chapter 6).

Untaxed interest/income from property   Interest received without tax being deducted (e.g. from National Savings) and income from property.

Court order   Includes maintenance you received from a court order made before 15 March 1988. If you're an ex-spouse, the amount shown will be the payments less the free-of-tax amount you're allowed (see p. 84).

Adjustments
Finally, your Notice of Coding may include other inform-ation about adjustments which need to be made.

Unpaid tax   If you owe tax for an earlier year (or years) the amount owed will be included here. A deduction from your allowances will be made to collect this tax. If you pay basic-rate tax a deduction of four times the tax you owe will be made; for higher-rate tax payers the deduction will be two and a half times the amount of tax owed.

Taxed payments   If you make covenanted payments and your tax bill is likely to be less than the amount of tax you have deducted, the difference will be included here.

Higher rate adj   If you pay tax at the higher rate and have investment income which has been taxed at the basic rate only, there may be an adjustment here to collect the extra tax owed.

Less total deductions
This is the total figure for all deductions and adjustments.

Allowances set against pay, etc.
This figure is reached by subtracting your total deductions from your total allowances and determines your PAYE code.

The number in your code
This is arrived at by knocking the last figure off the figure in **Allowances set against pay etc**. So if this figure is 950 (as in our example) your code number is 95. Because of the way rounding works, this code entitles you to tax-free pay of £959 instead – an extra £9 of tax-free pay. If it's zero, you have no free-of-tax amount to be deducted.

Inland Revenue
PAYE-Notice of Coding

Please keep this notice for future reference and let me know of any change in your address. Form P3(T) enclosed (or previously sent) explains the entries.

Issued by
H.M. Inspector of Taxes

Please use both lines of this reference if you write or call - it will help to avoid delay.		
347/WM9091/F		
JW	11	11	A

Date   14.02.93

Taxpayer's
name and address

This notice cancels any previous notice of coding for the year shown below. It shows the allowances which make up your code.
Your employer or paying officer will use this code to deduct or refund the right amount of tax under PAYE during the year shown below.
Please check this notice. If you think it is wrong please return it to me and give your reasons. If we cannot agree you have the right of appeal.
Please let me know at once about any change in your personal circumstances which may alter your allowances and coding.
By law you are required to tell me of any income that is not fully taxed, even if you are not sent a Tax Return.

See Note	Allowances		£	See Note	Less Deductions	£
12	RET ANNUITY RELIEF		700	25	BENEFITS (CAR)	4440
13	INTEREST HIGHER RATE		750	25	BENEFITS CAR FUEL	940
17	PERSONAL		3445	29	UNPAID TAX £114	285
17	MARRIED COUPLE'S		1720			
	Total allowances		6615		Less total deductions	5665
					Allowances set against pay etc. £	950

Your code for the year to 5 April 1993 is

95T

Please see
Part
overleaf

P2 (T)

The letter in your code

L if you get the personal allowance (£3,445).

H if you get the personal allowance (£3,445) plus the married couple's allowance (£1,720) or additional personal allowance (£1,720).

P if you get the full personal allowance for someone aged 65 to 74 (£4,200).

V if you get the full personal allowance for someone aged 65 to 74 (£4,200) plus the married couple's allowance for someone aged 65 to 74 (£2,465).

T under certain circumstances – e.g. if you get a personal allowance for someone aged 75 or more, or if you get a reduced amount of age-related personal allowance because your income is above a certain level. Your code will also include **T** if you have a company car or if you don't want your employer to know about your age or marital status.

F if the total deductions shown on your Notice of Coding come to more than your total allowances; the Revenue will have to collect tax under PAYE at a higher-than-normal rate. **F** will be replaced by **K** from 5 April 1993.

NT if no tax is due on your pay.

BR if all your allowances have been given elsewhere and all your earnings will be taxed at the basic rate. You're most likely to get this if it is a code for a second job.

D if all your allowances have been given elsewhere and all your earnings will be taxed at the higher rate. Again you're most likely to get this if it is a code for a second job.

If your PAYE code has the letters L, H, P or V, your employer will be told what changes to make to your code to take into account any changes to the personal and married couple's allowances announced in the Budget. With other letters or if any other allowances you may be getting are increased, a new code will take longer to come through.

PAYE enquiries

If you pay tax under PAYE, it's possible that your tax office is a long distance away. This may make resolving any tax problems you have more difficult. In this situation, check to see if there's a local tax office or Tax Enquiry Centre – look in the telephone book under *Inland Revenue*, or see *IR52*. If necessary, details of your tax affairs can be sent to the local office so that the people there can discuss your problems with you, give you advice and chase up matters (e.g. a long overdue tax rebate) for you.

Starting work

Your first job

If you've started work for the first time after full-time education (and haven't claimed unemployment benefit or income support) your employer will ask you to complete **form P46**. If your earnings are below the PAYE threshold (about £66 a week or £287 a month in the 1992–3 tax year) you won't pay any tax. If you are paid more than this you will be given an emergency code – 344L for the 1992–3 tax year – which assumes that the only allowance you're entitled to is the basic personal allowance. This code gives you £287.42 of tax-free pay each month (£66.33 each week) – i.e. roughly one-twelfth (or one fifty-second) of £3,449.

Tax won't be deducted until the free-of-tax pay since the beginning of the tax year has been used up. So, for example, if your first monthly pay-day is in the fourth month of the tax year, you are entitled to four months of free-of-tax pay on code 344L, i.e. £287.42 x 4 = £1,149.68. So on your first pay-day tax will be deducted only on any excess over £1,149.68. If your total pay for the month is less than this amount, the balance of the free-of-tax pay owing to you will be given to you on subesquent pay-days until it runs out. Note that if you don't complete form P46, the emergency code will be operated on a *Week 1* (or *Month 1*) basis. See *Returning to work* opposite for what this means.

As well as form P46, your employer also gives you a Coding Claim **form P15** to complete in case you're entitled to other outgoings or allowances. When you return it to the Revenue your proper code will be worked out. You will be sent a Notice of Coding and your employer will be told your new code. This new code may allow you a higher amount of free-of-tax pay than the emergency one. If so, any tax over-deducted will be refunded to you.

Working in the vacation

A student who gets a vacation job won't be taxed on weekly (or monthly) earnings even if these are more than £66 a week (£287 a month), if his or her earnings and other taxable income for the whole year won't exceed the personal allowance of £3,445. Both the student and the employer have to complete **form P38(S)** to get this exemption.

Returning to work

If you haven't worked for some years (e.g. because you've stayed at home to look after the children), the procedure is broadly the same as that described in *Your first job* on p. 135.

However, if your earnings for the 1992–3 tax year are more than £66 a week (£287 a month) your employer will operate the emergency code (344L for the 1992–3 tax year) on a *Week 1* or *Month 1* basis. This means that no account will be taken of any free-of-tax pay due from the beginning of the tax year to the time you started working, and tax will be deducted straight away. When the Revenue has received your Coding Claim (form P15), and allocated your proper code to you, any tax you've overpaid will be refunded to you.

Changing jobs

When you change jobs, your old employer should give you a **form P45**. This shows your PAYE code and details of the tax deducted from your total pay for the year to date. Give this to your new employer on your first day so that the correct amount of tax can be deducted from your pay.

If you don't do this, your employer will follow the procedure described above in *Returning to work* and you may pay too much tax for a while.

National Insurance contributions

If, in the 1992–3 tax year, you earn £54 or more a week (£234 or more a month), you'll have to pay Class 1 National Insurance contributions. These will be deducted from the whole of your pay on up to a maximum limit of £405 weekly earnings (or £1,755 monthly). These limits apply to each job, if you have more than one job.
Social Security Act 1975 s1–s4

Temporary work through an agency

If you work through an agency, e.g. as a temp, you will be treated as an employee (normally of the agency) and taxed

under PAYE. But there are exceptions to this rule: you may be able to work through an agency and be treated as *self-employed* if you're an entertainer, model, subcontractor in the building industry, or if all your work is done at or from your own home.
ICTA 1988 s134

Other temporary or casual jobs

Tax won't be deducted unless your earnings are more than £66 a week (£287 a month). If you are paid more than this amount, the basis on which you are taxed depends on whether or not you can give your employer **form P45**. With a P45, the procedure is as described under *Changing jobs* on the previous page. Without a P45, the emergency code (344L for the 1992–3 tax year) will be used on a *Week 1* (or *Month 1*) basis. Special rules apply to the building industry – see p. 116.

Interrupting work

Off sick

Statutory sick pay (SSP) paid by your employer and sick pay you get from your employer's own sick pay scheme are taxable under PAYE. But if the amount you get is lower than the amount of free-of-tax pay you are entitled to, your employer will refund some of the tax you've already paid, in each pay packet. You get statutory sick pay only for a limited period; then you may get state invalidity benefit. This isn't taxable, though tax will still be deducted from any sick pay you get from your employer's scheme.

Some employers have *sick pay insurance schemes* which pay out income when you're off sick. Tax will normally be deducted from payments you receive from these schemes. But if you contribute towards the insurance premiums, you'll be taxed only on the part of the payment attributable to your employer's contributions. If you've taken out your own sick pay insurance policy, income from it won't be taxed until it has been paid throughout a complete tax year. Then it's taxed as investment income.
ICTA 1988 s149

137

Maternity

Statutory Maternity Pay (SMP) and any extra maternity pay paid by your employer is taxable under PAYE. If either SMP or maternity pay is paid when (or before) you stop working, the tax deducted will depend on your PAYE code. If it's paid *after* you've stopped working, i.e. after you have received a P45, tax is deducted at the basic rate. This could mean too much tax is deducted. If so, claim a rebate.

State maternity allowance isn't taxable.
ICTA 1988 s150

Laid off, on short-time, on strike

In any of these situations, too much tax may have been deducted from your pay since the beginning of the tax year. If you've been laid off or put on short-time, any tax refunds due will be given on your normal pay-days by your employer. But strikers (or those involved in strikes) will have to wait until they return to work for their tax refunds.

Stopping work

Redundancy

If you're made redundant, earnings your employer owes you, e.g. normal wages, pay in lieu of holiday, pay for working your notice period, commission, paid when you leave your job, are taxed in the normal way under PAYE. But the following payments are tax-free:

- any lump sum for any injury or disability which meant you couldn't carry on your job
- compensation for loss of a job done entirely or substantially outside the UK
- gratuities from the armed forces (but if for early retirement, balance over £30,000 may be taxable)
- certain lump sum benefits from employers' pension schemes
- money your employer pays into a retirement benefit scheme or uses to buy you an annuity (if certain conditions are met).

Other payments are also tax-free if, added together, they total less than £30,000. These are:

- redundancy payments made under the government's redundancy payments scheme or a scheme 'approved' by the Inland Revenue
- pay in lieu of notice, in most circumstances, provided your conditions of service don't say you're entitled to it
- other payments made to you, as long as they are not payments for work done, not part of your conditions of service, and, technically at least, unexpected. This would normally cover redundancy payments over and above the government minimum.

Anything more than £30,000 is added to the rest of your income and taxed in the normal way.

Your employer has to deduct tax under PAYE on the excess over £30,000 before paying it to you. Unless a special, reduced tax payment is negotiated with your tax office, too much tax will be deducted because the Tax Tables don't allow for these special rules and you'll have to claim a rebate. If, on leaving a job, you received a lump sum of more than £50,000 between 6 April 1982 and 3 June 1986, you may have paid too much tax. This is because of a change in the interpretation in the law. So you should claim a rebate within six years of the end of the tax year in which you received the lump sum.

ICTA 1988 s188, s191, sch 11 (tax-free payments)

Employer going bust

Pay in lieu of notice is normally tax-free. But if you lose your job because your employer goes bust, and get pay in lieu of notice from the liquidator (or trustee in bankruptcy), basic-rate tax will be deducted from the whole amount. You can't claim a full rebate, but if this notional tax is more than the tax that would have been deducted if you'd received it as normal pay, you can get a refund of the difference. You get the refund from your local Redundancy Payments Office.

Dismissal

Earnings your employer owes you will be taxed under PAYE. In most circumstances pay in lieu of notice together with any other payments (provided they are not payments for work done, not part of your conditions of service and, technically, unexpected) totalling less than £30,000 are tax-free. Anything over £30,000 is taxed in the normal way.

If you are awarded compensation for unfair dismissal by an industrial tribunal, the amount you get for loss of wages will be paid after deduction of basic-rate tax, though any compensation for loss of your job would not be taxed. As with pay in lieu of notice paid by a liquidator (see above), the only tax rebate you can get is the difference between the amount actually deducted and any (smaller) amount that would have been deducted if you'd received the money as normal pay.

Refunded pension contributions

If you leave an employer's pension scheme within two years, you may be offered a refund of your contributions, but 20 per cent tax will have been deducted.

Spare-time income

Many people who have jobs in their spare time don't realise that they almost certainly need to tell the Revenue about the income they get. The most common examples of how you might get spare-time income are:

- you have a second job in the evenings, or at weekends (e.g. working behind the bar at your local pub), completely different from your main job
- you're someone with a skill (e.g. electrician, plumber, carpenter, motor mechanic), and you normally work full-time for an employer, but you get spare-time income doing work for other people, often for cash
- you're a professional person (e.g. schoolteacher, architect). Again, you use your professional skills and knowledge to get spare-time income (e.g. if you're a teacher, you may give private tuition)
- you have some extra income (e.g. commissions from running mail-order catalogues or income from foreign students)
- you own a second home or a caravan which you let out, or you let rooms in your house.

How the Revenue finds out about your activities

- If you are employed, your employer should tell the

Revenue that you have started work, and ask for a PAYE code for you to be able to work out how much tax to deduct from your pay.

- If your activities consist of a trade or business, or the letting of property, and you advertise in local or national papers, the Revenue has a department which monitors these ads and checks to see that the income has been declared.

- The Revenue has wide powers to compel employers to send details of payments they make to freelance staff, consultants, caterers, etc. – in short, any people who do work for them.

- The Revenue also gets a number of letters from informants – some of them anonymous, and a few of them paid by the Revenue. What they say may or may not be taken seriously, but it may tie in with suspicions the Revenue already has, or it may alert it to taking an interest in your affairs.

Since the Revenue can get to know of your income without your telling them, it makes it more important for you to report your income yourself. If the Revenue starts an inquiry into your affairs as a result of information received you're more likely to be charged penalties in addition to the tax due than if you disclose your income voluntarily.

TMA 1970 Part III, Part X

Telling the Revenue

If you get a Tax Return

If you get a Tax Return, you must list all your income on the Return. Where exactly on the form you need to show your spare-time income depends on what sort of income it is (e.g. from a second employer, or from renting out your house). If you're not sure where to show the income, don't worry too much: the important thing is for it to appear somewhere. The Revenue can, if need be, transfer it to the right heading. Broadly speaking, the income will probably fall under one of these headings:

- **income from employment** If you get a wage from your spare-time work (e.g. £20 a week for working in a chip shop in the evenings), enter the name and address of your employer and the amount of your earnings, including any tips, in the section of the Return dealing with employments. Enter any *allowable expenses* (see p. 122) separately.

- **income from trades, professions or other business activities** If your spare-time income comes from a trade or business (e.g. you put small ads in the newsagent's window saying that you decorate houses), use the section of the form dealing with trades, professions or vocations. Say what your trade or business is (e.g. painter and decorator), give the address from which you work (e.g. your home), and declare the amount of your profit for the tax year.
- **income from lettings** If you let a property or rooms, you should show (in the section dealing with property) the gross rental income due for the tax year and all the expenses you're claiming (see p. 218).
- **income from other activities** If your income doesn't fit under any of the headings above, there's a special section of the Return which asks for details of any other income or profits. Enter full details of your income and expenses.

See pp. 122 and 178 for details of the types of expenses which you can claim against your income.

If you don't get a Tax Return

If you don't get a Tax Return, you must still tell the Revenue about your income within one year of the end of the tax year in which the income arose – e.g. income earned in August 1992 must be reported to the Revenue by 5 April 1994 at the latest. If you fail to do this you can be charged a penalty of the amount of tax owed – in addition to the tax due – when you eventually tell the Revenue about the income, or it finds out about it from other sources. You will also be charged interest from the date on which the tax ought to have been paid to the date on which it was actually paid (see p. 66).
TMA 1970 s7, s88

How will your income be taxed?

Income from spare-time activities can be taxed in a number of ways:

- under Schedule E if your income is from an employment

- under Schedule D Case I or II if it amounts to a trade or business
- under Schedule A if your income is from the letting of property. (It will normally be taxed under Schedule D Case VI if the property is let furnished, and under Schedule D Case I if your letting of furnished accommodation counts as a trade)
- under Schedule D Case VI if the income doesn't fit in anywhere else, or arises from activities which do not amount to a trade or business, and are not an employment, e.g. a casual commission. Income charged under this Case will almost always be taxed as investment income.

For a more detailed explanation of the Schedules, see p. 38.

Why bother about the Schedules?

The most important reason is the type and level of expenses which you can claim. These differ from Schedule to Schedule. The rules for allowable expenses under Schedule E are more stringent than the rules under Schedule D Cases I and II. For example, the cost of travelling between your home and your place of work are not allowable under Schedule E. But if you're in business and work from your home, the cost of travelling to see your clients or customers is allowable under Schedule D Cases I and II.

8 *FRINGE BENEFITS*

If your employer lets you use a company car, provides you with a cheap meal in a canteen or pays for private medical bills insurance, fringe benefits are a part of your life.

Are fringe benefits worthwhile?

Yes, because the tax system treats most fringe benefits favourably compared with a rise in salary. Getting a fringe benefit can often be worth more to you than a salary rise costing your employer the same to provide.

But there are disadvantages to getting fringe benefits:

- no choice – you may find that your fringe benefits aren't the things you'd choose to spend your money on
- lower pension, life insurance and redundancy money – all these are often linked to your pay in £££, *excluding* the value of the fringe benefits you get.

A fringe benefit – or an expense?

Some payments which you might get from your employer are on the borderline between a fringe benefit, which is generally taxable and an allowable expense, which isn't. These include mileage allowance, removal expenses and overnight allowances, and are normally regarded as expenses because your employer is reimbursing you for money you have to spend in the course of your job. They are all tax-free as long as they count as *allowable expenses* – see p. 121.

Your employer may have what's called a *dispensation* for certain expenses and fringe benefits you get, such as a mileage or subsistence allowance. You don't have to pay tax on these expenses and benefits. If you get expenses and benefits for which there is no dispensation, your employer will give details to your Tax Inspector on **form P11D** if you

earn more than a certain amount – see below.
ICTA 1988 s166, s198

How are fringe benefits taxed?

Fringe benefits are taxed in one of three ways:

- some are tax-free
- some are taxed only if you count as earning £8,500 or more a year
- the rest are taxed whatever you earn.

See p. 147 for how individual benefits are taxed.

Swapping pay – a warning

No matter how much (or little) you earn, if you can swap some of your pay for a fringe benefit (or *vice versa*) the Revenue may tax you on the amount of pay you give up if this is more than the taxable value of the fringe benefit under the normal tax rules.

Heaton v. Bell 46 TC211; Tennant v. Smith 3 TC 158

Tax-free fringe benefits

There are many fringe benefits which you can get without having to pay any tax, provided certain conditions are met. Some of the more common ones include pension contributions from your employer, free life insurance and sick pay insurance, cheap or free drinks and meals.

Taxable fringe benefits

With these benefits, you pay tax on the *taxable value* of the benefit. This is also the amount you have to enter in your Tax Return. The taxable value will be the amount your fringe benefits cost your employer to provide, less anything you pay towards the cost (but see p. 154 for exceptions) *if you count as earning £8,500 a year*. If you don't, the taxable value will be the *second-hand value* of your fringe benefits – usually less than they cost your employer. In this case, the taxable value of fringe benefits which don't have a second-hand value (e.g. free hairdressing at work) is nil.
ICTA 1988 s156

Do you count as earning £8,500 or more?

For the 1992–3 tax year this will apply to you if you're paid at a rate of £8,500 or more a year. *At a rate of* means you'd be caught if, say, you were paid £4,500 for six months' work.

If you are paid at a lower rate than £8,500 a year, you will still count if the total of the following comes to more than £8,500:

- your earnings from your job
- your fringe benefits *valued as though you did earn £8,500 or more*
- any expenses reimbursed to you by your employer for which there is no dispensation (see p. 145), even if these count as allowable expenses.
  ICTA 1988 s167

If you have more than one job with the same (or an associated) company and your total earnings and expenses from these jobs come to £8,500 or more, you'll also be caught. This also applies to directors – see below.

Directors

A director is normally treated as earning £8,500 or more whatever he or she earns. But a director earning at a rate of less than £8,500 a year doesn't count if he or she:

- owns or controls five per cent or less of the shares in the company (together with close family and certain other associates), *and*
- is a full-time working director of the company, *or* works , for a charity or non-profit making company, *and*
- is not a director of an associated company.
  ICTA 1988 s167, s168 (8–12)

EXAMPLE 1

Joseph Jones is paid a salary of £7,800. His employer lets him use a new 1.3 litre car in which he drives over 18,000 miles on business. To find out if he counts as earning £8,500 or more, Joseph needs to add the taxable value of the car, assuming he does fall into this category, to his salary. This is £1,070 for the 1992–3 tax year, which takes him over the limit of £8,500. So Joseph does count as earning £8,500 or more.

How each fringe benefit is taxed

benefit	how it is taxed if you count as earning £8,500 or more	how it is taxed if you don't count as earning £8,500 or more
board and lodging, i.e. job-related accommodation (see also *living accommodation*) *ICTA 1988 s145, s163*	accommodation provided for you, tax-free; for other benefits, pay tax on what employer pays out *less* anything you pay towards employer's costs up to a limit – see p. 157	◀
company car, including use of the car for private purposes, employer pays costs, e.g. repairs, insurance *ICTA 1988 s156, s157, s158, s159, Sch 6*	pay tax on the taxable value of car – see p. 153	tax-free
clothes specially needed for work, e.g. overalls *Ward v. Dunn 52 TC 517*	tax-free	tax-free
crèche or day-nursery provided by employer *FA 1990 s20*	tax-free – but see p. 159 for cash payments or vouchers	◀
use of credit cards, charge cards *ICTA 1988 s142, s144*	taxed on what employer pays out *less* anything you pay towards employer's costs and *less* allowable expenses	◀
discounts on goods and services, if employers sell their own products cheap to employees	tax-free, as long as employer doesn't end up out of pocket, though a case yet to be decided may change this	◀
employees' outings, including Christmas party *ESC A70*	normally tax-free (up to £50 per person per year)	◀
fees and subscriptions to professional societies or associations *ICTA 1988 s201*	tax-free if society or association recognised by Inland Revenue and relevant to employment; if not, taxed on cost to employer	◀

147

benefit	how it is taxed if you count as earning £8,500 or more	how it is taxed if you don't count as earning £8,500 or more
food and drink – includes free or cheap meals, tea, coffee, etc. *ICTA 1988 s155 (5); ESC A74*	tax-free, if provided for all employees – even if separate facilities are provided on the employer's premises for different groups of employees	←
gifts, if they are genuinely personal, such as wedding or retirement gifts (but not a gift of money on retirement) *Herbert v. McQuade 4TC 489; Moorhouse v. Dooland 36TC 1*	tax-free	tax-free
gifts of things (not cash) from someone other than your employer *ESC A70*	tax-free, provided they cost £100 or less	←
gifts of something previously lent, e.g. furniture, TV *ICTA 1988 s156 (1), (2)*	pay tax on taxable value – see p. 159	pay tax on second-hand value
hairdressing at work *ICTA 1988 s156 (3), (4)*	pay tax on cost to your employer	tax-free
life insurance – cost of providing this under a scheme approved by the Inland Revenue *ICTA 1988 s155 (4)*	tax-free	tax-free
living accommodation, e.g. rent-free or low-rent home *ICTA 1988 s145, s146, s163*	sometimes tax-free – see p. 158	←
loans of money *ICTA 1988 s160, s161, Sch7; SI 1989/1297*	tax-free, if loan qualifies for tax relief; pay tax on taxable value of other loans – see p. 156	tax-free

benefit	how it is taxed if you count as earning £8,500 or more	how it is taxed if you don't count as earning £8,500 or more
loans of things, e.g. furniture *ICTA 1988 s156*	pay tax on taxable value – see p. 159	tax-free
long-service awards, e.g. gifts of things or shares (but not a gift of money) *ESC A22; Weston v. Hearn 25 TC 425*	tax-free, if given for service of 20 years or more with the same employer. The cost must not be more than £20 for each year of service and you must not have had such an award within the past 10 years	←
luncheon vouchers *ESC A2*	15p each working day is tax-free	←
medical bills insurance *ICTA 1988 s155(6)*	pay tax on cost to your employer (tax-free if insurance is to cover working abroad)	tax-free
mobile phones – including fixed car phones *ICTA 1988 s159A*	pay tax on fixed taxable value of £200	tax-free
mortgage – low-interest or interest-free *ICTA 1988 s160, s161, Sch 7*	tax-free, if interest qualifies, or would qualify, for tax relief	←
pension contributions your employer pays into an 'approved' or 'statutory' pension scheme for you *ICTA 1988 s590, s592*	tax-free	tax-free
petrol – if you get any for private use in company car *ICTA 1988 s158, s157(3), s167(2)*	pay tax on taxable value – see p. 153	pay tax on cost of petrol unless directly provided by employer – see p. 154

149

benefit	how it is taxed if you count as earning £8,500 or more	how it is taxed if you don't count as earning £8,500 or more
relocation allowances towards extra expenses in higher-cost housing areas *ESC A67*	tax-free if compulsorily transferred by employer provided certain conditions are met (but lump sum payments at time of transfer are taxable)	←
removal expenses (if reasonable) including solicitor's, surveyor's and estate agent's fees, stamp duty, removal costs, an allowance for carpets and curtains, temporary subsistence allowance, rent while you're looking for a new home and, in certain circumstances, the interest on a bridging loan even if the loan takes you over the £30,000 limit *ESC A5*	normally tax-free, if you have to move to take a new job or are transferred by your employer	←
scholarship and apprenticeship schemes awarded to you by your employer *SP 4/86*	tax-free if you are enrolled for at least one academic year and attend full-time for an average of at least 20 weeks a year. Rate of payment (including lodging, subsistence and travelling allowances but excluding tuition fees) must not be above £5,500 or the amount of a grant from a public body such as a research council, if higher – otherwise taxable in full. Payments for time at work taxable in normal way	←

benefit	how it is taxed if you count as earning £8,500 or more	how it is taxed if you don't count as earning £8,500 or more
scholarships awarded by your employer to your children *ICTA 1988, s154, s165*	normally pay tax on amount of scholarship. Amount is tax-free if scholarship awarded before 15 March 1983 as long as first payment was made before 6 April 1984 *and*, for payments made after 5 April 1989, your child is still at the same full-time school or college. Special rules apply if scholarship comes from a trust fund	tax-free
season ticket loans *ICTA 1988 s160, s161, Sch 7*	most are tax-free as the taxable value of the loan is usually nil – see p. 155	tax-free
shares bought cheap (or free) in your employer's company through an approved employee share scheme *ICTA 1988 s185, s186, s187, Sch 9, Sch 10, Sch 29*	tax-free – but see p. 161 and p. 162 for capital gains tax rules	←
sick pay insurance – cost of insurance paid for you by employer *ICTA 1988 s149, s154 (2)*	cost of insurance met by employer is tax-free if the scheme meets the Revenue's conditions. Income from scheme normally taxed as part of your earnings. If you pay some of the premiums, only the income provided by the employer's contributions is tax-free	←
social and sports facilities	normally tax-free	tax free
staff suggestion schemes – awards from schemes *ESC A57*	tax free up to an overall maximum of £5,000	←

benefit	how it is taxed if you count as earning £8,500 or more	how it is taxed if you don't count as earning £8,500 or more
training, e.g. attending a course or studying on normal pay; tuition fees *Humbles v. Brooks 40 TC 500; ESC A63* *ICTA 1988 s588, s589*	pay is taxed in the normal way. Books and tuition fees paid for by your employer for some external training courses in the UK are tax-free. Provided you're not away for more than 12 months, extra travel expenses and living costs met by your employer while on the course may not be taxable either. Similar expenses if you are leaving or have left your job for retraining in new work skills are also tax-free	←
transport between home and work for severely disabled employees who can't use public transport *ESC A59*	tax-free	tax-free
travel costs, e.g. for taxi, hire car for late-night journeys from work *ESC A66*	tax-free, provided you have to work to 9pm or later, doesn't happen regularly or frequently and public transport has ceased or would be difficult	←
travelling and subsistence allowance when public transport is disrupted by industrial action *ESC A58*	tax-free	tax-free
vouchers – such as travel voucher (e.g. British Rail season ticket) or any other voucher which can be exchanged for goods or services (e.g. a letter to a tailor telling him to give you a new suit) or for cash (e.g. a cheque) *ICTA 1988 s141, s143 s144*	pay tax on amount your employer pays out *less* anything you pay towards the cost. If you work for a transport organisation, any transport voucher under a scheme in operation on 25 March 1982 is tax-free	←

Some fringe benefits in more detail

We give here details of the special rules for:

- use of cars and fuel
- cheap loans
- living accommodation
- workplace nurseries
- loans of things and their subsequent gifts to you
- employee share schemes.

Cars and petrol

The taxable values of company cars are set each year. The table opposite gives these values if you count as earning £8,500 or more in the 1992–3 tax year. For other employees the taxable value is nil. The figures for petrol apply if you get *any* petrol for private use from your employer which you don't pay for in full – no matter how much or how little. (From 6 April 1992, the taxable value of fuel for diesel cars has been lower than for that of non-diesel cars.) If you don't count as earning £8,500 or more, you pay tax on the cost of the petrol unless it is provided directly by your employer. Travelling to and from work will normally count as *private use* of a car.

If you have a company car for only part of the tax year, the taxable values (both for the car and, if this applies, for petrol) are reduced proportionately. If you have to pay your employer a sum of money for private use of the car, you can subtract this sum from the value in the table. For electric cars and cars with rotary engines, ask your Tax Inspector for details of the taxable values.

If you cover at least 18,000 miles on business in the tax year, the benefit (both for the car and for petrol) is half the figure in the table. If you have the car for only part of the tax year, the 18,000 figure is reduced proportionately. If you drive no more than 2,500 miles on business during the tax year, the value for the car is 1.5 times that in the table (the charge for petrol stays the same).

If you have a second company car, the taxable value for the car you use least for business travel is 1.5 times the figure in the table whatever your business mileage. The charge for the other car, and for both cars' petrol, is the normal charge for cars of their engine size. If the second car is provided for another member of your family, these

153

rules still apply. But if you and another member of your family both earn £8,500 or more and each has a company car, each car is taxed as the first car whether or not you're both employed by the same company.

Motoring costs for a company car paid by your employer

If your employer pays certain costs, such as repairs, business petrol, insurance, direct (e.g. settling a company account), it doesn't affect your tax position. But if *you* pay them, claim the business part of what you pay as *allowable expenses* in your Tax Return, i.e. the proportion attributable to your business mileage. And if your employer reimburses you in full or in part (e.g. by a mileage allowance), also enter what you get under *expense allowances*, unless your employer has a dispensation (see p. 144).

If your company car has a telephone, you have to pay extra tax. And if your employer provides you with a telephone for your own private car, there'll be tax to pay on private use unless you reimburse your employer, see p. 153.

A free car-parking space provided at or near your place of work isn't taxable. And there will be no tax to pay if your employer pays for a parking space (or reimburses the cost). *ICTA 1988 s155(1A) s157, s158, s159A, Sch 6; ESC A71*

Pool cars

A pool car doesn't count as a fringe benefit and there is no tax to pay by the people who use it. To qualify as a pool car, the car must be made available to (and used by) more than one employee, and it mustn't normally be kept overnight at, or near, an employee's home. Any private use of the car must be incidental to business use – e.g. occasional travel between home and office as part of genuine business trips. *ICTA 1988 s159*

Cars, the value of which when new was up to £19,250

| size of engine | age of car at the end of the tax year | | charge for petrol | charge for diesel |
	under 4 years	4 years or more		
1400 cc or less	£2,140	£1,460	£500	£460
1401 to 2000 cc	£2,770	£1,800	£630	£460
more than 2000 cc	£4,440	£2,980	£940	£590

Cars, the value of which when new was £19,251 to £29,000

all sizes of engine	£5,750	£3,870	as above	as above

Cars, the value of which when new was more than £29,000

all sizes of engine	£9,300	£6,170	as above	as above

Cheap loans

If your employer lets you have a loan on which you pay little or no interest, there may be tax to pay. How much depends on whether or not the loan qualifies for tax relief.

Qualifying loans If the loan or part of it qualifies for tax relief, then the part which *does* qualify is a tax-free fringe benefit. So, for example, if you get a loan to buy your only or main home, the interest on the first £30,000 of it is a tax-free fringe benefit because it qualifies for tax relief. Interest on anything over £30,000 is a taxable benefit because it doesn't qualify for tax relief. If the loan is interest-free and you took out a second loan (e.g. from a bank or building society) at the same time as, or later than, the employer's loan. It's the second loan which counts towards the £30,000 limit and attracts tax relief. Any employer's loan over the limit counts as a taxable benefit. The excess over £30,000 is taxed in the same way as a loan not qualifying for tax-relief (see below).

Because tax relief on mortgages has now been restricted to the basic rate (see p. 202), higher-rate taxpayers will find interest on the first £30,000 of their cheap mortgage is no longer tax-free. But they'll only be taxed on the bit that doesn't attract tax relief – and so they'll pay tax of 15 per cent (the difference between basic-rate and higher-rate tax) on the benefit of their cheaper mortgage interest payments. The tax will be deducted from their salary through PAYE, see p. 115.

Other loans A cheap loan which doesn't qualify for tax relief counts as a taxable benefit, *unless* you don't count as earning £8,500 or more, in which case it is tax-free. The taxable value of such a loan is the difference between the amount of interest you pay and the amount you would pay if you were charged the *official rate of interest* – 10.5 per cent a year, at the time we went to press.

You don't have to pay tax if the value the Revenue puts on your loans adds up to £300 or less. If the value comes to £301 or more, you are taxed on the whole lot – not just on the amount over £300.

EXAMPLE 2

George Hamlyn borrowed £5,000 from his employer to buy some furniture. He will repay the loan in a lump sum after three years and will pay interest at a rate of four per cent – i.e. interest of £200 a year. George earns £19,000 and the interest on the loan doesn't qualify for tax relief. So he will pay tax for the 1992–3 tax year on the difference between the interest he pays his employer, i.e. £200, and the interest he would pay at the official rate, i.e. 10.5 per cent of £5,000 = £525. So he'll pay tax on £525 – £200 = £325. Note that George will pay tax on this whole amount, even though he's only just over the £300 tax-free limit.

Assuming the official rate stays at 10.5 per cent, you could have an interest-free loan of £2,845 for the 1992–3 tax year completely free of tax, if you paid it back in one lump sum at the end of the tax year. (The official rate of interest was 10.75 per cent for the first two months of the current tax year). In practice, you are likely to start repaying the loan sooner, for instance monthly, so the maximum amount you can borrow without paying tax will be more than £2,845. For example, if you have a loan for a whole tax year and pay it off with regular monthly instalments, you could borrow up to £5,230 before you hit the £300 barrier. Loans where the total average balance outstanding over the tax year is up to about £2,845 won't be taxed.

First method
Step 1   Work out the average of the amount you owe at the start and at the end of the tax year (or at the time you got the loan or paid it off if these fall within the tax year).

Step 2   Multiply the answer to Step 1 by the number of complete months for which you've had the loan during the tax year (months for this purpose start on the sixth day of the month).

156

Step 3 Divide the answer to Step 2 by 12.

Step 4 Multiply the answer to Step 3 by the official rate of interest for the year (or by the average rate of interest if the rate varied).

Second method
Interest is worked out on a daily basis, taking into account how much you owe each day and the official rate of interest at the time.

Depending on how your loan varies during the year, either method may give a higher amount. You or the Inland Revenue can elect to use the second method, though the Revenue is unlikely to do this unless it would come to a significantly higher amount. You should elect the second method if it works in your favour. Note that if you pay off a yearly loan by regular instalments, both methods should give the same answer.

If you are not sure about your loan, ask your employer whether there is a dispensation (see p. 144) for loans of the size given to you. If there is a dispensation you'll pay no tax.

In the case of a loan where its period and interest rate are both fixed and unvariable, and where you're charged interest at not less than the official rate which applied at the time you got the loan, there'll be no tax to pay if it begins to look 'cheap' simply because the official rate of interest has gone up.

If your employer lets you off paying back a loan, the amount you're let off paying counts as part of your income, and is taxed in the normal way.
ICTA 1988 s160, Sch 7; SI 1989/1297; ESC A5

Living accommodation

A rent-free or low-rent home can be a tax-free fringe benefit if one of the following applies:

- it is necessary to live in the home to do your job properly (e.g. you are a caretaker)
- living in the home enables you to do your job better, and it is customary for people doing your sort of job to live in such a home (e.g. you are a publican)
- there is a special threat to your security, and you live in the home as part of special security arrangements.

A home provided for a company director for either of the first two reasons above qualifies as a tax-free fringe benefit only if he or she owns five per cent or less of the shares in the company, *and* is a full-time working director *or* the company is non-profit making or a charitable body.

There are special rules for free or cheap accommodation abroad – see p. 168.

Even if the home does count as a tax-free benefit, if you count as earning £8,500 or more you will have to pay some tax on what your employer pays for heating, lighting, cleaning, decorating or furnishing (but the value put on these by your Tax Inspector cannot be more than 10 per cent of your earnings not including these benefits).

If a rent-free or low-rent home doesn't count as a tax-free fringe benefit, the Revenue values the benefit at either the *gross value* of the home (the figure the rateable value used to be based on, but with an adjustment in Scotland) or the rent your employer pays if greater, less any rent you pay. For properties which don't have a gross value (such as property built since the abolition of rates) your employer will estimate what the gross value would have been and agree a figure with the Revenue. This method of valuing the benefit applies whether or not you count as earning £8,500 or more.

If the home costs your employer more than £75,000 to provide, there will be an extra tax bill. The extra tax bill is worked out by finding how much the accommodation cost to buy and set up and deducting £75,000. You then multiply this figure by the *official rate of interest* on cheap loans – 10.5 per cent at the time we went to press. You must use the official rate at the start of the tax year i.e. 6 April 1992. But you can deduct any rent paid in excess of the *gross value*.

Agricultural workers whose employers give them free board and lodging may be able to take higher wages and arrange their own accommodation instead. That would normally make the value of their board and lodging taxable. But by a concession, agricultural workers who don't count as earning £8,500 or more will generally avoid the tax.
ICTA 1988 s145, s146, s163; ESC A56, A60

Workplace nurseries

In the 1990 Budget, the Chancellor announced that from 6 April 1990 the cost of workplace nurseries provided by employers would no longer be a taxable benefit for those who count as earning £8,500 or more. The exemption applies to nurseries run by the employer at the workplace or elsewhere and to nurseries set up jointly with other employers, voluntary bodies or local authorities (provided the employer participates in the cost and management of the scheme). Facilities provided for older children after school or during school holidays are also tax-free.

Any cash payments or vouchers provided by an employer to cover child care (e.g. childminders or private nurseries) are still taxable for all employees. Any child-care places bought by an employer in other companies' schemes where the employer is not involved in the management are also taxable.

FA1988 s155

Loans of items and their subsequent gift to you

If you count as earning £8,500 or more and your employer lends you something like furniture or a TV, your Tax Inspector will value it at 20 per cent of the market value at the time your employer first loaned the thing out, *less* anything you pay for the use of it. For items first loaned out before 6 April 1980, the 20 per cent figure becomes 10 per cent. Anything your employer pays for servicing (or any other costs) is added to the taxable value.

If your employer gives you something previously lent to you, your Tax Inspector will value it at the market value at the time your employer first loaned it out, *less* anything you've paid towards it, and *less* any amount you've already paid tax on (e.g. under the 20 per cent rule). But if this value is lower than the market value when the item is given to you, you'll be taxed on the higher (market) value, *less* anything you've paid towards it. And if the item was first loaned out before 6 April 1980, its value is taken as the market value when the item was given to you (*less* anything you've paid towards it).

If you count as earning £8,500 or more and you use something for which your employer pays rent (e.g. a flat, a TV) your Tax Inspector can value the benefit at the amount your employer pays in rent, running costs, etc., *less* anything you pay, if this comes to more than the value using the normal method.

If you don't count as earning £8,500 or more, there's no

tax on a loan; and you're taxed on the *second-hand value* of a gift.
ICTA 1988 s156

Employee share schemes

An employee share scheme is organised by an employer and is a way in which an employee can get a stake in the company he or she works for. The following sorts of schemes have considerable tax advantages if they are *approved* by the Revenue:

- profit-sharing schemes
- share option schemes
- SAYE share option schemes.

Profit-sharing schemes
Under an *approved* scheme you can get shares in your employer's firm free of tax. The yearly limit is £3,000 worth of shares, or 10 per cent of your earnings, whichever is higher, with an overall limit of £8,000-worth of shares a year. To get approval, the scheme must meet various conditions. For example, the shares must be held in trust for you. They can't normally be handed over to you from the trust for at least two years (unless you reach retirement age, are made redundant, or stop work through injury or disablement). And if you withdraw your shares from the trust within five years of getting them, there will normally be some income tax to pay (unless the shares are withdrawn because you die).

If you sell the shares for more than their value at the time you were given them, the gain you make counts as a chargeable capital gain, and there may be capital gains tax to pay (see p. 264). And any dividends you get count as part of your income for the tax year in which you get them.
ICTA 1988 s186, s187, Sch 9, Sch 10

Share option schemes
A share option scheme gives you the right (or *option*) to buy shares in your employer's company at some future date, but at today's market price. There is no income tax to pay on any gain you make when you exercise your option, if the scheme is an *approved* one. Instead, any gain you make when you sell (or give away) the shares will count as a chargeable capital gain. In addition, employers have the

discretion to offer the option to buy shares at a discount of up to 15 per cent, for options granted on or after 1 January 1992 – but only if the scheme is open to all employees.

Any tax will be based on the difference between the price you paid to buy the shares, and the price when you sell (or give away) the share – see p. 264. To get approval, the scheme must meet certain conditions. For example, you can't get an option of more than the greater of £100,000-worth of shares (valued at the time the option is granted) or four times your earnings (see p. 121) excluding the taxable value of your fringe benefits and after deduction of any contributions you make to your employer's pension scheme in the current tax year. The preceding year's earnings are used if they are greater.

When you exercise your option, you must be able to do so at the market price at the time the option was made. The option must be taken up at some time between three and ten years, but this can only be done at three-yearly intervals, i.e. three times during the seven years. Employees who work at least 20 hours a week (directors, 25 hours a week), are allowed to get an option under these rules.

From 18 March 1986 you are liable for income tax on anything you receive for agreeing *not* to exercise the option or for granting someone else an option over the shares.

If you are in a share option scheme which is not *approved*, you will pay income tax on the difference between the market value when you exercise your option and the cost to you of the shares, including any amount paid for the option. You might have to pay capital gains tax when you sell (or give away) your shares, based on the difference between their market value when you exercise your option and their value when you dispose of them.

ICTA 1988 s135, s185, s187, Sch 9

Savings-related share option schemes

Your company can run a savings scheme giving you the option to buy its shares some years in the future at a price fixed now. Provided the scheme is an *approved* one and you buy the shares with the proceeds of an SAYE scheme – which normally runs for five or seven years – there will usually be no income tax to pay when the option is given to you, nor on the difference between the value of the shares when you buy them and the price you pay for them (which must not be less than 80 per cent of their market value at the time the option is given). But if you sell (or give away) the shares,

there could be capital gains tax to pay based on the difference between the price you buy at and the market value when you sell or give them away. The maximum saving is £250 a month and the minimum can't be more than £10.
ICTA 1988 s185, s187, Sch 9

Company takeovers and share option schemes

It is now possible for employees in a company which is taken over to exchange their existing share options under an approved share option (including savings-related schemes) for options to buy shares in the company which takes over. The replacement options can only be granted if certain conditions are met to ensure that the employees concerned will be no better or worse off than if the takeover had not happened.
ICTA 1988 Sch 9(15)

Single-company PEPs

Shares acquired under an all-employee profit-sharing and savings-related share option scheme can now be transferred, tax-free, into a single-company Personal Equity Plan (PEP, see p. 000). Shares with a value of up to £3,000 can be invested in a single-company PEP, in addition to the usual yearly limit of £6,000. The transfer into a single-company PEP must be made within 42 days of the employee acquiring the shares.
ICTA 1988 s333

9 WORKING ABROAD

If you want to keep the Revenue's hands off your hard-earned guilders, dinars or even pounds, you'll have to earn them abroad. But just earning them abroad isn't enough. You'll have to be absent from the UK for at least a year to get your earnings free of UK tax.

Where you live – according to the Revenue

In general, the UK tax system aims to tax all earnings made in the UK, and all earnings paid to people who are *resident* and *ordinarily resident* in the UK, even if the money is earned outside the country. But if you're paid money abroad and aren't allowed to take it out of the country (because of a ban on doing so, or a war, say) you can ask the Revenue to let you off paying tax on it until it is possible for the money to be sent to the UK. You'll then have to pay tax on the income whether or not it is sent to the UK.

The terms 'resident' and 'ordinarily resident' have not been defined by Act of Parliament, so their interpretation is up to the courts. Whether you are resident and/or ordinarily resident is decided separately for each tax year. But you will always be treated as resident if you're in the UK for at least six months (183 days) of the tax year. The 183 days may be made up of one visit or a succession of visits. Under current Revenue practice, the day of your arrival and the day of your departure do not normally count towards the 183 days. You're also likely to be treated as resident if:

- over a four-year period, you come to the UK for an average of three months or more each year, *or*
- you visit the UK at all during the tax year, and have accommodation for your use here (even if you don't own it). This doesn't apply if you work wholly abroad full-time. But if you're married, and your husband (or wife) doesn't work abroad full-time and comes back to the UK

163

with you, he (or she) could count as resident, even though you don't.

The term 'ordinarily resident' is less clear-cut and is to do with your intentions and way of life. If you are treated as being resident in the UK year after year, you are likely to count as ordinarily resident too.

A person can be resident (or ordinarily resident) in two or more countries at the same time – or even none at all. *ICTA 1988 s334–s336, s19(1) (2), s192; IR20*

Domicile

You'll generally be considered to be *domiciled* in the UK if this is where you have your permanent home and where you're likely to end your days. If you're considered to be domiciled in the UK, it will largely affect your liability to capital gains tax and inheritance tax, even if you're currently living abroad.

How you're taxed

If you're resident and ordinarily resident in the UK, you'll be taxed on all you earn abroad unless you qualify for a *100 per cent deduction*. If you do qualify, all your earnings from abroad will be treated as free of UK tax.

The 100 per cent deduction

If you're abroad for a continuous period of 365 *qualifying days* (see opposite) or more (not necessarily coinciding with a tax year), all your earnings will be tax-free. Where possible (e.g. you work for a UK company which has sent you abroad) the deduction is given in your PAYE code, and if the Revenue is satisfied you'll get the 100 per cent deduction, you'll get a 'No Tax' code (see p. 134) for those earnings.

Even if you come back to the UK during your 365 days, you may still qualify for the 100 per cent deduction. The Revenue adds together:

- the continuous days abroad immediately *before* your UK visit
- the number of days in your UK visit
- the number of days abroad immediately *after* your UK visit.

If the number of days in your UK visit comes to more than one-sixth of this total *or* to more than 62 days, the continuity of your 365 days is broken at the end of your first period abroad. And a new period of 365 days starts at the beginning of your second period abroad. But if your UK visit is one-sixth of the total above (or less) and not more than 62 days, the whole time, including the days in the UK, counts towards your 365 days. If you come back to the UK for another visit, the whole period which counted towards your 365 days is included when working out the continuous days immediately before your second UK visit, and the total number of days that you've spent in the UK in previous visits is added to the number of days in your latest visit – see the example below. The 62-day limit doesn't apply to the cumulative total for UK visits. The process is repeated for each UK visit.

Note that the 100 per cent deduction applies only to work done entirely abroad, unless your work in the UK is regarded as *incidental* to the overseas employment. Things like getting further instructions, or reporting to head office, would be treated as incidental; beyond this the Revenue deals with each case on its merits.

ICTA 1988 s132(4), s193(1)

Qualifying days

A qualifying day of absence is a day abroad spent mainly working, and at the end of which you are absent. The day you leave the UK to travel to your job also counts, but the day of your return doesn't. Aircrews and seafarers count as working abroad during trips that take them to or from (or between) places abroad.

ICTA 1988 s132(4), s193(1), Sch12(4)

EXAMPLE

Angela Tavistock and Brian Duckworth work for the same company. They both have to go abroad three times in the next 16 months or so, for a total of 400 days away. They know when they have to be away and when they will come back for UK visits, so they work out if they are entitled to the 100 per cent deduction.

Neither of Angela's UK trips exceeds the limits, so her earnings will be free of UK tax.

165

Brian's first visit to the UK breaks the one-sixth rule, and his second and third trips abroad (including the 20 days of his visit to the UK) don't add up to 365 days. So he can't claim the 100 per cent deduction. If Brian could arrange another working trip abroad which linked to his third trip abroad without breaking the one-sixth rule, and he then met the 365-day requirement, he could claim the 100 per cent deduction for his second and third trips abroad and the final one that took him over the 365-day requirement.

If Angela's work (other than work incidental to overseas employment) was done partly in the UK during visits home, she would not get the 100 per cent deduction from all her earnings. It would be given against earnings shown to be *reasonable* given the nature of the duties, the time devoted to them in the UK and abroad, and all other relevant circumstances.

Angela	days	1/6 limit exceeded?	**Brian**	days	1/6 limit exceeded?
1st trip abroad	100		1st trip abroad	100	
1st UK visit	20		1st UK visit	60	
2nd trip abroad	150	no (20/270)	2nd trip abroad	150	yes (60/310)
2nd UK visit	60		2nd UK visit	20	
3rd trip abroad	150	no (80/480)	3rd trip abroad	150	no (20/320)*

*but Brian hasn't met the 365-day requirement since the beginning of his second trip abroad.

When the normal rules don't apply

It can happen that your visit to the UK is either caused, or extended, for reasons beyond your control. For example, you may have been working in one of the Gulf states at the outbreak of the Gulf crisis in 1990 and had to return to the UK for safety reasons. Maybe you were already on a visit to the UK and could not return abroad because of the outbreak of a crisis or because you were ill. Days spent in the UK because of exceptional circumstances won't be taken into account in working out how long you have stayed in the UK, so long as you intend to resume full-time employment abroad. However, these days will be taken into account when it comes to the 183-day rule (see p. 163) *SP 2/91*

Servants of the crown

Servants of the crown (e.g. UK diplomats and members of the armed forces) working abroad are, for most income tax purposes, taxed as if they worked in the UK. But any extra allowance paid for working abroad isn't taxable. *ICTA 1988 s132, s319*

Personal allowances while you're away

If you're resident in the UK, you'll get your full personal allowance for the tax year. So if, say, you get the 100 per cent deduction you'll be able to use all your personal allowances against other income you get in the UK – e.g. National Savings interest, dividends, UK earnings.

Travelling expenses

You don't have to pay tax on what your employer pays towards the cost of travel to a job abroad (and back again when you've finished), or between countries where you're working. If your employer doesn't pay, you can claim such costs you incur as *allowable expenses* – see p. 121.

You can now make any number of visits to the UK, paid for or reimbursed by your employer, without being taxed on the travel expenses, providing your job can be performed *only* outside the UK and you go abroad purely for work purposes. And, providing you've worked abroad continuously for at least 60 days and there are no more than two return trips for each person per tax year, what your employer pays towards some other journeys is tax-free too:

- visits by your wife (or husband) or children under 18
- return trips that you make to visit them.

But if *you* pay for these trips, the costs cannot count as *allowable expenses*. There's no tax to pay on costs, met by your employer, of travel in the UK at the beginning or end of your journey, e.g. from a UK home to the airport. *ICTA 1988 s193, s194, s195*

167

Board and lodging abroad

If your job is done wholly abroad, and your employer pays (or reimburses) the cost of board and lodging which enables you to carry out your duties, there'll be no tax to pay on this fringe benefit. But you *will* be taxed on the cost to your employer of board and lodging for your husband or wife and children, and of any board and lodging for a holiday abroad. If your employer doesn't pay, you can't claim any board and lodging as an *allowable expense*.

If your job is done partly in the UK and partly abroad, there'll normally be no tax to pay on what your employer pays towards *your* board and lodging, and if your employer doesn't pay, you may be able to claim the cost as an allowable expense. See p. 121 for details.
ICTA 1988 s193

Golden handshakes

If you're a UK resident, redundancy payments you get after working abroad may be wholly tax-free, even if they're over £30,000 (see p. 138). Payments you get are tax-free if any of the following apply:

- you worked abroad for at least three-quarters of the time you did the job
- you worked abroad for all of the last 10 years
- you did the job for over 20 years, and at least 10 of the last 20 years *and* at least half the total time was spent working abroad.

Where the payment isn't wholly tax-free, part may be. An amount will be deducted from the payment equal to:

$$\frac{\text{number of years you worked abroad} \times \text{the amount which would otherwise have been taxable}}{\text{total number of years' service}}$$

You count as working abroad if you weren't ordinarily resident or if you got the 100 per cent deduction (see p. 164).
ICTA 1988 s188, sch 11

Double taxation relief

If you pay local income tax on what you earn abroad, you may be eligible for *double taxation relief*. The UK has a number of double taxation agreements with other countries, which prevent you paying tax both abroad and in the UK on the same income. This is done either by making certain types of income (e.g. earnings, dividends, business profits) taxable in one country and other types taxable in the other or by reducing the UK tax bill by the smaller of the overseas tax liability and the UK tax liability.

If there is no double taxation agreement, you can claim *unilateral relief* if you're a UK resident earning income which has been taxed abroad. You'll be allowed to offset the tax you paid abroad against your UK tax bill.
ICTA 1988 s788–s790; IR6

Tax if you're non-resident

As a non-resident, you pay UK income tax on only your UK earnings – at the lower rate and the basic rate and higher rate if your UK income is high enough. You'll also have to pay tax on your UK investment income. But there may be relief given under a double taxation agreement – see above. (Note: some British Government stocks have a tax-free return for non-residents. And you won't normally have to pay UK tax on bank and building society interest.)

Becoming non-resident

If you work abroad full-time (so that any work you do in the UK is *incidental* to your work abroad – see p. 165), you'll count as non-resident and not ordinarily resident providing your visits back to the UK don't exceed the limits on p. 164 *and* providing your trip abroad spans a complete tax year or more. You'll count as non-resident from the day after you leave to the day before you come back.

If you're not employed full-time abroad, in addition to meeting the requirements above, you'll have to produce some evidence to support your claim to non-residence – e.g. selling your home in the UK and setting up a permanent home abroad. If you can do this, your claim may be accepted provisionally. It will normally be confirmed when you've been away for a complete tax year during

which visits back to the UK have not amounted to more than an average of three months a year. If you're unable to provide sufficient evidence, the decision is delayed for three years, and your tax liability will be worked out provisionally as though you were still resident (except for any tax year in which you don't set foot in the UK at all). After the three years are up, you'll be able to claim back any overpaid tax if it's confirmed that you're non-resident.
IR20; ESC B13 (untaxed interest)

Personal allowances

You can claim personal allowances as if you were resident in the UK, and a non-resident husband can give unused married couple's allowance to his wife in most cases.
ICTA 1988 s278

10 WORKING FOR YOURSELF

Being self-employed includes all sorts of occupations – owning a shop, being a wholesaler, working as a doctor, barrister or writer, and so on. Most of this chapter is for people in business on their own ('sole traders', in the jargon), but we also tell you something about partnerships on p. 196. Casual earnings are dealt with in Chapter 7 on p. 140.

Self-employed people can generally claim more in expenses to reduce their tax bills. Tax is not deducted from the earnings of the self-employed before they are paid, as it is for employees. And they do not have to pay the tax they owe until some time – up to 20 months – after they have received the money. This is because they are taxed under the rules for Schedule D Case I or Case II, rather than as employees under Schedule E (see p. 40).

Do you count as self-employed?

To be treated as self-employed, you must convince the Revenue that you are genuinely in business on your own account. If you own a shop or offer a mobile car mechanic service, say, provide all your own equipment and find all your own customers, there is little doubt that you are self-employed. But there can be circumstances in which, though you may regard yourself as self-employed, the Revenue says you are not.

In general, you are on dangerous ground if all (or nearly all) your work comes from just one source – from one company you have a contract with, say – and you are paid on a regular basis without having to send in an invoice. The Revenue may decide you are an employee with a *contract of service* rather than a self-employed person with a *contract for services*. If the Revenue says you have a contract of service, you may be taxed under Schedule E as an employee and the company will have to deduct tax from your pay under the Pay-As-You-Earn system. This is particularly likely to happen if all the work you do is carried out on the company's premises.

Each Inland Revenue and DSS local office has someone responsible for saying whether or not you will be treated as self-employed, and who will confirm decisions in writing if you wish. Also, see Inland Revenue leaflet *IR56*.

If you are a director of a limited company, no matter how small, you are an employed person, not self-employed.

What is trading?

You may be taxed as if you're a business, even if you don't think you are, if your Tax Inspector says you are *trading*. You might be said to be trading if, among other points:

- you frequently buy and sell similar items
- you sell items which you haven't owned for very long
- you alter the items so that you can sell them for more
- your motive in buying and selling is to make a profit.
  ICTA 1988 s18, s832

A simpler system?

The Inland Revenue issued proposals in August 1991 aimed at producing 'a simpler system for taxing the self-employed'. The new system has not yet been introduced, but it is claimed that the changes should reduce the self-employed taxpayer's dealings with the Revenue and create a more streamlined system, e.g. by changing from the preceding year basis for taxing profits (see below).

When profits are taxed

A big advantage of being taxed as self-employed is that there can be a considerable delay before you have to pay tax on the profits you make. There are two things you can do to get the longest delay you can:

- choose your *accounting year-end* carefully, and
- use the rules about which profits are taxed when your business starts – see Table 1 on p. 174.

When your business has been going for two complete tax years, tax will normally be charged on a *preceding year basis* (see Table 1) – i.e. your tax bill for the 1992–3 tax year will be based on the profit you made in your accounting year ending in the 1991–2 tax year. This tax will have to be paid in two equal instalments on 1 January 1993 and 1 July 1993.

Occasional or spare-time earnings

If your 'business' is simply occasional freelance or spare-time work, it will normally be taxed on a *current year basis* – i.e. your tax bill for the 1992–3 tax year is based on the profit you make during that tax year. For more details, see p. 140.
ICTA 1988 s69

Starting a business

Choice of accounting year

Your accounting year need not run from 1 January to 31 December, nor need it coincide with the tax year. If you choose your accounting year carefully, e.g. end it a little after the start of the tax year, there could be as much as 20 months before you start to pay tax on the profits you've earned. As long as your profits are rising, this could be an advantage, because you will be paying tax on lower profits than you are currently making.

EXAMPLE 1

Accounting year end		dates tax due	time lag
31 December 1992		1 January 1994	12 months
	and	1 July 1994	18 months
31 March 1993		1 January 1994	9 months
	and	1 July 1994	15 months
30 April 1993		1 January 1995	20 months
	and	1 July 1995	26 months

Your first accounting 'year' doesn't have to cover exactly 12 months, but once you have chosen a date to make your first accounts up to, you should normally stick to that date in the following years as the rules about changing are very complicated – see Inland Revenue leaflet *IR26*. But if you think you may benefit by changing the date, get advice from an accountant. If you're certain that the profits for your first accounting period will be low, it can pay you to make your first accounting period longer than a year – see Example 2, opposite.

Table 1: What your tax bill is based on in the opening years of a business

	Tax is initially based on	But for some years, there is a choice
First tax year you are in business	*Actual profit* [1] in that tax year	no choice this year
Second tax year	Profit in your first 12 months of operation	**your choice**: you can choose to have your tax bills for the second and third tax years (but not just one of them) based on the *actual profit* [1] for each of these tax years. **Do so if this would make the total tax bill for the two years smaller**
Third tax year	Profit in your accounting year ending in the preceding tax year (or, if your first accounting year hasn't come to an end, normally your first 12 months' profit)	
Fourth and subsequent tax years	Profit in your accounting year ending in the preceding tax year (i.e. *preceding year basis*)	no choice for these years

[1] Your *actual profit* for any tax year is the proportion of your profits (worked out on a time basis) which will be attributed to that tax year. Suppose your accounting period doesn't coincide with the tax year. If you need to attribute your profits, do it on this basis:

profits in accounting year × number of months of accounting period in tax year ÷ number of months in accounting period

If your first accounting period is more than 12 months, the taxable profits for your third and fourth tax years may be a proportion of the taxable profits you make in your first accounting period – see example below. Your Tax Inspector may insist that you apportion profits on a daily basis.

Note that if you want to choose to have your tax bills for the second and third year based on actual profits, you have to choose within six years after the end of the third year of assessment.

EXAMPLE 2

Henry Haswell started in business on 6 November 1991. He decided to make his first accounting period last 18 months and end on 30 April 1993. He expected his taxable profits to be low for that period – £10,000, say. Assuming that he does in fact make taxable profits of £10,000 in his first accounting period, his assessments of taxable profits for the first five tax years are likely to be as follows:

tax year

1991–2	$^5/_{18} \times$ £10,000 = £2,778
1992–3	$^{12}/_{18} \times$ £10,000 = £6,667
1993–4	$^{12}/_{18} \times$ £10,000 = £6,667
1994–5	$^{12}/_{18} \times$ £10,000 = £6,667
1995–6	profits in accounting year on 30 April 1994

If Henry had decided to end his accounting period on 31 March his assessment for the 1994–5 tax year would be based on his accounting year ending on 31 March 1994.

You and your Tax Inspector

When you've been in business for nearly a year, your Tax Inspector will ask you for your accounts for your first accounting period. If you can't provide them – because, for example, your first accounting period isn't finished – the Inspector will shortly send you an assessment of tax. You will receive two assessments, one for each of the first two tax years. When you get the assessments, if you don't agree with them you can appeal and apply to postpone payment. You normally need to do this within 30 days – see p. 61. If it turns out in the end that more tax is due than is shown on the assessment, interest can be charged on the extra tax due, as well as on any tax you've postponed paying.

After your first accounting period is over, send your accounts showing your taxable profit to your Tax Inspector. You don't always need to send a balance sheet and you don't need to have your accounts audited. If your total turnover is less than £15,000 a year, you only have to submit *three line accounts* giving your total turnover, total business purchases and expenses, and your net profit. But you must be able to back up your accounts with proper records, if your Tax Inspector should challenge them. You

175

need written receipts for as many items as possible. Keep a record of your cash payments in and out of your bank account and your petty cash box.

There are some simple rules to cut down the chances of being investigated by the Revenue (see p. 65):

- find out the profit margin for people in similar businesses, and if yours is lower send a note saying why
- if the income you take out of the business is very low, e.g. because you are living on savings, tell your Tax Inspector why this is so
- try to send your accounts in on time
- don't miss out simple things, such as National Savings Investment account interest, from your Tax Return
- if possible, send a balance sheet and list of fixed assets as well as a profit and loss account
- if you've made a loss, explain it.
  ICTA 1988 s60–s63; TMA 1970 s31, s55, s86

Checklist: starting a business

- decide whether to register for VAT – see p. 194
- inform the Department of Social Security
- inform your local Tax Inspector
- make a list of fixed assets, e.g. office equipment, car
- get cash books to show cash paid into (and taken out of) the bank, and a book for petty cash
- set up an accounting system (e.g. in a book – or books) to show details of sales and purchases. Sort the purchases into different types, e.g. stationery, travel, heating and lighting
- if you need stocks of raw materials and other goods, keep records of what you've bought, what you've sold, and what has gone from stock
- get written receipts and file them in date order
- get a notebook to record items for which there's no receipt
- plan how you are going to pay your tax bill – e.g. by putting money aside each month
- if a car is used partly for your business, keep a record of business mileage, petrol, and all running costs
- if you are going to use items you already own in your business, e.g. a car, typewriter, computer, include them in your accounts. You will be able to claim capital allowances on them (and you may be able to recover the VAT)
- choose your accounting year-end to take advantage of delay in tax payments – see p. 173
- if profits are likely to be low in first year, take advantage of the rules about starting in business – see p. 173
- consider employing your spouse or making your spouse partner – see p. 193

- ask for any expenditure before you start business to count as pre-trading expenditure – see p. 179
- if you make a loss in the first year, remember you can set it off against other income – see p. 192
- make sure you have adequate life insurance and pension cover. Think about *permanent health insurance* in case you're ever too ill to work.

Closing a business

In the last tax year in which you're in business you are taxed on the *actual profit* – see [1] on p. 174 – you make in that tax year. In your last-but-two and last-but-one tax years your Tax Inspector can choose how to work out your tax bills. The Inspector can either base the bills on your profit in your accounting year ending in the preceding year. Or when you tell the Revenue that you've closed down your business, the Inspector can choose to base your tax bills for both years (but not just one of them) on the *actual profit* – see [1] on p. 174 – for each of these tax years. The Inspector will do this if it will make the total profits for the two years greater.

Income after you close a business

If you get any income after you have closed your business, it will be taxed under Schedule D Case VI (see p. 42) as earned income of the tax year in which you get it. However, if you get it within six years of closing the business, you can choose within two years to have it treated as income you got on the last day of your business. Your final assessment will be adjusted.

ICTA 1988 s103 s104, s108

Working out taxable profits

The taxable profit of your business is the amount on which you are going to pay tax. If you were working out your taxable profit from scratch, it would be your takings during your accounting year, i.e. cash received during the year for the sales you make, plus:

- money owed *to you* at the end of the accounting year
- money owed *by you* at the beginning of the year

- the increase in value of your stocks during the year (see p. 183)
  less the following deductions:
- allowable business expenses – see opposite
- money owed *to you* at the beginning of the year
- money owed *by you* at the end of the year
- capital allowances – see p. 184
- losses – see p. 189
- half of any Class 4 National Insurance contributions payable for the year of assessment – see p. 194.

In practice, you may start off by working out your profit under normal accounting rules. You then turn this into your taxable profits by adding back things which aren't allowable business expenses (e.g. depreciation and your wages) and deducting things on which you can get tax relief (capital allowances).

In a very few cases (e.g. a barrister) your sales figure may be taken as the cash you receive during your accounting year for work done – regardless of when you actually did the work. So you can ignore money owed at the start or end of the accounting year.

If you take items out of stock for your own use you normally have to include these in sales at the normal selling price.

CIR v. Gardner Mountain & D'Ambrumenil 29 TC 69; Sharkey v. Wernher 36 TC 275

Other income

If you have any other income which is not part of your trading income, it is not part of the taxable profits of your business. How any non-trading income is taxed depends on where it comes from. For example, bank interest is taxed as investment income.

Allowable business expenses

An expense is allowable only if incurred *'wholly and exclusively'* for the business. Table 2 on p. 180 lists expenses you will probably be allowed and those you will not. But business needs vary widely and an expense allowable for one business may not be for another. If in doubt, claim.

Note that the *'wholly and exclusively'* rule does not mean that you can't claim anything if, for example, you sometimes use your car for business, sometimes for private purposes. If the car is used wholly for business purposes on some occasions, then you can normally claim the proportion of car expenses which is attributable to business use; you'll have to agree the proportion with your Tax Inspector. You can usually claim the same proportion of your car expenses as your business mileage bears to your total mileage. However, if you use the car for a trip which is part pleasure, part business, you may not be able to claim any of the costs of the trip as an allowable expense. This is known as the *dual purpose rule*. For example, you can't normally claim the expenses of a business trip which is combined with a holiday. However, if you attend a conference during the trip, the conference fee will be allowable.

You can normally claim part of your home expenses, e.g. heating, lighting, insurance, if you use part of your home for business. Home expenses are usually shared out on the basis of the number and size of rooms. If you claim costs of using your home for business, beware of a possible capital gains tax bill if you sell your home – see p. 207.

Capital expenditure, e.g. what you spend on buying cars, machinery, improving property, is not an allowable expense, nor is depreciation, such as that on cars. But you may get capital allowances – see p. 184.

ICTA 1988 s74

Pre-trading expenses

If you spend money, e.g. rent and rates on your business premises, before your business actually starts, it will probably count as pre-trading expenditure. It will be treated as a loss in your first year of trading, and you can get loss relief – see p. 192.

ICTA 1988 s401

Table 2: Business expenses

	Normally allowed	Not allowed
Basic costs and general running expenses	Cost of goods bought for resale and raw materials used in business (see p. 181 for how much to claim). Discounts allowed on sales. Advertising. Delivery charges. Heating. Lighting. Cleaning. Business rates. Proportion of the standard community charge ('poll tax') on a second home if let out or used for business. Telephone. Rent of business premises. Replacement of small tools and special clothing. Postage. Stationery. Relevant books and magazines. Accountants' fees (mostly). Bank charges on business accounts. VAT if you're not registered (see p. 196).	Initial cost of buildings, machinery, vehicles, equipment, permanent advertising signs – but see *Capital allowances*, on p. 184.
Use of home for work	Proportion of telephone, lighting, heating, cleaning, insurance. Proportion of rent and domestic rates for periods prior to their abolition (they have not been abolished in Northern Ireland) if you use part of home *exclusively* for business – but watch out for capital gains tax (see p. 207).	Personal community charge ('poll tax') paid on your main home.
Wages and salaries	Wages, salaries, redundancy and some leaving payments paid to employees. Pensions for ex-employees and dependants.	Your own wages or salary, or that of any business partner.
Workplace nurseries	Cost of some types of child care provision for employees' children.	Cost of premises and equipment – but see *Capital allowances*, on p. 184.
Tax and National Insurance	Employer's National Insurance contributions for employees. VAT on allowable expenses if you're not a registered trader for VAT (and, sometimes, even if you are – see p. 195).	Income tax. Capital gains tax. Inheritance tax. Your own National Insurance – but see p. 194.

	Normally allowed	Not allowed
Entertaining	Entertainment of own staff, e.g. Christmas party.	Any business entertainment.
Gifts	Gifts costing up to £10 a year to each person so long as the gift advertises your business (or things it sells).	Food, drink, tobacco, gifts or vouchers for goods given to anyone other than employees.
Travelling	Cost of travel and accommodation on business trips. Travel between different places of work. *Running costs of own car*: whole of cost, excluding depreciation, if used wholly for business, proportion if used privately too. Provided trips are exclusively for business purposes, the cost of travel to and from the UK to carry on business performed wholly outside the UK.	Travel between home and business. Meals, except the reasonable cost of evening meals and breakfast on overnight trips. Cost of buying a car or van – but see *Capital allowances*, on p. 184
Interest payments	Interest on, and costs of arranging, overdrafts and loans for business purposes – see p. 30.	Interest on capital paid or credited to partners. Interest on overdue tax.
Hire purchase and leasing	Hire charge part of payments (i.e. the amount you pay *less* the cash price). Rent paid for leasing car or machinery, for example.	Cash price of what you're buying on hire purchase (you may get *capital allowances* on cash price – but see p. 184).
Hiring	Reasonable charge for hire of capital goods, including cars. [1]	
Insurance	Business insurance, e.g. employer's liability, fire and theft, motor. Life insurance, personal accident insurance, permanent health insurance and private medical insurance for employees.	Your own life, accident, permanent health and private medical insurance.

[1] But charges for cars costing more than £12,000 will be restricted.

	Normally allowed	Not allowed
Trade marks, designs and patents	Fees paid to register trade mark or design; or to obtain a patent.	Cost of buying a patent from someone else – you may get *capital allowances*, see p. 188.
Legal costs	Costs of recovering debts; defending business rights; preparing service agreements; appealing against rates on business premises; drawing up a partnership agreement; forming a company; renewing a lease, with the landlord's consent, for a period not exceeding 50 years (but not if a premium is paid).	Expenses (including stamp duty) for acquiring land, buildings or leases. Fines and other penalties for breaking the law. Costs of fighting a tax case.
Repairs	Normal repairs and maintenance to premises or equipment.	Cost of additions, alterations, improvements.
Debts	Specific bad debts and, in part, doubtful debts.	General reserve for bad or doubtful debts.
Subscriptions and contributions	Payments which secure benefits for your business or staff. Genuine contributions to approved local enterprise agency. Payments to professional bodies which have arrangements with the Revenue (in some cases only a proportion). Contributions to Training and Enterprise Councils.	Payments to political parties, churches, charities (but small gifts to *local* churches and charities may be allowable).
Training	Subject to certain conditions, cost of training employees to acquire and improve skills needed for their current jobs; cost of training employees who are leaving or who have left in new work skills.	
Secondments	Cost of seconding employees on a temporary basis to certain educational bodies, including local education authorities and institutions maintained by them, and to charitable institutions.	

ICTA 1988 s74; Coltness Iron Co v. Black 1 TC 287 (machinery); ICTA 1988 s577; FA 1988 s72 (entertaining); ICTA 1988 s577 (gifts); Newsom v. Robertson 33 TC 452, Caillebotte v. Quinn 1975, 50 TC 222 (subsistence when travelling); TMA 1970 s90 (interest on overdue tax); Darngavil Coal Co v. Francis 77 TC1 (hire purchase); ICTA 1988 s83, s520 (trade marks, patents, etc.); Smith's Potato Estates Ltd v. Bolland 30 TC 267 (legal costs); ICTA 1988 s79, s577; ICTA 1988 s86, s588 (training and secondments); FA 1988 s155 (workplace nurseries)

Stock

You can claim as an allowable expense the cost of raw materials you use in your business, and the cost of things you buy for resale. But you can claim only the cost of business materials which you actually sell during your accounting year – i.e. the value of your stocks of these things at the start of the year *plus* anything you spend on buying more during the year, *minus* the value of your stocks at the end of the year. So an *increase* in the value of stocks will normally increase your taxable profits for the year. A *decrease* in the value of stocks reduces your taxable profits.

If you have stocks which can only be sold for less than you paid for them, you will normally be allowed to value them at what they would fetch if sold now. This means for tax purposes that you can value stock *at the lower of cost or market value*. No other method of valuing stock is allowed by your Tax Inspector, regardless of what is allowed under accounting rules.

When you value your stocks at the start and end of the accounting year, you need to add in the value of *work-in-progress*. This is the value of work which has begun, but which isn't completed, e.g. products half-way through the manufacturing process, or part-completed work if you're a builder, solicitor, engineer, etc. Work-in-progress can be valued in one of the following ways:

- cost of raw materials used
- cost plus overheads
- cost plus overheads plus profit contribution.

Once you've chosen a way of valuing work-in-progress, this is how it must be valued each accounting year.

If you are closing a business, your stock will be valued either at the price it's sold at, if sold to someone else in business, or at the price it would fetch if sold in the open market.

183

Capital allowances

When you work out your taxable profits, you can't deduct anything you spend on capital assets or equipment, e.g. machinery or cars. Money spent in this way is not an allowable business expense. But you can still get tax relief on these sorts of things by claiming capital allowances on:

- plant and machinery (e.g. vans, machines, typewriters, computers)
- motor cars
- buildings (e.g. industrial, agricultural, hotels, in enterprise zones)
- patents, know-how and scientific research.

To get a capital allowance, expenditure must be '*wholly and exclusively*' for the business. But again, on anything used partly for business, partly privately, you will get a proportion of the capital allowance, depending on the proportion of business use.

If you buy equipment for private use, and then use it in your business, you can claim a capital allowance on its market value at the time you start using it. Detailed rules are given below.

How you pay for the equipment doesn't make any difference to the capital allowance. If you pay by a loan or by bank overdraft, the interest is an allowable business expense, not part of the cost of the asset. In the same way, hire purchase charges are a business expense.
CAA 1990

VAT
For how to deal with VAT on items on which you claim a capital allowance, see p. 194.

Plant and machinery

You can get a capital allowance of up to 25 per cent of the cost of plant and machinery for the accounting year in which you buy it. The rest of the cost is written off over the following years at up to 25 per cent of the remaining value each year. This is how it works.

The cost of plant or machinery you buy goes into a *pool of expenditure*. At the end of the year, you can claim up to 25 per cent of the value of the pool as a *writing-down allowance* – this can be deducted from your profits for that year.

The pool is reduced by what you claim: what's left is known as the *written-down value*, and becomes your pool for the start of the next accounting year. Any purchases in the next year are added to the pool, and at the end of the year you can claim 25 per cent of whatever the pool is now worth. Note that you can claim less than the full 25 per cent writing-down allowance (see Example 4, overleaf) – you deduct only what you claim from your pool.

If you sell something on which you have claimed capital allowances, the proceeds (up to the original cost of the item or sometimes the market value) must be deducted from your pool of expenditure before working out your writing-down allowance for the year in which you sell. If the proceeds come to more than the value of your pool, the excess (the *balancing charge*) is added to your profit.

You can claim capital allowances in full only on expenditure which is 'wholly and exclusively' for the business. Things bought partly for business, partly for private use, should be kept separate from other business assets in their own pools. You can claim a proportion of the maximum capital allowances, in line with business use.
CAA 1990 s24, s25, s140, s141

EXAMPLE 3

Herbert Hughes works out what he can claim in capital allowances for his accounting year ending on 30 April 1992. His pool of expenditure at the start of the year was £6,782. During the year, Herbert had bought a new van, costing £8,880, trading in his old van for £2,650. He also bought some shelving for his stock room for £960.

Herbert first adds the new purchases to his pool of expenditure: £6,782 + £8,880 + £960 = £16,622. He then subtracts the trade-in value of his old van: £16,622 − £2,650 = £13,972; this is the value of his pool of expenditure on 30 April 1992. He can claim a writing-down allowance of 25 per cent of his pool of expenditure, i.e. 25 per cent of £13,972 = £3,493.

The value of his pool of expenditure at the start of his next accounting year is £13,972 − £3,493 = £10,479.

EXAMPLE 4

Mary Worsley bought some machinery costing £10,000 in her accounting year to 30 June 1991. She could claim a writing-down allowance of 25 per cent of this, i.e. 25 per cent of £10,000 = £2,500. However, her taxable profit for the year is just £6,000, while her outgoings and allowances come to £4,000. Assuming that she has no other taxable income, she will pay tax on £6,000 − £4,000 = £2,000 of taxable income. If she claims the full £2,500 capital allowance, she will have wasted £500 of allowances. So she decides to claim just £2,000 of capital allowances, 20 per cent of her pool expenditure.

That leaves £8,000 as the written-down value of Mary's pool of expenditure, to be carried over to next year.

Leasing

If, instead of buying an asset, you choose to lease it, you can claim the lease rental as an allowable expense, as long as you are using the asset in your own business. The person or company from whom you lease can normally claim the capital allowances.

Cars

As with plant and machinery, you can claim a writing-down allowance of up to 25 per cent for each year in which you own the car. Cars must go into a separate pool of expenditure. Lorries and vans do not count as cars – they can go into the pool with other plant and machinery.

If the car cost more than £12,000, it has its own pool of expenditure (i.e. separate even from other cars). In this case, the maximum writing-down allowance in any year is £3,000.

CAA 1990 s34–s36, s41

Assets with a life of less than five years

With things like computers which last for only a few years, you could find yourself still claiming capital allowances for the cost after you had got rid of them. Suppose, for example, you bought a personal computer for £1,000, and claimed the full 25 per cent capital allowance on it each

186

year. The following table shows what the written-down value would be year by year:

Year	25 per cent allowance	Written-down value at end of year
1	£250	£750
2	£188	£562
3	£140	£422
4	£106	£316
5	£79	£237

If you scrapped the computer after four years, there would still be a written-down value of £316 in your pool of expenditure, and you'd only write this off over several more years.

With equipment which you expect to scrap or sell within five years, you can opt for special treatment which allows you to write off the value of the equipment when you get rid of it. You must keep each such *short life asset* in its own pool of expenditure. If you sell it for less than its written-down value, the difference can be subtracted from your profits for the year, as a *balancing allowance* (if you scrap it, you can claim the whole written-down value as a balancing allowance). If you sell it for more than its written-down value, the difference is added to your profits as a balancing charge (see p. 183). And if you've still got the equipment after five years, its written-down value is added to your main pool of expenditure as if it had never been treated separately.
CAA 1990 s37, s38

Computer software
The yearly writing-down allowance of 25 per cent for plant and machinery is normally available for software bought at the same time as computer hardware. And a new rule means that even if software is bought separately from the hardware, you can usually treat it as a capital allowance.

Buildings
You can claim writing-down allowances on various types of buildings at four per cent of their original cost excluding land:

- industrial buildings, e.g. factories, warehouses
- homes built for letting on assured tenancies, provided certain conditions are met

187

- agricultural buildings, including farmhouses, farm buildings, cottages, fences, roads
- hotels or hotel extensions of 10 bedrooms or more which meet certain conditions.

With industrial buildings and hotels in enterprise zones, you can claim 100 per cent of the cost in the first year, including the cost of fixed plant or machinery in the buildings. If you claim less than 100 per cent, you can claim a writing-down allowance of up to 25 per cent of the original cost, starting the following year.

CAA 1990 s1–s21 (industrial buildings and hotels); s84–s97 (homes let on assured tenancies); s122–s130 (agricultural buildings)

Patents, know-how and scientific research

You can claim a 25 per cent writing-down allowance on the cost of buying a patent to use in your business, in the same way as for plant and machinery. Note that you cannot claim an allowance for the cost of creating and registering your own patent (though you may be able to claim expenses for these – see p. 182).

You can get 25 per cent allowances for the cost of know-how – any industrial information or techniques likely to assist in manufacturing, mining, agriculture, forestry or fishing. And you can claim 100 per cent of the cost of capital expenditure for the purposes of scientific research (though not on land or houses), in the year of expenditure only.

ICTA 1988 s520–s533; CAA 1990 s136–9

New (and closing) businesses

You can get a capital allowance on all expenditure which qualifies, but you can't have more than one allowance on the same expenditure.

It becomes confusing working out capital allowances when you start (or close) a business because some profits may be taxed twice and others not at all. The rule is that you get the allowances in the first tax year available (and not in the following tax year if the assessment is based on the same taxable profits).

If you've bought something in an accounting period and the profits for that period are *not* assessed for tax purposes, you get the allowance as if you had bought the equipment in the following accounting period. But if the following

accounting period is the last year of the business (because you're closing it down), you get the allowance in the preceding year.
CAA 1990 s147, s160

Losses

If you make a loss in your business there are several things you can do with it. Your choice depends on whether the business is new, a business closing down, or one which has been going for a few years and which you don't intend to close.

Losses in an established business

Strictly speaking, with a loss in an accounting year which doesn't coincide with the tax year, you should apportion it to the correct tax years. In practice, your Tax Inspector will normally let you treat it as a loss for the tax year in which your accounting year ends. And losses can be set off only against the income of the person who incurred them.

You have three options, given below, as to how to treat your loss.

Option A: set the loss against future profits from the same business   You start by setting the loss against profits in the same business in your following accounting year. Any losses left over can be carried to the year after, and so on.

The advantage of doing it this way is that it is relatively straightforward. The disadvantages are:

- the loss can only be set off against profits from the same trade
- there may be quite a time before the loss can be translated into a cash saving – see Example 6, opposite
- the whole loss has to be set off against the profits available which means you may not be able to take advantage of any outgoings or allowances you may be entitled to.

If you decide to set off losses in this way, you need to do so within six years after the end of the year in which you want the relief.
ICTA 1988 s385

Option B: claim immediate relief You can ask for the loss to be set off against any *other income* you have for the tax year in which your accounting year ends. This could include profits made in your *preceding* accounting year, because these profits will be counting as income for tax purposes in the current year. It could also include income received and taxable in the current year, such as earnings from a job, or dividends from shares. You can now also set trading losses against capital gains.

If you ask for losses to be set off in this way, the whole of your losses have to be set off before you can set off any other outgoings or allowances you may have. So some of your outgoings and allowances may be unused because the losses could reduce your tax bill to zero. If you don't have enough income to cover your losses, you can carry forward the excess to the next tax year and get relief then against other income for that year – see Option C.

If you decide to set off losses in this way, you need to do so within two years after the end of the year in which you want the relief.
ICTA 1988 s380 FA 1991 s72

Option C: set the loss off against other income for the following tax year Examples of this are earnings from a job or dividends from shares. You can choose to do this rather than set losses off against other income in the same tax year, if you'd prefer it. You can't use Option C unless your business is still being carried on in the following tax year. If there are still any losses left over they can be carried forward, but not set against other income, only against income from the same business.

If you decide to set off losses in this way, you need to do so within two years after the end of the year in which you want the relief.
ICTA 1988 s380

EXAMPLE 5

Suppose you have other income of £10,000, and outgoings and allowances of £4,000. In this case your taxable income will be £6,000. If you have losses of £8,000, and ask for them to be set against other income, the whole of the £8,000 will be set off first against your other income, even though you only need £6,000 in losses to reduce your tax bill to zero. You will not be able to carry forward the remaining losses to the future, so you will have lost the benefit of £2,000 of outgoings and allowances.

EXAMPLE 6

Jessica Jones has a job as a part-time bookkeeper from which she earns £10,000 a year. She has outgoings and allowances of £4,000 a year.

Jessica also runs a business on the side as a theatrical costumier. In the accounting year ending on 31 December 1991 her taxable profits were £10,000. But, in the following year, she makes a substantial loss of £20,000. Then, in the following years, she makes profits of £10,000 a year.

Her Tax Inspector allows Jessica to treat all the loss for the accounting year ending on 31 December 1992 as a loss for the 1992–3 tax year (strictly speaking the Inspector could insist that she splits the loss between tax years). As Jessica is taxed on a preceding year basis, she has no income from her business to be taxed in the 1993–4 tax year.

Jessica has to decide the best way of getting relief for her loss. She can set her loss off against future profits from her business (Option A); she can claim immediate relief against other income she has – i.e. from her job and income from her business for the preceding year (Option B); or she can set the loss off against other income of the next year (Option C). Here's how the options affect her tax bill:

	1992–3 tax year	1993–4 tax year	1994–5 tax year	1995–6 tax year
Income:				
business	£10,000	nil (loss of £20,000)	£10,000	£10,000
job	£10,000	£10,000	£10,000	£10,000
Option A	**Setting off loss against future profits**			
income [1]	£20,000	£10,000	£10,000 (from job)	£10,000 (from job)
allowances	£4,000	£4,000	£4,000	£4,000
tax to pay [2]	£3,900	£1,400	£1,400	£1,400

191

	1992–3 tax year	1993–4 tax year	1994–5 tax year	1995–6 tax year
Option B	Claiming immediate relief against other income			
income [1]	nil	£10,000	£20,000	£20,000
allowances	*nil* [3]	*£4,000*	*£4,000*	*£4,000*
tax to pay [2]	nil	£1,400	£3,900	£3,900
Option C	Setting off loss against following tax year's other income			
income [1]	£20,000	nil	£10,000 (from job)	£20,000
allowances	*£4,000*	*nil* [3]	*£4,000*	*£4,000*
tax to pay [2]	£3,900	nil	£1,400	£3,900

[1] after setting off losses – for how losses can be set off, see previous page
[2] at 1992–3 rates
[3] with no income, Jessica's allowances can't be used

Although Option A would mean Jessica would pay less tax in total over the years, she decides that her best choice is Option B, claiming immediate relief. It cuts her tax bill at the time she makes the loss. Option A or Option C would mean waiting a long time to get relief, and in this example would mean £3,900 to pay in tax in the year in which she makes the loss.

Losses in a new business
If you make a loss in any of the first four tax years of your business, you can set it against other income (including earnings from a job) in the three years before the year in which the loss was made – and so get a rebate. You start by setting the loss off against the earliest year first. Note that you don't get this relief unless you can show that your business could reasonably have been expected to make profits in that period or within a reasonable time.

With losses in a new business, you will have to apportion between tax years if your accounting year doesn't coincide with the tax year.

If you want to set off your losses in this way, you need to do so within two years after the year when the loss occurred. *ICTA 1988 s381*

Losses in a closing business

If you're closing down a business which has made a loss in its final 12 months, you have two options. You can set the loss against profits from the same business in the three preceding tax years, starting with the latest year first. Or, you can set the loss against *other income* of the same tax year. If the loss is large enough, you can do both. Ask your Tax Inspector for more details.
ICTA 1988 s380, s388

You as an employer

When you employ staff on a permanent basis you have several duties as an employer. These include:

- acting as a collector of taxes and deducting income tax and Class 1 National Insurance contributions from your employee's pay (assuming your employee earns more than a certain amount – £54 or more a week in the 1992–3 tax year)
- paying National Insurance as an employer – see box overleaf for rates.

Your spouse

You may be able to save tax by employing your spouse. If he or she has no other income, you can pay your spouse up to £3,445 in the 1992–3 tax year before any tax is due on it. But if weekly earnings exceed a certain amount (£54 a week – equivalent to £2,808 a year – in the 1992–3 tax year) both of you will have to pay National Insurance contributions.

National Insurance rates for employers

There's no National Insurance to pay on earnings below £54 a week. Above £54, rates are on a graduated scale. For earnings:

- from £54 up to £89.99 a week, 4.6 per cent on all earnings
- from £90 up to £134.99 a week, 6.6 per cent on all earnings
- from £135 up to £189.99 a week, 8.6 per cent on all earnings
- from £190 a week, 10.4 per cent on all earnings with no upper limit.

Note that rates are different where an employer runs a *contracted-out* pension scheme.

For employee rates, see p. 301.

Your own National Insurance contributions

You will have to pay Class 2 National Insurance contributions (unless your earnings from self-employment will be less than £3,030 for 1992–3) and you may also have to pay Class 4 contributions depending on your earnings.

Class 2 contributions are payable each week. Class 2 is a flat rate payment of £5.35 a week for the 1992–3 tax year. You can pay it either by buying a special stamp each week from the post office and sticking it on to a contribution card, or by direct debit. Paying Class 2 contributions entitles you to most contributory benefits, but not unemployment benefit or the earnings-related portion of the retirement pension.

Class 4 contributions are earnings-related and collected along with your tax payments. You get tax relief on half the Class 4 contributions you pay. For the 1992–3 tax year the Class 4 contribution is 6.3 per cent of the amount by which your 'profit' exceeds £6,120 – up to a maximum contribution of £941.22. Your 'profit' for Class 4 purposes will normally be your taxable profit before deducting half your Class 4 National Insurance, but in certain situations you can make further deductions – see leaflet *IR24*. Paying Class 4 contributions doesn't entitle you to any benefits over and above those you get by paying Class 2.

There are special rules to prevent you paying more than a certain amount in all classes of National Insurance – see DSS leaflet *NP18*.

Value added tax

The current rate of value added tax (VAT) is 17½ per cent. There are some goods on which the rate is zero, e.g. most food, books, newspapers, children's clothing and transport. And some goods are *exempt*, e.g. land, insurance, postage, education, and so on. But if you buy any goods or services for your business, it's likely that on some of those things you will be paying VAT. If you are registered for VAT, you will be able to claim that tax back once every three months. By doing this, you are lowering your costs. However, you must add VAT on to all the bills you send out or sales you make if, of course, they are items on which VAT is payable at 17½ per cent. By doing this you are increasing your selling prices, but not your income, because you have to hand over the VAT to Customs and Excise.

Handing over VAT on income you haven't yet received can cause cashflow problems. But businesses with a yearly turnover below £300,000 have the option of handing over VAT only on income actually received. (This is known as *cash accounting* by Customs and Excise.)

Registering for VAT

At present, you have to register for VAT if, at the end of any month, the value of your taxable supplies in the last year exceeds £36,600. You must also register if at any time you think it likely that the value of your taxable supplies over the next 30 days will exceed £36,600. Taxable supplies in this case means any supplies which are not exempt – so it includes zero-rated goods and services.

Below these levels, you can choose whether or not to register. Your choice depends upon:

- how much you can cut your costs by claiming VAT back on things you buy for use in your business (which you can do if you register)
- whether your customers will be able to claim back VAT which you must add to your selling prices, and
- how tedious you find the record-keeping necessary to be registered for VAT.

For more information about VAT, contact your local VAT office (under *Customs and Excise* in the telephone book).

Keeping records

If you are registered, you have to:

- give your customer a bill (and keep a copy yourself) which shows, among other things, your VAT registration number, your name and address, the amount payable before VAT and the amount of VAT due. (If you're a shopkeeper and the bill, including VAT, is £50 or less, you needn't show all these)
- keep a VAT account in your books which shows the amount of VAT you are reclaiming and the amount of VAT you are handing over
- fill in a form (VAT return) every three months (normally) and send it to Customs and Excise, showing what you are claiming and what you are handing over. Businesses which have been registered for VAT for at least a year,

195

pay VAT regularly and have a yearly turnover of below £300,000 can opt for a yearly return (but you have to pay an estimated amount of VAT monthly by direct debit).

If you have charged more VAT on your sales than you can claim on your purchases, then you have to send the difference to the VAT Collector. If you can claim more on what you've bought than you can charge on what you have sold, the VAT Collector will pay you the difference.

Business expenses and capital allowances

If you *are not* a registered trader for VAT, include any VAT when claiming the cost of allowable business expenses. Also include VAT in the cost of any 'machinery or plant' on which you can claim a capital allowance.

If you *are* a registered trader for VAT, *don't* include VAT when claiming business expenses or capital allowances. However, you should include in your claim for expenses or capital allowances any VAT which you can't claim back through the normal VAT system, e.g. because it relates to part of your sales exempt from VAT.

But with cars (unless you're a car trader), include VAT in the cost you base your claim on for business expenses and capital allowances. The reason is that VAT on cars you buy can't be reclaimed, even if the expense is related to part of your business liable to VAT. From 1 August 1992, however, private taxi and self-drive hire firms and driving schools are permitted to recover the VAT they pay on cars purchased for their businesses.

Partnerships

If you are a business in a partnership with others, much of what has gone before about expenses and capital allowances is relevant. But there are special rules for working out the tax on partnership profits.

How partnership profits are taxed

Partnership profits are worked out in the same way as profits for a trade or business. But when it comes to working out how much tax to pay on those profits, the rules can, in some cases, be strange:

- **Rule one**   All partners are *jointly and severally liable* for all tax on the profits from the partnership. This means that if one partner doesn't pay up, the others can be made to pay up instead
- **Rule two**   Rule one doesn't apply to the capital gains of a partnership, and it doesn't apply to non-trading income (e.g. interest from a bank deposit account). In these cases, each partner pays the tax on his or her share, and if one doesn't pay, the others don't have to
- **Rule three**   The amount of tax charged on the partnership profits depends on the rates of tax paid by the individual partners. For example, a partnership might have very modest profits – £2,000, say. But if one of the partners is paying tax at a top rate of 40 per cent, part of the profits (in normal cases) will be taxed at 40 per cent
- **Rule four**   When the Revenue works out the bill on the partnership profits, the profits are divided between the partners in the same proportion as the partners themselves are sharing the profits in that tax year. So if the profits are £2,000, and there are two partners sharing the profits equally, the £2,000 will be divided equally between them. If one partner pays tax at 25 per cent, and the other at 40 per cent, the tax bill on the profits will be 25 per cent of £1,000 *plus* 40 per cent of £1,000 = £250 plus £400 = £650
- **Rule five**   Partnership income is normally taxed on a preceding year basis – i.e. in any tax year, the partnership pays tax on profits from its accounting period ending in the previous tax year
- **Rule six**   The partners can agree to pay the tax in any proportions they like – they don't have to pay the tax on their share of the profits.

The effect of rules four and five
Rule four is based on the division of profits in the current tax year. But the income taxed in that year will – because of rule five – be from an earlier year, and may have been divided quite differently.
ICTA 1988 s277

EXAMPLE 7

Alice, Barbara and Caroline are in partnership. In the 1991–2 tax year, they decide to split the income of the partnership equally between them. But the tax bill for the 1991–2 tax year is based on the profit for their accounting period ending in the *previous* tax year (i.e. the 1990–1 tax year). Those profits *weren't* shared on an equal basis. Alice took half the profits, and Barbara and Caroline took 25 per cent each. The profits amounted to £30,000.

In the 1991–2 tax year, Alice pays tax at a top rate of 25 per cent (the basic rate of tax for 1991–2). The other two both pay tax at a top rate of 40 per cent. Here's how tax is calculated on the £30,000:

Total partnership profits for the 1991–2 year of assessment [1] £30,000

partner	received	share [2]	equals	tax rate	tax
Alice	£15,000	one-third	£10,000	25%	£2,500
Barbara	£7,500	one-third	£10,000	40%	£4,000
Caroline	£7,500	one-third	£10,000	40%	£4,000
	£30,000		£30,000		£10,500

So the partnership has to pay £10,500 in tax.

[1] i.e. the profits from the accounting period ending in 1990–1
[2] Divided on the 1991–2 basis of sharing

It looks as though Alice has done very well – £2,500 in tax on her share of £15,000. But of course the partners can divide up the tax bill in any way they like (see rule six). If they wish, they could agree that Alice pays half the £10,500 (£5,250) and Barbara and Caroline a quarter each (£2,625) – or any other split.

A new partner

Each time a partner joins (or leaves) the partnership, the partnership can come to an end. In fact it *will* come to an end, unless everyone who was a partner before the change *and* everyone who is a partner after the change agrees that it should continue (technically, by making a *continuation election* to the Revenue), *and* at least one of the partners before the change is still a partner after the change. If a partnership continues, the calculation of tax on partnership profits can be even more bizarre.
ICTA 1988 s113(2)

EXAMPLE 8

Alice, Barbara and Caroline make a profit of only £9,000 in their 1991–2 accounting year. This is split equally between them (see Example 7), so they each get £3,000. They decide they need an injection of capital, and so a new partner, Daphne, joins them after the end of the 1991–2 accounting year. The arrangements are that Daphne will take two-thirds of the profits in 1992–3 and the other three will take one-ninth each. They all agree that the partnership should continue. The tax bill for the 1992–3 tax year is worked out on the profits for the accounting year ending in the 1991–2 tax year (rule five) and on the way the profits are shared in 1992–3 (rule four). So let's look at what happens to the tax bill on the £9,000. Alice, Barbara, and Caroline have a top rate of tax of 25 per cent (the basic rate of tax for 1992–3). Daphne's top rate tax is 40 per cent.

partner	received	share	equals	tax rate	tax
Alice	£3,000	one-ninth	£1,000	25%	£250
Barbara	£3,000	one-ninth	£1,000	25%	£250
Caroline	£3,000	one-ninth	£1,000	25%	£250
Daphne	nil	two-thirds	£6,000	40%	£2,400
	£9,000		£9,000		£3,150

So although Daphne actually received none of the £9,000, the tax on the partnership is worked out as though she received £6,000.

If a partnership ceases

The same rules for opening and closing years apply to partnerships to sole traders – see pp. 173 and 177. But if the membership of the partnership changes (i.e. someone leaves or joins) and this results in the partnership being treated as coming to an end, special rules apply.

If all the partners before and after the change *do not* make a continuation election, the tax on the new partnership's profits will be assessed on a current year basis for the year of the change and the following three tax years. So the tax bills will be based on the actual profits earned each year. This will result in higher tax bills if profits are rising.
ICTA 1988 s61(4), s62(4)(5)

199

Partnership losses

Partnerships have much the same options as individuals for dealing with losses – see p. 189. If a partnership makes a loss, the individual partners 'own' the losses in the same proportion as they would have actually received the profits. Carrying back of losses isn't allowed, except for a new partner. And carrying back isn't allowed if the new partner is married to an existing partner and the partnership continues.

Individual partners can treat losses in different ways – i.e. they don't all have to treat them in the same way. So, for example, one partner could set his or her losses against other income or capital gains for the same tax year; another could carry them forward against future profits from the partnership.

EXAMPLE 9

Suppose Example 8 is unchanged, except that the £9,000 profit becomes a £9,000 loss. Alice, Barbara and Caroline 'own' the losses in the same proportions as any profits would actually have been received: i.e. they each 'own' £3,000 of losses. They can each treat these losses in one of three ways.

- set them against other income of the tax year in which the loss was made (i.e. the 1991–2 tax year in this example).
- set them against future profits from the partnership
- set them against other income or capital gains for the tax year in which the profits of the partnership (if there had been any) would have been taxed (i.e. the 1992–3 tax year in this example).

There is no need for them to treat their losses all in the same way: each of them could use the losses in a different way from the other two.

Limited partners

The amount of losses a limited partner can set against other income is limited broadly to the amount of capital he or she has contributed to the business.
ICTA 1988 s117

Pension for partners

There are special rules where a pension is paid to a partner who has retired on the grounds of age or ill-health, or to the widow or dependant of a partner who has died. In brief the rules are:

- take the partner's *actual profits* – i.e. what he or she actually declared in the Tax Return – for the last seven years in which he or she spent substantially the whole of his or her time in acting as a partner in that partnership (or in a collection of partnerships)
- separately for each year, multiply the profits by the Retail Prices Index (RPI) for December in the final tax year and divide them by the RPI for December in the year in which the profits were charged to tax
- take the average of the three highest figures and divide by two.

The result is the maximum pension which counts as earned income. Payments above that limit are investment income. The payments reduce the partnership's income for tax purposes, but payments *within* the limit can't reduce the partnership's (or anyone else's) investment income.
ICTA 1988 s628

11 *Homes and Land*

In this chapter, we explain the tax rules that apply to owning and renting a home – whether you live there, work there or let it. We also look at the rules that apply if you employ someone in your home – a housekeeper, say.

Tax relief for buying your home

Buying a home is by far the largest transaction most people enter into, and few can afford to pay for their home outright. The availability of basic-rate tax relief on loan interest makes borrowing cheaper than it otherwise would be, as our table shows. (Until 5 April 1991, higher-rate tax relief was also available but this has now been abolished.)

Cost of a £30,000 interest-only mortgage with tax relief

gross interest rate	7%	8%	9%	10%	11%	12%	13%	14%	15%
gross yearly cost £	2,100	2,400	2,700	3,000	3,300	3,600	3,900	4,200	4,500
net interest rate	5.25%	6%	6.75%	7.5%	8.25%	9%	9.75%	10.5%	11.25%
net yearly cost £	1,575	1,800	2,025	2,250	2,475	2,700	2,925	3,150	3,375
net monthly cost £	131.25	150	168.75	187.50	206.25	225	243.75	262.50	281.25

In general, you can get tax relief on the interest you pay on up to £30,000 of loans used to buy your home. If you have more than one home, you normally get tax relief only on loans used to buy your *main* home. In most cases, this is the one you in fact live in most of the time.

You can be away from this home for up to a year at a time and still get tax relief, and you can be away for longer if your employer requires you to live elsewhere, or if you live in a home which counts as a tax-free fringe benefit, or if you're self-employed and have to live in accommodation provided under the terms of your business – see *Your home and your work* on p. 213.

EXAMPLE 1

Richard Powell owes £40,000 on his mortgage. In the 1992–3 tax year he is charged £4,200 interest, and he gets tax relief on

$$\frac{30,000}{40,000} = \frac{3}{4}$$

of this – i.e. on £3,150. His tax relief will be 25 per cent of £3,150 = £787.50, so the cost of the interest to him will be £4,200 − £787.50 = £3,412.50.

If you take out more than one loan on the same day, they are treated as a single loan. If you're taking out two loans which total more than £30,000 (e.g. a building society mortgage and a more expensive top-up loan) try to arrange things so that you take out the more expensive loan at least a day before the cheaper loan. You'll then get tax relief on more of the total interest you pay.

When you can exceed the £30,000 limit

You will be able to get tax relief on the interest you pay on loans in excess of £30,000 in the following cases.

- **Getting married** If you get married, and each partner has a home with a mortgage, see p. 77 for the extra relief for which you may be eligible.
- **Moving home** If you have to take out a loan (e.g. a mortgage or a bridging loan) on the house you are buying before you've sold your old home, you can continue to get tax relief on the old home. The loan on the old home is ignored when working out how much tax relief you're entitled to on the new loan. For 12 months (longer in deserving cases) you can get tax relief on both loans. It doesn't matter which of the two homes you live in during these 12 months. In addition, if you were a higher-rate taxpayer on 5 April 1991 and were entitled to receive higher-rate relief on the loan on your old home, you could continue getting the extra relief on the loan on the old home (even though higher-rate relief for other loans was abolished in the 1991 Budget). This applied if the loan for the new home was made by 5 April 1991. It also applied if the loan for the new home was

taken out after 5 April 1991, provided that, by 5 April 1991, a lender had made an offer of such a loan and there was a binding contract to buy a property.

- **Joint purchases before 1 August 1988** Before 1 August 1988, each individual and each married couple could get tax relief on the interest on their share of a loan(s) of up to £30,000 even when they were buying a property with other people. This meant that, for example, two single people buying a property together could get tax relief on the interest on loans of up to £60,000. Since 1 August 1988 the £30,000 limit has been applied to each individual property for new loans. If you are still getting multiple tax relief because you took your loan out before the deadline, beware of re-mortgaging. You will lose tax relief. Two joint owners who get married will also lose relief.

- **Arrears** If at some time in the past you didn't pay all the interest which was due and it has been added to what you owe the lender, you can get tax relief on interest on up to £1,000 of arrears added to the outstanding capital.

- **Buying property to let** You can normally get tax relief on the interest you pay on a loan to buy a home which you let (and which isn't also your main home). The rules on this are quite separate from the rules for tax relief on your main home; the £30,000 limit doesn't apply. For details of letting property, see p. 221.

- **If you are over 65** If you are 65 or over, in addition to the normal £30,000 limit, you can get tax relief on the interest on further loans up to £30,000 to buy an annuity. The loan(s) must be secured on your home. A home income plan is an off-the-peg scheme combining loan and annuity. For more about annuities and home income plans, see pp. 100–107.

Loans taken out before 6 April 1988

Certain loans were eligible for tax relief until 6 April 1988:
- home improvement loans
- loans to buy a home for a dependent relative
- loans to buy a home for a former spouse.

Such loans taken out before that date will continue to get basic-rate tax relief, but will count towards the £30,000 limit. Beware of re-mortgaging; you'll lose the tax relief.
ICTA 1988 s353, s355, s357, s367; FA 1991 s26

Which loans qualify for relief?

Interest on a loan qualifies for tax relief only if you spend the money you borrow on:

- buying the home, or
- buying an *interest* in the home (e.g. buying a half share, or buying someone else's stake).

Part of the loan can be spent on the cost of acquiring the property, e.g. solicitor's fees, surveyor's fees, stamp duty, removal costs. The loan doesn't have to be secured on the home you're buying. Nor does it matter if you have other savings or made a profit on your previous home which made it unnecessary for you to borrow – see Example 2. But note: if you own your own home outright (or have a mortgage of less than £30,000) you can't get yourself a cheap loan (i.e. one that attracts tax relief) by arranging an artificial sale of the property to, say, your spouse or some other accomplice and then buying it back.

EXAMPLE 2

Bill and Linda Adams plan to sell their London flat for £70,000 and pay off the £25,000 owing on their mortgage. Their new home in Norfolk will cost them £50,000, and their moving expenses will come to nearly £5,000. They have £70,000 − £25,000 − £5,000 = £40,000 to pay towards their new home, so need a loan of only £10,000. But they decide to get a £30,000 mortgage and keep the extra £20,000. They will get tax relief on the interest on the whole £30,000.

The interval between getting the loan and acquiring the interest in the property must not normally be more than six months (it doesn't matter which comes first). If you get the money before acquiring the interest in the home, you mustn't spend it on anything in the meantime, though you can place it on deposit and get interest. If interest becomes payable on the loan in this period, you can claim tax relief on it when the purchase is completed. You can also claim tax relief on interest you've paid to the vendor because you haven't paid the full price, or because you moved in before completion.

If you pay off a qualifying loan (or part of it) and, within six months, replace it with another loan on the same property, you get tax relief on the interest you pay on the new loan. But if the new loan is bigger than the amount you paid off, you don't get any relief on the interest you pay on the excess (unless the new loan is taken out within six months of buying the home). It doesn't matter if the loan you pay off was interest-free.

You can't get tax relief on a loan which has to be repaid within 12 months of being taken out, unless the interest is paid in the UK to a bank, stockbroker or discount house. Nor is there any relief on a bank overdraft or a credit card debt (except as a business expense) though you can get relief if you convert to another type of loan within 12 months.

ICTA 1988 s354(1), s355(5), s367(2); IR11 (1968)

Which homes qualify?

The home must be in the UK or Republic of Ireland. It can be freehold or leasehold. A caravan or mobile home can qualify, as can a houseboat, if it has been designed or adapted for living in.

ICTA 1988 s354, s367(1); FA 1991 s28

How you get tax relief

Tax relief is given on most loans by the borrower paying a reduced amount to the lender under the system known as MIRAS (Mortgage Interest Relief At Source). You get this 'tax relief' even if you pay little or no tax. The government pays the difference between the net amount you've paid and the gross amount direct to the lender.

Most lenders have government approval to operate MIRAS, but a few don't. If your lender is not in the MIRAS scheme you'll have to pay the gross amount to the lender and claim the relief you're entitled to from the Revenue. You'll then get the tax relief in your PAYE coding or by getting a lower tax bill. You cannot normally get tax relief under MIRAS if you let more than one-third of your home. If your loan is in MIRAS and you start letting more than one-third of your home, you should tell both your lender and your tax office straight away.

With a loan which takes you over the £30,000 limit, lenders calculate your payments so that you pay the correct

net amount of interest on the first £30,000 of the loan and the gross amount of interest on the rest.
ICTA 1988 s353, s369, s373, s376

Claiming tax relief

If your loan comes under MIRAS, the forms you fill in when you get the loan will entitle you to get your tax relief by making reduced payments. The lender will tell you the net amount to pay. If the loan doesn't come under MIRAS, or you need to claim higher-rate tax relief for a bridging loan (see p. 203), get a *Certificate of Interest Paid* from the lender at the end of each tax year and send it to your Tax Inspector. If you are not in MIRAS and are on a low income, you may not pay enough tax to receive all the tax relief you would otherwise get. You may still be able to get the relief by writing to MIRAS Central Unit, St John's House, Merton Road, Bootle, L69 9BB with details of your mortgage.

Your home and capital gains tax

Any gain you make when you sell your home is normally exempt from capital gains tax. Exceptions are listed on p. 208. Any gains on other homes or land you own will normally be liable to capital gains tax.

A 'home' means a freehold or leasehold house, flat or maisonette. A caravan or a houseboat won't normally be liable to capital gains tax, whatever the circumstances (though the land on which a caravan stands won't be exempt unless you can show that the caravan was your only or main home for the whole time you owned the land).

For general details of capital gains tax (including how the indexation rules are applied), see Chapter 14, p. 264.
TCGA 1992 s272, s223(1)

More than one home

If you have two or more homes it's only your 'main' home which is exempt from capital gains tax. (In certain cases, homes bought for relatives before 6 April 1988 can be exempt in addition to your main home. See leaflet CGT4 for the exact rules.)

You can choose which home you want to be regarded as your main one – it doesn't have to be the one you spend the most time in though in most cases you must live in it at some stage. And it needn't be the one with a mortgage you get tax relief on. It's best to nominate the one on which you think you'll make the largest *chargeable gain* (see p. 267 for what this means).

Make your choice by writing to the Revenue within two years of acquiring the second home. You can alter the choice at any time, simply by telling the Revenue. Your new choice can be backdated by up to two years. A married couple must both sign these letters, unless all the homes are owned by one of you.

If you don't tell the Revenue within the two-year period which is your 'main' home, it will be decided for you. If the decision doesn't suit you, you can appeal within 30 days but you will have to prove that the home selected is *not* in fact your 'main' home.

If you live mainly in a rented home – or in one which goes with your job (e.g. as a caretaker or clergyman) – but also own a home where you spend some of your time or intend to live eventually, it is vital that you nominate the one you *own* as your main home. If this has applied for more than two years the Revenue may accept a late request. *TCGA 1992 s222 (5), (6)*

When your only or main home isn't exempt

You may not get full exemption from capital gains tax on your only or 'main' home in any of the following cases:

- the home wasn't your main one for capital gains tax purposes for all the time you owned it
- you lived away from home
- you let all or part of the home out
- you used part exclusively for work
- you converted it into self-contained flats and then sold them
- you built a second home in your garden and then sold it off
- you sold the house on its own, and the land around it afterwards
- the garden (including the house area) was bigger than half a hectare
- the home was one of a series of homes you bought, or spent money on, with the object of making a profit.

The detailed rules are given in the next three pages

(except that aspects to do with your work are covered on p. 213 and property you let is covered on p. 224). In many cases, only *part* of the gain you make when you sell your only or 'main' home will be taxable – see p. 210.
TCGA 1992 s222–s224

If you have lived away from your only or 'main' home

The capital gain you are assumed to have made during periods when you were living away from your only or main home will normally not be exempt from CGT. For example, if you have lived away from the home for 7 years out of the 15 you owned it, ⁷/₁₅ of the gain you made would not be exempt from CGT. But there are six situations in which absence from the property is ignored:

- **Before 6 April 1982**   Generally, only gains made after 31 March 1982 are subject to capital gains tax, so any absence before this date becomes irrelevant. For the rules on when you might want to take account of the value of your house before this date, see p. 269.
- **The first year**   If you can't move into your new home straight away because you're having a new home built on a plot you've bought, or because you're having the home altered or redecorated, or because you can't sell your old home, you will still get exemption from capital gains tax for up to a year (longer if there's a good reason). You must live in the home immediately afterwards.
- **If you live in job-related accommodation**   A home which you (or your husband or wife) own and which you intend to live in one day can be exempt from capital gains tax while you are living in a home which goes with your job, or are self-employed and have to live in accommodation provided under the terms of your business – see pp. 215 and 216.
- **Because of your work**   Certain periods when you have to be away from home because of your job are exempt – see p. 213.
- **The last three years**   Any absences in the last three years before you dispose of a home which has been your only or main home at some time are always exempt. It doesn't matter why you're away, or if you have another home which you've nominated as your main home during this period. If you're away for more than three years

before you sell, the gain for the excess over three years won't be exempt unless one of the other exemptions applies.

• **Any other absences** for any reason totalling up to three years will not affect exemption, as long as you use the home as your main one for a time both before the first such period and after the last one.

Except in the first year or last three years, you can't get the exemptions above if any other home of yours is exempt. None of the exemptions above is lost if you let the home while you're away.
SPD4; ESC D3, D4; TCGA 1992 s223

If you divide the property, or change its use

Exemption from capital gains tax for your only or main home is likely to be partly lost if you divide up the property or use part of it for something other than living in. For example, if you convert part of your home into self-contained flats, part of the gains you make when you sell the flats would not be exempt (see *Working out the chargeable gain*, on p. 212. If you build a second home in your garden, the gain you make when you sell it would not be wholly exempt. If you use part of the property exclusively for a trade or business or some other non-residential use, you may also lose exemption on that part. The amount of the gain which is not exempt is whatever the Commissioners (see p. 63) consider to be just and reasonable, but will normally be based on the proportion of the property affected. For example, if you bought a home for £37,000 (after deducting buying costs) and spent £8,000 having part of it done up to sell, the cost of acquiring the whole home is taken to be £37,000 + £8,000 = £45,000. If you sell part for £40,000 when the whole home is worth £90,000, the cost of acquiring the part you sell is taken to be four-ninths of £45,000 = £20,000. So the gain (before allowing for selling costs or indexation) on the part you sell would be £40,000 − £20,000 = £20,000. Not all this gain is chargeable. The chargeable amount is the gain *less* what the Commissioners reckon your gain would have been (on that part) if you hadn't spent money improving the property. So if, without the additional expense, the gain would have been £15,000, the chargeable part is £20,000 *less* £15,000 = £5,000.

If what you get for part of a property is no more than £20,000 and its market value is not more than 20 per cent of the value of the whole property, you can elect for the sale not to be treated as a disposal until you sell the rest of the property.
TCGA 1992 s42, s224(2), (3), s242, s244

Your garden

The garden of your main home is not normally liable to capital gains tax even if you sell off part of it while you still own the home. But if it's over half a hectare, the gain on the excess will not be exempt unless the Revenue considers that a larger garden is appropriate for that house.

If you sell the home and retain some of the land, the gain you make on the land from the time when it stopped being part of your garden may be liable to capital gains tax.
TCGA 1992 s222(1)–(4); Varty v. Lynes, 1976; 3 All ER p. 447

The profit motive

If there is evidence that you bought your home wholly or partly with the object of selling it at a profit, you get no exemption from capital gains tax – even though it was your only or main home. Of course, it's not easy to prove what was in your mind when you bought it, but if you moved frequently from house to house – buying them in a derelict state and improving them, say – it would look as though your main aim was profit. The Revenue might even class you as a property-dealer, and tax your gain like income.

If you make major changes to your home (such as converting it into flats, buying the freehold if it's leasehold) in order to increase the price you get for it, the *extra* gain you make may not be exempt.
TCGA 1992 s224(3); ICTA 1988 s18(1)–(4)

Compulsory purchase

If part of your property is compulsorily purchased, special rules apply for working out any capital gains tax bill.
TCGA 1992 s245

Working out the chargeable gain

In many cases, only *part* of the gain you make when you sell your home will be chargeable. For example, normally only gains made after 31 March 1982 are liable for capital gains tax. If you have let your home while you lived away for a few years (unless you lived away for one of the reasons listed on p. 209), or nominated another home as your main one for part of the period you owned this one, you will be liable for tax on the part of the gain you are assumed to have made in that period. In general, the Revenue assumes the value of your home has increased by even monthly steps from the price you paid for it to the price at which you sell.

First, the gain over the whole period is worked out as outlined in Chapter 14, p. 267. Broadly speaking, this is the amount you sold the home for *less* the amount you paid for it – but certain *allowable expenditure* (see below) may reduce your tax bill, as will the indexation rules (see p. 270). The Revenue then works out the chargeable gain for the period when the home was *not* exempt from capital gains tax by the *time apportionment method*. This gain is:

$$\text{Gain over whole period} \div \text{Total number of months you owned it} \times \text{Number of months it was liable for tax}$$

See Example 3 for how this works in practice.

Allowable expenditure normally includes:

- any costs of acquiring *and* disposing of the home (e.g. commission, conveyancing costs, stamp duty, valuation)
- capital expenditure which has resulted in an increase in the value of the home (e.g. improvements, but not ordinary maintenance).

There are special rules for limiting the chargeable gain arising from letting your only or 'main' home – see p. 224. *TCGA 1992 s38, s223(2), s224*

EXAMPLE 3

Sarah Keighley bought her home in May 1987 and sold it in May 1992 for £76,000, making a total gain of £20,000 (after deducting buying and selling costs, and after indexation).

Because Sarah lived in another home which she had nominated as her main home during 1988, the home she bought in 1987 was not exempt for those 12 months. She owned the home for a total of 60 months. Her chargeable gain is £20,000 ÷ 60 × 12 = £4,000.

Your home and your work

If you work for an employer

If you work at home

You may be able to claim a proportion of heating and lighting costs, and, possibly, of telephone, cleaning and insurance costs as an allowable expense to set against your earnings. If you use part of your home *exclusively* for your work, you may be able to claim a proportion of your rent. But it's unlikely you'll be able to claim *any* of these expenses unless it's an express or implied condition of your employment that you carry out some of your duties at or from your home.

Using part of your home exclusively for your employment should not mean you lose your home's exemption from capital gains tax, even if you are allowed tax relief for your expenses.

ICTA 1988 s198

Working away from home

If you're getting tax relief on the mortgage on your only or main home, you're allowed to be away from the home for up to a year at a time before you stop getting relief. And if your employer *requires* you to live away from home, you continue to get tax relief if you're likely to return to that home within four years. If you don't move back within four years (or if you sell the home without moving back) you don't lose any of the tax relief you've had. But there's no further tax relief for that home until you move back. If you move back for at least three months, you can have another four years' absence.

Being away from the home you've nominated as your 'main' home for capital gains tax purposes may not mean you lose exemption. Any periods when you were employed (but not self-employed) and all your duties were carried on outside the UK are exempt from capital gains tax, however long they are; taking leave in the UK or elsewhere doesn't

213

affect this exemption. In addition, you can be away from your home for up to four years without losing exemption if you have to live away because of the location of your job. If you are away for more than four years in total, the excess won't be exempt (unless another exemption on p. 209 applies, e.g. it was the last three years you owned the home). To get any of the exemptions on account of your work, you must have lived in the home as your only or main home at some time before the first absence, and, unless you can't return home because your job requires you to work away from home again, you must also live in it after the last absence. A married couple still get these exemptions even if one partner owns the home and the other has the job causing the absence.

ESC A27 (interest relief); TCGA 1992 s223; ESC D3, D4 (capital gains)

EXAMPLE 4

In September 1992 Hamish MacDonald was trying to sell his home in Edinburgh which he bought in December 1973. He didn't always live in his home, and when he was away he let it.

- The first absence: from August 1976 to May 1979 he lived in Wales.
- The second absence: from September 1982 to February 1983 he lived abroad where he was employed.
- The third absence: from March 1984 to February 1989 he was working in London.
- The fourth absence: in September 1992 he bought a new home in London where he now lives. He is trying to sell his empty Edinburgh home.

How do the absences affect his exemption from capital gains tax?
- The first absence is prior to 1 April 1982 and irrelevant to the calculation. Any tax bill would be based only on the rise in value (taking account of indexation) after 31 March 1982, so Hamish would have to find out what the house was worth then. But if there is a tax bill, the time apportionment method will take account only of the period Hamish has owned his home since then. In fact, Hamish probably won't have to pay any tax.

- The second absence will be exempt because he was employed abroad.
- The third absence: the first four years will be exempt because Hamish had to live nearer his job in London; the last year will be exempt because he is allowed to be absent for periods totalling three years for any reason, so long as he lived in the home after the absence (which he did, from March 1989 to August 1992).
- The fourth absence will be exempt provided he sells within three years of September 1992 (even though he has now nominated his London home as his main home).

If you live in job-related accommodation

You can get tax relief indefinitely on a loan used to buy a home which you (or your spouse) own and in which you intend to live. And, if you nominate the home you own as your 'main' one for capital gains tax purposes, any gain you make when you sell the home is exempt from capital gains tax so long as you are living in a home which goes with your job. It doesn't matter if you change your mind and sell the home without ever living in it, as long as you intended to live in it at some stage. To qualify on either count, at least one of the following must apply to your job-related accommodation:

- you need to live there to do your job properly (e.g. you're a social worker living in a children's home)
- living where you do enables you to do the job better *and* it is common for people doing your sort of job to live in such a home (e.g. you're a caretaker)
- you live there because there is a special threat to your security.

A director can qualify for the first two reasons above only if he or she owns or controls five per cent or less of the shares in the company, *and* is a full-time working director of the company *or* works for a charity or non-profit-making company.

ICTA 1988 s356 (interest relief); TCGA 1992 s222(8) (capital gains)

If you're self-employed

If you work at home
If you're self-employed (or do some freelance or spare-time work) and do part of your work at home, you can claim as an allowable expense the proportion of the cost of running your home that's attributable to business use – see p. 180.

But if you use part of your home *exclusively* for your business, the part you use will not be exempt from capital gains tax for the period you use it. The exact *proportion* of the gain you make when you sell the house which will be liable to tax will have to be negotiated with your Tax Inspector (in one of the same ways as would be adopted if you had let part of your home – see p. 224). However, if your business is on a modest scale, and if you've got an understanding Tax Inspector, you may be able to get the best of both worlds by using a room *almost* exclusively for business – enough to be allowed heating and so on as an expense, but not so exclusively as to risk a capital gains tax bill.

Even if there is a chargeable gain when you sell the home, you won't be liable for any tax at the time if you use the proceeds from selling the part of the home you used for your business to buy another property where you will carry on the same business or a similar one. The new building counts as replacement of a business asset, and the gain is *rolled over* (see p. 279). If you don't use all the proceeds in this way, only the part you use can qualify. If you eventually qualify for *retirement relief* (see p. 280), you may avoid a capital gains tax bill entirely.
ICTA 1988 s74 (expenses); TCGA 1992 s224(1), s152, s163 (capital gains)

Accommodation provided under the terms of your business
If you live in accommodation provided under the terms of your business (e.g. you're a licensee publican) and you're buying a home elsewhere which you intend to live in one day, you can get tax relief on your mortgage and exemption from capital gains tax as if you were an employee in job-related accommodation (see p. 215).
ICTA 1988 s356

Letting property

If you let land or property, there are two main points to consider:

- how rents you receive are taxed, and what expenses and interest you can set against the income
- capital gains tax when you sell the property. If a property is not your only or main home, the gain you make will be liable to capital gains tax. If you let part of your own home, the gain on the let part may be liable to tax, unless you were away from the home on a qualifying absence (see p. 209).

Income from property and land you let

In most cases, income from land or property you let is treated as investment income, and taxed under Schedule A. This includes rents you receive, ground rents, feu duties and premiums on leases. The main exceptions are:

- income from furnished property is generally taxed under Schedule D Case VI – see p. 42 – but receipts of a hotel or guesthouse are treated as earnings from a business and taxed under Schedule D Case I. Income from certain furnished holiday lettings is also treated as earnings from a business, although it remains assessable under Schedule D Case VI
- income from land and property abroad is taxed under Schedule D Case V, usually on a preceding-year basis
- if you're entitled to rent from a property as a privilege of a job, the income is taxed under Schedule A but treated as earned income.

There are certain rules for premiums on leases – check with your tax office.

The Case or Schedule under which your income is taxed may affect you if you have a loss on any property – see pp. 38 and 220.

Other income from land and property

Most other income you get as a result of owning land, having an interest in it or rights over it is treated as investment income and taxed under Schedule A. The main exceptions are:

- mineral rents and mining royalties are taxed under Schedule D Case I.

Letting land and unfurnished property

In any tax year, you are taxed on the income you are entitled to receive in that year. This applies even if you haven't yet received the income, but not to debts you've tried unsuccessfully to recover, or ones you've waived to avoid hardship. Alternatively, you can ask to be taxed on your profits for your accounting year ending in the tax year, as long as they meet certain conditions. Once this is decided, you can't change back. You are allowed to deduct certain expenses and interest (see below) which you have actually paid during the tax year when you work out your profits. If the expenses and interest come to more than your income, you will have made a loss. For how losses are treated, see p. 220.

Tax on income from property is due on 1 January in the tax year (e.g. the tax on all the property income you are entitled to receive in the 1992–3 tax year is due on 1 January 1993). If you pay tax through PAYE and your taxable rental income is small, your PAYE code may be adjusted to collect the tax you owe.

In many cases the Revenue will ask you to pay only the basic-rate tax on 1 January, and will ask for any higher-rate tax later. As the Revenue is collecting the basic-rate tax before you've received all the income, it has to make an estimate of how much you should receive and what your expenses will be in the tax year. It uses last year's figures for this estimate, and adjusts your assessment when the actual amount is known. If you know that your income (before deductions) will be less than it was last year because, say, you've sold off some property, you can ask the Revenue before 1 January to reduce the initial assessment.

If you are letting UK property while you live abroad, your tenants have to deduct basic-rate tax from the rent if it is paid directly to you. If, however, it is paid to an agent, the collection of any tax will depend on your residence status in the UK. Check your position with your tax office.
ICTA 1988 s22

Allowable expenses
You can deduct certain expenses from your income from letting when you work out your profits. If you let only part

of your home, or let it for only part of each year, you and the Revenue will have to agree on the proportion you can claim. You can't claim anything for your own time. The most common allowable expenses are:

- water rates, ground rent, feu duty (in Scotland)
- normal repairs and decoration, but not repairs necessary when you bought the property, nor improvements, additions or alterations to the property
- management expenses as a landlord (e.g. stationery, telephone bills, accountant's fees, cost of rent collection)
- cost of insurance and any necessary valuation for insurance
- legal fees for renewing a tenancy agreement (for leases of up to 50 years)
- estate agent's fees, accommodation agency fees, cost of advertising for tenants
- rent you pay for a property which you, in turn, sublet
- cost of lighting common parts of property
- cost of services you provide including wages of people who provide such services (e.g. cleaners, gardeners)
- cost of maintenance and repairs made necessary by improvements you've made, as long as you haven't changed the use of the property
- cost of maintaining roads, drains, ditches etc. on an estate you own, if for the benefit of tenants.

You can also deduct interest you pay on a loan used to buy or improve property – see p. 220. If you buy any machinery or equipment (e.g. a lawnmower or ladder) for upkeep or repair of property, you can either claim *capital allowances* as if you were self-employed (see p. 184), *or* claim on a *renewals basis* (see *Wear and tear* on p. 222). Once you have decided which basis to use you must stick to it.

If you incur expenses while the home isn't actually occupied by a tenant, they still qualify for tax relief as long as you let the home out at *full rent* straight afterwards and (unless you'd just bought the home) you had been letting it immediately beforehand. 'Full rent' means an amount which, over the years, is enough to cover all your expenses and the interest you pay (though you might still make a loss in any individual year).

ICTA 1988 s25–s28

Interest

You can get tax relief on interest on a loan (other than an overdraft or credit card debt) used to buy or improve a home you let out. In any 52-week period, you can get tax relief as long as it's let at a commercial rent for more than half the 52-week period, and provided that for the rest of the period it is available for letting or used as your only or main home (unless building or repair work is going on).

The interest you pay can be set off against any income from property but not against any other income. These loans don't count towards your £30,000 limit (see p. 203) except when the property is being used as an only or main home when the rules for loans to buy your main home apply – see *Tax relief for buying your home*, p. 202.

ICTA 1988 s354(1), s355, s367

Losses

Any part of a loss which consists of interest can be set off against any income from property. If you haven't enough other property income to set it all against, you can carry what's left forward and set it against any income from property in future years, as long as you're still letting the property you made the loss on.

The way a loss resulting from allowable expenses is treated is more complicated and depends on the type of lease:

- If the lease is at *full rent* (see p. 219) and you are responsible for all or some of the repairs (*normal lease*), any loss can be set against income from other properties you let on a normal lease. If such income doesn't use up the whole loss, you can carry what's left forward and set it against income of the same type in future years.
- If the lease is at full rent but the tenant pays for all or substantially all repairs (*tenant's repairing lease*), the loss can be set against income from any properties on a *normal* lease in the same or future years, *or* carried forward and set against future profits on the *same* property only.
- If the lease is at a nominal rent (e.g. to a relative paying you little or no rent), a loss can only be carried forward and set against future income from letting the same home to the same person.

ICTA 1988 s25, s355(4)

Letting furnished property

Income from letting furnished property is normally treated as investment income. But if you run a hotel or guest-house, the whole of your income will normally count as earnings from self-employment. For furnished holiday lettings, see p. 224.

If you let furnished accommodation to a tenant who pays you separately for services you provide (e.g. meals, cleaning, laundry), the amount you get for these services may count as earnings from a business and be taxed under Schedule D Case I. What you get for the rooms counts as investment income and is taxed under Schedule D Case VI.

If you pay someone else to provide such services in furnished accommodation, the wages you pay count as an allowable expense deductible from the rent you get. For the person you pay, they count as earnings. So if your husband or wife, say, provides the services, what you pay will be his or her earnings (as long as the amount you pay is appropriate for the work done). This can be useful if your husband's or wife's other income is less than the full amount of the personal allowance (£3,445 for someone under 65 in the 1992–3 tax year). See Example 5, p. 222.

Income taxed under Schedule D Case VI is taxed in the same way as income from the land and unfurnished property (see p. 217) except that you're taxed on the amount you actually receive in the tax year instead of the amount you're entitled to.

You can ask (within two years of the end of the tax year) for the part of the rent which comes from the *premises* (as opposed to the furnishings or any services you provide) to be taxed under Schedule A instead of under Class VI of Schedule D. This could be useful if you have made a loss on furnished lettings which you want to set off against income from unfurnished property being taxed in the same tax year (or vice versa) in order to reduce your tax bill immediately. As well as apportioning the rent you get between the premises and for the furnishings, you'll have to apportion your allowable expenses. See Example 6, p. 222.

ICTA 1988 s18

EXAMPLE 5

Brian Wallis lets out three furnished flats and gets £10,000 a year in rent. His student son provides the tenants with an evening meal, cleans the flat twice a week and collects the rents. Brian pays his son £3,900 a year for this (but has to deduct some tax and National Insurance from what he pays). As his son has no other taxable income, £3,445 (the personal allowance) of this will be tax-free. Brian deducts the £3,900 wages from his letting income of £10,000, and will be taxed on £6,100, less the National Insurance he pays, and less any other allowable expenses.

EXAMPLE 6

Brian Wallis also lets out an unfurnished house. In the 1992–3 tax year the mortgage interest and allowable expenses on the house come to £400 more than the rent he gets. As Brian wants to reduce his tax bill immediately, he asks for the income he gets from letting the *premises* of his furnished flats (see Example 5), which he reckons on being £4,700 after expenses on the property, to be taxed under Schedule A. He can now set the £400 loss on the unfurnished home against it, and be taxed on only £4,700 − £400 = £4,300.

Allowable expenses

When working out your profits, deduct all the expenses allowable for unfurnished property (see p. 218) *plus*:

- heating, lighting and tenants' telephone bills you pay
- wear and tear of fixtures and fittings (see p. 223), cost of specific repairs to furniture
- cost of preparing an inventory.

Where possible, keep receipts for the expenses you are claiming. If your total rents before deducting expenses are £10,000 or more, you will have to submit a detailed statement of your expenses figure with your tax return.

If you take in a lodger or get paid separately for services you provide, the income counts as earnings from a business, and you can deduct other allowable expenses from it – see the table on p. 180. In these circumstances, you can claim capital allowances on furnished property. The tax due on business earnings is payable in two instalments, on 1 January and 1 July – see p. 173. Check with your tax office whether your income from a lodger counts as business earnings. See also *Providing furnished accommodation tax-free*, p. 224.

Wear and tear
You can claim an allowance for wear and tear on fixtures, furniture and furnishings – e.g. chairs, cookers, lampshades, beds and sheets. You can claim *either* the actual cost of fixtures, furniture, etc. you replace during the year (called *renewals basis*), *or* a proportion (normally 10 per cent) of the rent *less*, if you pay them, service charges and water rates. Once you've chosen a basis, you must stick to it.
SP/A19

Interest
Interest you pay on a loan to buy or improve the property can also be deducted from the income you get. If the rent counts as investment income, the same rules apply as with unfurnished property (see p. 220).

If part of the income you get counts as earnings from a business, interest you set against it counts as a business expense (see p. 178). The rules on p. 205 don't then apply, so you could get tax relief on an overdraft or credit card debt, for example.

Losses
If the income is taxed under Schedule D Case VI, any part of a loss which consists of interest can be set off against any other income from property. But any part which results from the allowable expenses can be set off only against other income taxed under Schedule D Case VI – e.g. other income from furnished lettings, or freelance earnings you've received. If you haven't any (or enough) other income of the right type in the same tax year, you can carry the loss forward and set it against any income of that type in future tax years.

If the income on which you've made a loss counts as earnings from a business and is taxed under Schedule D Case I, you have the options outlined on p. 189 for offsetting this loss.
ICTA 1988 s380–s389

Providing furnished accommodation tax-free

From 6 April 1992, tenants and owner-occupiers can take advantage of the rent-a-room scheme. If you let furnished accommodation in your only or main home you can receive a gross rental income of £3,250 (£62.50 a week). If your rental income exceeds £3,250, you can choose *either* to pay tax on the excess, without any relief for allowable expenses; *or* to pay tax on the whole lot but claim expenses in the normal way. If you choose to claim the £3,250, you must tell your tax inspector within one year of the end of the relevant tax year. Your choice will remain in force until you decide to change to the normal method of assessing rental income. There is no need to make this choice if your rental income is £3,250 or less. If two or more people receive rental income, the tax-free limit is £1,625 for each person. Note that the definition of 'only or main home' is not the same as the one used for capital gains tax (see p. 207). It is the home which is, *in fact*, your main home – for example, the one for which you're entitled to MIRAS.

Furnished holiday lettings

Income from letting property (including caravans) which is let as furnished holiday accommodation for part of the year is treated as earnings from a business, even though it is assessed under Schedule D Case VI.

To qualify, both the following must apply:

- the property is available for letting to the general public at a commercial rent for at least 140 days (which need not be consecutive) during each 12-month qualifying period (not necessarily a tax year)
- it is actually let out as holiday accommodation for at least 70 of those days, and during at least seven months of the 12-month period it isn't normally occupied by the same tenant for more than 31 days at a stretch.

If you let more than one unit of accommodation, you can average the days they're actually let to pass the 70-day rule.

If a furnished letting counts as holiday accommodation, all the income you get from it in the tax year counts as earned income. But if only part of the let accommodation counts as furnished holiday lettings only a proportion of the income counts as earned income.

ICTA 1988 s503, s504

EXAMPLE 7

Winston Fry started letting out a furnished bungalow in Skegness for holidays on 1 June 1992. It will count as a furnished holiday letting for the 1992–3 year of assessment, as long as it's available to the public at a commercial rent for 140 days during the 12 months from 1 June 1992 to 31 May 1993, and as long as he lets it out for 70 of those days, mainly for periods of 31 days or less.

Capital gains on let property

If a home has been your only home or nominated as your main one for the whole time you've owned it, the whole of your gain will be exempt from capital gains tax even if you've let it out while you were away, as long as all your absences count as qualifying absences (see p. 209). But the gain attributable to any other period you let it while you were away (worked out by the time apportionment method shown on p. 212) won't be exempt.

If you let part of your only or main home, you don't lose any exemption for having lodgers share your living rooms and eat with you. In other cases it depends on whether you have occupied the part of the home you've let at any time. If you haven't, the gain on the part you let will not be exempt from capital gains tax. The chargeable gain will normally be based on the number of rooms you let or the floor area of the part you let, but could alternatively be based on the rateable value of the part you let, or on its market value. It's up to you and the Revenue to agree which method to use; if you don't agree, you can appeal to the General or Special Commissioners (see p. 63).

If you have lived in the part of the home you've let out, the gain on the let part is apportioned according to the period you've let it. In addition, this gain (after allowing for indexation – see p. 270) will remain exempt from capital gains tax if it's not more than the (exempt) gain attributable to your occupation of the home (after allowing for indexation), *and* if it's not more than £40,000. If either limit is exceeded, the excess (the larger excess if both limits are exceeded) is liable to capital gains tax – see Example 8. To get this exemption, the let part must be lived in by someone, but must not be a completely separate home (e.g. not a self-contained flat with its own access from the street) and you

225

should not have had more than minor alterations made to the home.

TCGA 1992 s223; FA 1980 s80; SP14/80

EXAMPLE 8

Elizabeth Kerr bought a house in Belgravia in May 1984 and sold it eight years later in May 1992. Her gain, after deducting selling costs and her indexation allowance, was £200,000. Throughout this time the house was her main home for capital gains tax purposes. For the first two years she lived in the whole house, but then she let out two-thirds of the house as living accommodation. The first two years of ownership (when she lived in the whole house) are exempt. The last three years of ownership are also exempt (see p. 209). Of the remaining three years, only one-third of the home is exempt. So the exempt part of the gain is 2 (first two years) + 3 (last three years) + 1 (one-third of three years) ÷ 8 = ⁶⁄₈. £200,000 × ⁶⁄₈ = £150,000. The gain attributable to the let part is therefore £50,000. This is £10,000 more than £40,000, so £10,000 will be a chargeable gain.

The first £5,800 of gains made in the 1992–3 tax year are exempt from capital gains tax. Elizabeth will have to pay tax on £10,000 − £5,800 = £4,200. She is a higher-rate taxpayer, so the tax bill will be £4,200 × 40% = £1,680. She will also have to pay tax on any other chargeable gains in that tax year, as her annual exemption has been used up on her house sale.

If the letting counts as a business

If the let property counts as furnished holiday accommodation (see p. 224) or if (unusually) income from the letting counts as earnings from a business because of services you provide, you may not have to pay tax when you sell the home even if a taxable gain arises. If you use the proceeds from selling the home (or from the part you let) to buy another property where you continue to provide similar accommodation and services, the new property can count as replacement of a business asset and the gain can be *rolled over* (see p. 279). If you don't use all the proceeds in this way, only the part you use can qualify.

Doing this only defers your tax bill, as you would normally have to pay capital gains tax on rolled-over gains when you finally sell up and cease letting. However, if you don't do this until you reach 55 (or retire earlier through ill-health) you qualify for *retirement relief*, which exempts part of the gains – see p. 280.

TCGA 1992 s152–s158 (Rollover relief), s163–s164, Sch 6 (Retirement relief); ICTA 1988 s503, s504 (2)–(9)

Employing someone in your home

If you employ someone, it's your responsibility to collect income tax and National Insurance contributions from them under the PAYE system – assuming that the amount of pay the employee gets will mean that tax and National Insurance are payable. This section tells you how to collect the money if you are employing someone in the home – e g a housekeeper, nanny and so on.

Another duty you have as an employer is to give your employee a payslip. This should show the amount of pay and the amount of the deductions – see p. 116.

If your employee earns £54 or more a week in the 1992–3 tax year, National Insurance will have to be deducted from his or her pay. Depending on his or her income and personal circumstances, tax may need to be deducted too. Write to the local Tax Inspector (look up *Inland Revenue* in the phone book) and state:

- your employee's full name, type of work, National Insurance number and address
- the date your employee will start work, the amount of pay and whether it's to be paid weekly or monthly
- the name and address of the previous employer (if any).

You should also pass this information on to your local DSS office.

The forms you get

You will be sent:

- **P12 – Simplified Deduction Card** This is where you will record all the details of pay and deductions
- **P16 – Simplified Tax Tables** These can be used for an employee who is paid a fixed amount each week or month. The tables show how much tax you need to deduct for different levels of taxable pay
- **P37 – Employer's Annual Declaration and Certificate** You will be sent this at the end of each tax year (i.e. 5 April). You need to fill this in and send it to the

Collector of Taxes, plus the Simplified Deduction Card, by 19 April
- **CF391 – Contribution Tables**   These show the amounts of employee's and employer's National Insurance contributions.

The first three are sent by the local tax office; the last by the local DSS office.

Board and lodging
There's no tax for the employee to pay on living accommodation provided, as long as the job is one in which accommodation is normally available – e.g. nanny, nurse, housekeeper. And there's no tax to pay on free or cheap meals if they're provided to all employees you may have.

Paying tax

You have to pay the Collector of Taxes at the end of each quarter (i.e. 5 July, 5 October, 5 January, 5 April) the amount deducted in tax from your employee's pay, and the amount of National Insurance contributions due from you and your employee.

If, during the quarter, you have paid any Statutory Sick Pay or Statutory Maternity Pay, you can deduct this amount from the National Insurance contributions.

When an employee leaves

You should complete the Simplified Deduction Card up to the date of leaving and send what's due in tax and National Insurance to the Collector of Taxes, together with the completed Deduction Card. If you know the name and address of the new employer, you should fill that in the space provided for it on the Card. Note that you don't need to give your employee a **form P45** (which shows earnings and tax to date – see p. 136).

Leaflets

P7 – Employer's Guide to PAYE
NI270 – Statutory Sick Pay Manual for Employers
NI257 – Statutory Maternity Pay Manual for Employers
NI269 – National Insurance for Employers
NI268 – Quick Guide to Statutory Sick Pay, Maternity Leave and NI Contributions

---

12 *INVESTMENTS*

What counts as investment income might surprise you. For tax purposes, investment income is income which isn't *earned* – broadly speaking, any income which isn't from a job, business or pension. So as well as income you get from your investments, income you get from, for example, a covenant, maintenance agreement and from letting property may count as investment income.

There are two main taxes which apply to investments:

- **capital gains tax** If your investment is the sort where its value can fluctuate there could be capital gains tax to pay when you sell (or give away) the investment. But for the 1992–3 tax year, the first £5,800 of net chargeable gains is tax-free. Anything above that level is taxed at the same rate as if it were your income – 20, 25 or 40 per cent. For more on capital gains tax, see p. 264.
- **income tax** Any investment income you get (such as interest or share dividends) is added to your earned income. You then deduct your outgoings (see p. 28) and your allowances (see p. 34), leaving your taxable income on which you pay tax. For the 1992–3 tax year, income tax is charged at 20 per cent on the first £2,000 of your taxable income, at the basic rate of 25 per cent on the next £21,700, and at the higher rate of 40 per cent on any of your taxable income above £23,700.
ICTA 1988 s833

How investment income is paid

Investment income can be paid in one of three ways:

- it can be tax-free (no tax to pay) – see list on p. 231
- it can be paid gross, i.e. before any tax has been deducted – see p. 232
- it can be paid with basic-rate tax (or its equivalent) already deducted – see p. 234 for how this works.

Note that if you choose to have the income credited to your investment, the tax treatment is the same as if it's paid out to you. For tax purposes, you get income when it is paid or credited to you, even if the interest is worked out more frequently.

Husband and wife

Until independent taxation was introduced on 6 April 1990, any income which came from a wife's investments was always counted as the husband's for tax purposes, even if the couple had chosen to have the wife's earnings taxed separately. Now, husband and wife are taxed independently for both their investment income and their capital gains. See Chapter 4 for more information.
FA 1988 s32

Which investment for which investor?

Here we give some guidelines on the types of investments which suit non- and higher-rate taxpayers. For basic-rate taxpayers, there are no particular investments which stand out from a tax point of view. If the highest rate of tax you pay on your income from investments is 20 per cent, your choice is much the same as for a basic-rate taxpayer. The difference is that where basic-rate tax is deducted at source, you will be able to claim back the difference. So if £25 has been deducted from a gross amount of interest of £100, for example, you will be able to claim back £5, i.e. 25 per cent of £100 less 20 per cent of £100. But don't consider tax alone. Look at other aspects, too, e.g. the after-tax return you get, risk, and for how long you want to invest.

Non-taxpayers

You should consider:

- investments which can pay income gross, before any tax is deducted – bank and building society accounts, high-income British Government stocks bought through the National Savings Stock Register, National Savings Investment Accounts and National Savings Income and Capital Bonds
- investments where income is paid with basic-rate tax already deducted but where the tax can be claimed back from the Revenue, such as shares and unit trusts.

Higher-rate taxpayers

You should consider:

- investments which are tax-free, e.g. Tax Exempt Special Savings Accounts (TESSAS), National Savings Certificates, National Savings Yearly Plan, SAYE schemes, Personal Equity Plans (PEPs).

People receiving age-related allowances

If your income is in the region where each extra £ of 'total income' loses you age-related allowances (see p. 95), you should consider:

- tax-free investments – e.g. Tax Exempt Special Savings Accounts (TESSAS), National Savings Certificates, National Savings Yearly Plan, SAYE schemes, PEPs.

All taxpayers

If you're prepared to take a risk, you can make £5,800 in capital gains free of tax in the 1992–3 tax year. Consider:

- investments which you hope will give a capital gain rather than income, e.g. low-income British Government stocks, index-linked British Government stocks, ordinary shares, ordinary shares in unquoted companies bought under the Business Expansion Scheme, unit trusts.

Tax-free investment income

Income or proceeds from the following investments are tax-free:

- Save-As-You-Earn (SAYE schemes)
- National Savings Certificates (and, in most cases, Ulster Savings Certificates if you live in Northern Ireland)
- National Savings Yearly Plan
- National Savings Children's Bonus Bonds
- qualifying regular-premium investment-type life insurance (if held for at least 10 years, or three-quarters of the original term, whichever is shorter) – but the company pays tax
- proceeds from some friendly society plans
- Premium Bond prizes (which don't really count as income)

- first £70 interest each year from a National Savings Ordinary Account
- income from a covenant dated after 14 March 1988
- interest on a tax rebate
- interest to do with delayed settlement of damages for personal injury or death
- return on investments held in a Personal Equity Plan
- the proceeds of a Tax Exempt Special Savings Account (TESSA).
  ICTA 1988 s46, s325, s326, s329, s464, s487

Investment income not taxed before you get it

This type of income is paid to you *gross* – i.e. before any tax has been deducted. Examples of income paid this way include interest from bank and building society accounts (if you're registered as a non-taxpayer, see p. 236), National Savings Investment Accounts and National Savings Income and Capital Bonds and interest from deposits at non-UK branches of UK and overseas banks.

If you've been getting interest of this type for a few years, it will normally be taxed on a *preceding year basis* – i.e. your tax bill for the 1992–3 tax year will be based on the interest paid (or credited) to you in the 1991–2 tax year. This bill must normally be paid by 1 January 1993 or within 30 days of the date on the Notice of Assessment you'll get, whichever is later. But if your interest isn't very substantial and doesn't vary much from year to year, and you pay tax under PAYE, the tax on it will probably be collected along with tax on your earnings – so you'll pay some of the tax sooner.

The first and last years

Special rules apply to the first three years and last two years in which you get interest without tax being deducted. See the tables opposite and on p. 234 for details.

Changes in amount of interest

If there is a big change in the amount of interest you get from a single source, e.g. if you greatly increase or decrease the size of your National Savings Investment Account, your Tax Inspector may treat such interest as coming from a new source and apply the special rules. You won't need to worry about these rules if your interest is much the same from year to year. Note that if you get interest from more than one source which is paid without tax deducted, your Tax Inspector will normally apply the special rules to each source separately.

Working the rules

If the amount of this type of interest which you get varies from year to year, you may be able to reduce your tax bill:

- If the amount of interest in year 3 is lower than the interest you got in year 2, tell your Tax Inspector that you want your tax bill for year 3 to be based on the interest you actually got in year 3. (You can make this choice at any time within six years of the end of year 3.)
- If the amount of interest in years 2 and 3 is high compared with the interest in year 4, consider closing your account (e.g. your National Savings Investment Account) just before the end of year 4, and re-opening it a week or so later (after the start of the next tax year). That way, your tax bill for year 4 will be based on the interest you actually got in that year, rather than on the higher amount of interest you got in year 3.
ICTA 1988 s18(2–4), s64, s66

Your Tax Return

You enter in your Tax Return the amount of before-tax interest you receive in that tax year. So if you are filling in your Tax Return for income in the 1992–3 tax year, you put in the interest you get in that tax year.

Your tax bill for the first three years

	tax is initially based on:	but for some years, there's a choice.
First tax year in which you get interest from this source (year 1)	interest you get in first tax year (*current year basis*)	no choice this year
Second tax year (year 2)	interest you get in second tax year (*current year basis*)	no choice this year [1]

233

	tax is initially based on:	but for some years, there's a choice:
Third tax year (year 3)	Interest you got in second tax year (*preceding year basis*)	**your choice:** you can choose to have tax based on interest you get in third tax year (*current year basis*). Do so if this is less than interest you got in second year [1]
Fourth and subsequent tax years . . .	interest you got in preceding tax year (*preceding year basis*)	no choice for these years

[1] But if this source of interest started on 6 April in year 1, tax for year 2 will normally be based on the interest you got in year 1 (*preceding year basis*), and you can choose to have tax for year 2 based on interest in year 2 instead (*current year basis*). Consider doing this if interest in year 2 is lower than interest in year 1. Note, in this case, you have no further choice in year 3.

Your tax bill for the last two years

	tax is initially based on:	but for some years, there's a choice:
The last-but-one tax year in which you get interest from this source	interest you got in preceding tax year (*preceding year basis*)	**the Revenue's choice:** when you tell the Revenue, at the end of the next year, that you've closed your account, your bill may be revised. It will be based on the interest you actually got in the last-but-one tax year (*current year basis*) if this comes to more than your original bill
last tax year in which you get interest from this source	interest you get in this tax year (*current year basis*)	no choice this year

Investment income taxed before you get it

Investments taxed in this way include share dividends, unit trust distributions and interest on some British Government

stocks. When you get the income, basic-rate tax has already been deducted. This type of income is taxed on a *current year basis* – i.e. your tax bill for the 1992–3 tax year is based on the income paid (or credited) to you in that tax year. Covenants (p. 239) and maintenance payments (p. 241) are treated somewhat differently.
ICTA 1988 s1(2b), s4

Non-taxpayers

If you don't pay tax, even allowing for income of this type, you can claim tax back. You can get the right form (R40) from your Tax Inspector.

20-per-cent taxpayers

Tax on this income is deducted at a rate of 25 per cent, but you will be able to claim a repayment of the difference between 25 and 20 per cent.

Basic-rate taxpayers

If you are liable for basic-rate tax only, tax due on this income is automatically met by tax deducted or credited.

Higher-rate taxpayers

If you pay tax at the higher rate, you will have to pay extra tax, worked out on the gross (before-tax) income. Any extra tax due on interest received in the 1992–3 tax year is due on 1 December 1993 (or within 30 days of the date on your Notice of Assessment, if later). Tax may be deducted under PAYE, in which case you pay some of the tax earlier – but you can choose to pay in a lump sum instead.

Your Tax Return

You should enter the gross (before-tax) amount of the interest received in your Tax Return. With share dividends and unit trust distributions, you enter the amount received and the amount of the tax credit. For interest with composite-rate tax deducted, enter the amount of interest that is actually paid or credited to you – your tax office will work out the gross amount.

How each type of investment is taxed

Alternative investments

If you invest in antiques, silver, gold coins or other tangible objects of this type, you will be hoping to make a capital gain. For how this is taxed, see p. 264.

Annuities

With annuities which you buy voluntarily, part of what you get back is treated as being a return of your original investment and is tax-free. The rest is taxed as investment income. For more details, see p. 100. The *whole* of income from annuities bought compulsorily, e.g. as part of a pension scheme, is taxed as earned income.

Bank and building society interest

When you get interest from building societies, banks and other 'authorised institutions' such as finance companies you don't have to pay basic-rate tax on it. This is because, at the moment, these institutions pay basic-rate tax direct to the Inland Revenue before paying out the interest to you.

If you pay tax at 20 per cent, you can claim back the difference between 20 and 25 per cent. To work out the amount of tax you can reclaim, divide the amount of basic-rate tax deducted by 5.

If you pay tax at higher rates, you will have to pay extra tax on your interest. When working out your tax bill, the Tax Inspector will include the *gross* amount of interest (see p. 36) as part of your income. If you got £375 interest, say, from a building society, this will be grossed-up to work out your taxable income. So if the basic rate of tax is 25 per cent, the grossed-up interest is £375 ÷ 0.75 = £500. You will have to pay tax at your highest rate of tax on this grossed-up amount of interest. But you are treated as having already paid basic-rate tax on the interest – so you only have to hand over the difference. See the example below.

Since 6 April 1991, non-taxpayers have also been able to have their interest from bank and building society accounts paid gross. To qualify, you need to tell each bank or building society with which you have an account by sending them a completed registration form (**form R85** – available

from Post Offices, bank and building societies and Tax Offices). Alternatively, you can reclaim the tax from the Inland Revenue, see p. 235.
ICTA 1988 s477A, s480A

EXAMPLE 1

Charlie Carter gets £675 interest from his building society in the 1992–3 tax year. As he pays some higher-rate tax, he realises he'll have to pay extra tax on this interest. He works out the grossed-up amount of interest, i.e. £675 ÷ 0.75 = £900.

He adds this to his other income and finds he's liable for tax at 40 per cent on the £900 grossed-up interest, i.e. £360 tax in total. But he's treated as having already paid tax on this interest at the 25 per cent basic rate, i.e. 25 per cent of £900 = £225. So he has to hand over the difference on £360 − £225 = £135 to the Inland Revenue.

British Government stocks

Interest on Government stocks is paid with basic-rate tax deducted, except for:

- interest on War Loan
- interest on any stock which gives you less than £2.50 gross interest each half year
- interest on stocks bought through the National Savings Stock Register (a leaflet from your post office lists these stocks)
- the discount or profit on sale or maturity of Treasury Bills.

Note that with stock issued by certain nationalised industries and stock issued by certain foreign governments which pay interest in the UK, the interest is paid with basic-rate tax deducted.

Index-linked British Government stocks are treated in exactly the same way for tax purposes as other British Government stocks.

Buying British Government stocks can be a useful way of investing for a capital gain. If you buy at a price which is less than the price at which the stock will eventually be redeemed or sold you'll make a capital gain which is free of

237

capital gains tax. If you buy *low coupon* stocks – i.e. stocks which pay relatively low amounts of yearly interest – then you can invest for a return which is largely made up of a capital gain. But don't let tax considerations force you into investments which would otherwise be unsuitable.
ICTA 1988 s18(3), s44–s52

Business Expansion Scheme

The Business Expansion Scheme (BES) was set up to encourage investment in new or small companies, which find it difficult to raise money. So it's a risky investment, in spite of the tax advantages.

Under the scheme, you buy newly issued ordinary shares in such a company and get tax relief on what you invest at your top rate of tax – i.e. up to 40 per cent in the 1992–3 tax year. The shares are also free of capital gains tax on the first occasion they are sold (or given away) if they were issued after 18 March 1986. But losses won't count for capital gains tax purposes, and the investment reduces your taxable income but normally *not* your 'total income' (see p. 37).

The maximum investment you can get relief on in any one tax year is £40,000, and to get full tax relief you must invest for at least five years. If you sell the shares earlier, the relief is reduced by the amount of the sale proceeds. The relief is also lost if the sale is not at 'arm's length', e.g. the proper commercial price is not paid, or if you get 'value' from the company, e.g. fringe benefits, or if the company in which you invested ceases to qualify under the scheme in the first three years.

The shares of most types of unquoted company qualify, unless it is a bank or finance company dealing in land or shares, a company holding collectable items, e.g. wines or antiques, purely as investments, or a company with substantial assets in land or buildings (except for companies specialising in some types of residential lettings). And you can't invest in a company of which you (together with your family and business partners) own more than 30 per cent, or a company which employs you (except in rare cases).

You can invest either directly (with a minimum invest-ment of £500 per company) or through an investment fund which spreads your money over several companies (with no minimum unless the fund managers impose one). To get relief, you need a certificate from the company stating that the necessary conditions have been met. Send this to your tax office. You generally get relief either through your PAYE coding (see p. 127) or by getting a lower tax bill. You get the relief for the tax year in which the shares are issued, except that you can carry back half of the BES investments you make in the first half of the tax year – i.e. before 6 October – to set against your income in the previous tax year, up to a £5,000 maximum.

The scheme is due to stop after the end of 1993.
ICTA 1988 s289–s312

EXAMPLE 2

John Jarvis invests a total of £12,000 in a BES company in August 1992. He can carry back half of his investment (but only up to the £5,000 limit) to set against his income in the 1991–2 tax year. He invested just £10,000 in BES in 1991–2 tax year so the £5,000 carried back won't take his total investment for that year over the £40,000 limit. He now qualifies for tax relief on up to £33,000 further BES investments in 1992–3, as only £12,000 − £5,000 = £7,000 so far invested counts against the £40,000 limit for the 1992–3 tax year.

Company loans and loans to individuals

Interest on company fixed-income loan stocks or debentures is paid with basic-rate tax deducted. But interest on loans to private individuals will be paid without tax deducted.

For company loans bought after 13 March 1984, the proceeds are normally free of capital gains tax.

Note that if the loan is not repaid when it is due, and not likely to be repaid in future, you can set the loss off against gains for capital gains tax purposes if the loan was a loan stock or a loan or guarantee made to a UK-resident trader for use in his business. Otherwise you can't set the loss off.
ICTA 1988 s234, s348; TCGA 1992 s251, s253; FA 1984 s64

Commodities

How any profits you make from investing in commodities will be taxed is far from certain.

Profits from buying and selling *physical* commodities are likely to be treated as trading profits, and so taxed as earned income. A loss might count as a trading loss and you could set it off against the total of your income from all sources, but not against capital gains.

Just one isolated venture into the commodity *futures* market is likely to be treated as giving rise to a capital gain (or loss). But if you make a profit from a series of transactions, or invest as a member of a syndicate run by brokers or by a professional manager, this is likely to be treated as investment income, which may mean that you don't benefit from your capital gains tax-free slice.

Covenants

Payments under a deed of covenant dated before 15 March 1988 are made with basic-rate tax already deducted. If you're a non-taxpayer you can claim back the tax deducted. And normally, there's no higher-rate tax to pay, even if you're a higher-rate taxpayer. Income from post-14 March 1988 covenants is tax-free.

Friendly society policies

Some societies have tax advantages such as paying no income tax on the fund's income or capital gains tax on any gains made in the fund. Since 1 September 1990, you've been able to invest £150 a year in a friendly society policy of 10 years or more without paying tax on what you get back at the end. Before this date the limit was £100.
ICTA 1988 s460; FA 1990 s41, Sch6

Income and growth bonds

These bonds are set up in different ways, often consisting of one or more life insurance policies and one or more annuities. The tax treatment of any bond will depend on how it's set up. Bonds can include various life insurance products, such as deferred annuities with a cash option, immediate temporary annuities, single-premium endowment policies or regular premium endowment policies.

Very briefly, the tax treatment is as follows:

- deferred annuity with cash option – proceeds are liable to tax at your highest rate on the profit you make (but you may be able to get top-slicing relief) – see p. 253

- immediate temporary annuity – the income you get is treated as income from a voluntarily purchased annuity. The company normally deducts basic-rate tax before paying it out to you – see p. 98
- endowment policies – at the end of the term, proceeds are taxed as a gain on a life insurance policy (if the policy is a non-qualifying one). Income from any bonuses cashed are treated as cashing-in part of a life insurance policy – see p. 256.

Investment trusts

Investment trust companies are companies quoted on the Stock Exchange. Their business is investing in the shares of other companies. The dividends they pay out are taxed in the same way as for any other company's shares – see p. 243.

Let property

In general, income from letting property is taxed as investment income. But, in some cases, part or all of the income from furnished property can count as earnings from a business – see p. 217.

Life insurance policies

With regular-premium policies, there is normally no tax to pay on the proceeds as long as you don't cash the policy in before ten years or the first three-quarters of the term, whichever is the shorter. For more details, see p. 249. And for the rules on tax relief for policies taken out before 14 March 1984, see p. 259. With single-premium bonds, there's no basic-rate tax to pay when you cash them in, but there could be higher-rate tax – see p. 252.

Local authority investments

Interest on local authority loans made after 18 November 1984 is paid with composite-rate tax deducted. Interest on local authority stock and yearling bonds is paid with basic-rate tax deducted. Any gain you make when you dispose of stock or bonds is liable to capital gains tax – see p. 264.

Maintenance payments

Payments can be *voluntary* (if you can't be made to pay up) or *enforceable* (if you are legally obliged to – under a Court Order, say). Voluntary payments and enforceable payments under an agreement made after 15 March 1988 are tax-free. Enforceable payments under an agreement made before 15 March 1988 (or applied for before that date and in place by 30 June 1988) should be paid to you with no tax deducted. The first £1,720 of payments you get in the tax year is tax-free. You may have to pay tax on the rest – but see p. 84.

National Savings investments

With National Savings Investment and Ordinary Accounts, and National Savings Capital Bonds, Income Bonds, Deposit Bonds and Children's Bonus Bonds, interest is paid without deduction of tax, and is normally taxed on a *preceding year basis* (see p. 232). With National Savings Certificates and Yearly Plan, index-linked SAYE and Premium Bonds, the proceeds are free of income tax and capital gains tax.

With National Savings Ordinary Account, the first £70 of interest is tax-free – for husband and wife, it's £70 each. Anything more than that is taxed at lower, basic and higher rates, if applicable. Any one person is allowed only £70 free of tax, however many National Savings Ordinary Accounts he or she has. Note that if you and your spouse have separate accounts and you have, say, £100 interest and your spouse has £20, you will have to pay tax on £30 (i.e. £100 − £70) of your interest, even though the combined interest isn't more than 2 × £70 = £140. If you and your spouse have a joint account, however, you can have £140 interest free of tax.

In July 1992, FIRST Option Bonds were introduced. Interest is earned with basic-rate tax deducted. If you're a non-taxpayer or pay tax at the lower rate, you need to apply for a refund from your tax office.
ICTA 1988 s18 (2–4), s46, s325, s326

Personal Equity Plans (PEPs)

These are a way of investing in shares in UK companies, unit trusts and investment trusts without having to pay tax on dividend or distribution income or on any capital gains.

They are run by plan managers, e.g. banks or investment companies who take care of the administration.

You can invest in only one 'general' PEP each tax year, up to a limit of £6,000, provided you invest in shares in UK or other EC companies, and/or 'qualifying' unit or investment trusts. A qualifying unit or investment trust is one which holds at least half its investment fund in UK or EC shares. If a trust isn't a qualifying trust, you can invest only £1,500 of your total PEP investment. In addition to the present £6,000 in a general PEP, you'll be able to invest up to a further £3,000 in a PEP in which you hold the shares of just one company. So for the tax year ending 5 April 1993 it will be possible to invest up to £9,000 in PEPs.

If you don't invest the maximum, you can't carry your unused allowance forward to the next tax year. A husband and wife can each invest the maximum in their own PEP, but you have to be aged 18 or over and resident in the UK for tax purposes to qualify for a PEP.

Share dividends and distributions from unit trusts are usually paid with the equivalent of basic-rate tax already deducted. Whether or not that income is paid directly to you or reinvested in your plan, the plan manager will reclaim the tax for you and reinvest it in your PEP. Any capital gain you make on your investments in the PEP is free of capital gains tax. This is on top of the normal limit for exemption from capital gains tax – £5,800 in the 1992–3 tax year. However, any cash held in a plan (which can be as much, within the overall limit, as you like) will have basic-rate tax deducted in the same way as building society interest. If you're a higher-rate taxpayer, you must declare on your Tax Return any interest received on cash withdrawn if the interest is £375 or more (after deduction of composite-rate tax).

You can invest in shares, unit trusts and investment trusts in the same plan, and you can now transfer certain new issues of shares into your PEP (ask your plan manager). *ICTA 1988 s333*

Shares

When you get dividends from UK companies there is no basic-rate tax to pay. With the dividends you get a tax credit. Your gross (before-tax) income is taken to be the amount of the dividend plus the amount of tax credit. The tax credit for the 1992–3 tax year works out at 25 per cent of the gross income. So if, say, the dividend is £75, the tax credit will be £25 and the gross income £100. A basic-rate taxpayer has no more tax to pay and a non-taxpayer can claim tax back. If you pay tax at 20 per cent, you can claim back a fifth of the tax which has been paid. If you pay tax at the higher rate, you will have to pay extra tax, but the tax credit counts as tax already paid. For the 1992–3 tax year, any higher-rate tax is due on 1 December 1993 (or within 30 days of the date on your Notice of Assessment, if later). In your Tax Return you should enter both the amount of the dividend and the amount of the tax credit.

When you sell your shares, any increase in value counts as a capital gain – see p. 264 for more details.

If the company gives you more shares as a result of a *bonus* (or *scrip*) issue, you are not liable to income tax unless you've chosen to have the shares instead of a cash dividend (a few companies give you the choice). If this is the case, you are liable to income tax on the cash equivalent of the shares.

If you hold your shares in a Personal Equity Plan, see p. 242. If your shares qualify for the Business Expansion Scheme, see p. 238.

For details of share option or profit-sharing schemes, see p. 160.

ICTA 1988 s20, s231

Tax vouchers

You get a tax voucher from the company (or unit trust – see opposite) showing the amount of the dividend (or distribution) and the amount of the tax credit.

With other types of income taxed before you get it, including distributions from unit trusts which specialise in British Government stocks, you normally get a tax voucher or other document from the payer. This tells you the gross (before-tax) amount of income, the tax deducted and the actual sum you get.

Keep any tax vouchers as proof that tax has been credited or deducted.

TESSAs

Since January 1991, banks, building societies and other financial institutions have been able to offer Tax Exempt

Special Savings Accounts (TESSAS). Provided the savings are left in the account for five years, the interest earned on a TESSA is paid tax-free.

Most institutions will allow you to withdraw interest from your TESSA, but only an amount equivalent to the interest you'd receive after the deduction of basic-rate tax. The remainder must stay in your account. Any interest withdrawn is treated as your taxable income for the year of withdrawal.

If you touch the capital in your TESSA the account will be closed and you'll pay tax on the interest you've earned at your highest rate.

The most you will be able to invest in a TESSA is £9,000 over the five years – up to £3,000 in the first year, and up to £1,800 in each later year, provided you don't exceed the £9,000 overall maximum. Alternatively, you will be able to save a regular amount of up to £150 a month.

ICTA 1988 s326A–s326C

Trust income

Trusts pay tax on their income – in the 1992–3 tax year, at 35 per cent if they are discretionary trusts, at the basic rate of 25 per cent otherwise. Trusts do not benefit from the new 20 per cent rate of tax. This applies whether the income is kept by the trust or paid out to beneficiaries. With income paid out by the trust, you get a tax credit of the amount of tax deducted.

If you are a beneficiary of a discretionary trust, and the highest rate of tax you pay is less than 35 per cent, consider asking the trustees to pay out to you as much of the trust's income as possible. You'd be able to claim tax back from the Revenue. For more on trusts, see p. 339.

ICTA 1988 s660–s670, s686, s687

Unit trusts

With distributions from most unit trusts, each distribution is accompanied by a tax credit. Your gross (before-tax) income is taken to be the distribution *plus* the tax credit (see *Shares* on p. 243).

With the *first* distribution you get from a unit trust you're likely to get an *equalisation* payment. This is a return of part of the money you first invested, so doesn't count as income and isn't taxable.

With an *accumulation* unit trust (where income is automatically reinvested for you) the amount reinvested – apart from any equalisation payment – counts as income and is taxable.

In your Tax Return you should enter the amount of the distribution and the amount of the tax credit.

If you buy unit trusts within a Personal Equity Plan, the income will be tax-free – see p. 242.
ICTA 1988 s20, s468, s469

Which Schedules?

Investment income comes under the following Schedules:
Schedule A – income from letting property in the UK
Schedule C – income from government stocks, UK and foreign, paid through a UK paying agent, such as a bank
Schedule D, Case III – interest, annuities or other annual payments
Schedule D, Case IV – income from foreign securities
Schedule D, Case V – income from foreign possessions
Schedule D, Case VI – income not assessable under any other case or schedule (includes rents from letting furnished property)
Schedule F – distributions and dividends of a UK resident company.

Income regarded as yours during the administration period of a will

Any income which is regarded as yours during the administration period of a will or intestacy (i.e. while the details of who gets what are being worked out), will be paid to you with basic-rate tax deducted.
ICTA 1988 s695, s696

Tax on income from overseas investments

The tax treatment of income from abroad can be extraordinarily complicated, and if you have a substantial amount of such income you'll need to get specialist advice – and look at Inland Revenue leaflets *IR6* and *IR20*.

In general, if you're resident and ordinarily resident in the UK (see p. 163), all your income is liable to UK tax, whether or not it is brought into this country. However, income from overseas investments is often taxed in the country in which it originates – so two lots of tax could be charged on one lot of income. The UK government has made agreements with a wide range of countries to limit the extent to which income may be taxed twice. Under one of these *double taxation agreements*, the amount of tax which a foreign government deducts from income before it reaches you is reduced. The tax which is actually deducted is allowable as a tax credit against the UK tax on the same income.

Suppose, for example, that you're entitled to £1,000 in dividends from the US. Tax at 30 per cent would normally be held by the US before paying over the dividends to non-US residents. However, because of our double taxation agreement with the US, only 15 per cent is withheld – i.e. you get £850. If, say, you're liable for tax in the UK at 40 per cent on your £1,000 gross dividends, there'd be £400 tax to pay. But the £150 you've paid in tax to the US would be allowed as credit against the £400 of UK tax you're liable for – so you'd have to hand over to the Revenue £250, not £400.

If you are liable for no UK tax (or less than has been deducted under a double taxation agreement) there'll be no further UK tax to pay – but you can't claim back the extra foreign tax you've paid.

How to get your relief

If your foreign income is paid to you through an agent (e.g. a bank) in the UK, who passes it on to you after deducting basic-rate tax, the agent should allow for any double taxation agreement when doing the sums. But if the income is paid direct to you from abroad, you have to apply for double taxation relief yourself. To get the foreign tax reduced, get an application form from the Inland Revenue, Inspector of Foreign Dividends, Hinchley Wood, Lynwood Road, Thames Ditton, Surrey KT7 0DP. To get a credit for the foreign tax withheld, apply to your Tax Inspector.

When UK tax is due

Your tax bill is normally based on the foreign income you get in the preceding tax year – i.e. your tax bill for the 1992–3 tax year would be based on the foreign income you got in the 1991–2 tax year. Special rules apply in the first

three and last two years in which you get foreign income of this type – see p. 233. Note, however, that income from Eire is always taxed on a current-year basis.
ICTA 1988 s18(2–4), s65–s68, s123, s788–s790

Remittance basis

If this applies, you are taxed only on what income you bring into the UK. You can claim remittance basis if you're resident but not domiciled in the UK, or if you are a British subject or a citizen of Eire *and* you are resident but not ordinarily resident in the UK.
ICTA 1988 s65

Offshore funds

Any gain which you get when you sell an investment in an offshore fund is liable to income tax at your highest rate, unless the fund has *distributor status*, in which case only its income is liable to income tax. An offshore fund can get distributor status if, for example, it distributes all its income.
ICTA 1988 s757–s763

13 *LIFE INSURANCE*

Life insurance at its simplest is a way of providing for your dependants when you die. But as you can see from the table overleaf, policies have gone beyond this simple form. Apart from insurance policies which pay out only when you die, there are policies which are mainly investments. Many of these were designed to make use of the premium subsidy available for qualifying policies – see p. 259. Though you can still get this subsidy on policies taken out on or before 13 March 1984, those issued after that date don't benefit.

Tax on the proceeds

You won't have to pay tax on the proceeds of *any* life insurance policy if (even with the policy gain added to your income) you pay tax at no more than the basic rate. And even if you're a higher-rate taxpayer there'll be no tax to pay on the proceeds of a *qualifying policy* if you keep it for long enough – see below. Otherwise you may have to pay higher-rate tax on any gain you make. How you work out the gain depends on whether the policy has come to the end of its term or you're cashing in all or part of it early.

Note that there's normally no capital gains tax to pay on the proceeds of a life insurance policy – but see pp. 252 and 258.

Qualifying policies

When a qualifying policy reaches the end of its term or pays out due to death of the person insured, the proceeds are free of income tax. So, for example, if you've kept a qualifying endowment policy till it matures there's no tax to pay. If you've kept the policy for at least 10 years (or three-quarters of the term if this is less), there won't be income tax to pay either – see p. 255 for more details.

Finding your policy

Policy type	Term	Whole-life
Investment or protection?	protection	either or both
Qualifying policy? [1]	yes, if term one year or more	yes
How you pay	regular premiums	regular premiums
The benefits	**level-term** – pays out a lump sum if you die before a fixed date. If you don't die nothing is paid out normally. **decreasing term** – as with level term but cover decreases over the years. Commonly used to pay off a mortgage if you die *(mortgage protection policy)*. **family income benefit** – pays out a tax-free income to your dependants (if you die) over the remaining years of the term. **flexible term insurance** – as with term insurance but you have various options (e.g. to increase the cover each year, to renew the policy, to convert it to an investment-type policy) without further medical checks. But watch out if you get the premium subsidy as you could lose it if you take up an option – see p. 260.	**whole-life** – pays out a lump sum when you die, however far in the future. Policies can be *without-profits* which guarantee a fixed sum, or *with-profits* where the amount paid out increases over the years as the company adds bonuses. With some policies you stop paying premiums at a certain age (65, say). You can cash in the policy before you die. **unit-linked whole-life** – your premiums buy units in fund run by the life insurance company. Some of the units are cashed each month to pay for a whole-life policy – units left are your investment. You can cash in the policy before you die. With *flexible cover plans* you can choose the amount of life cover you get and therefore how much of your premium are used for investment.
What the policies are useful for	• protecting your dependants from suffering financially if you die during the term of the insurance – see p. 261 • paying a large inheritance tax bill if the giver dies within seven years – see p. 348.	• protecting your dependants from suffering financially when you die – however far in the future • possibly, building up a lump sum. If for your heirs, see p. 261 • paying inheritance tax when you die – see p. 348

[1] Individual policies may not meet all the qualifying requirements even where we say yes – check with your insurance company

Endowment/friendly society	Other investment type
either or both	investment (level of life cover may be low)
yes, if term 10 years or more	no – but see *The benefits* (below)
regular premiums	single premium

all pay out a lump sum at a fixed date or if you die before then.

endowment – policies can be with or without profits (see *whole-life*). You can cash in the policy early.

unit-linked savings plans – part of each premium goes to buy term insurance, the rest buys units in one or more investment funds. The level of life cover may be low. You can cash in the policy early.

friendly society savings plans – the level of life cover is low, and you can't pay more than £200 a year in premiums (10 per cent of the premiums are ignored if premiums are paid more often than once a year). You can cash in the policy early but the most you'll get back is the premiums paid (plus the subsidy if you got it – see p. 259).

unit-linked single-premium bonds – pay out a lump sum when you cash them in, or if you die before then. Your premium buys units in a fund run by the insurance company. You can cash in early.

income bonds – pay out a fixed income for a set number of years, and then return your original investment. Bonds are based on *annuities* and maybe *endowment policies* (which can be qualifying). Bonds will pay out if you die before a fixed date. With some bonds you can't cash in early. See p. 240 for more details.

growth bonds – pay out a lump sum at a fixed date, or if you die before then. Bonds are based on *annuities* and/or *endowment policies* (which can be qualifying). With some bonds you can't cash in early. See p. 240 for more details.

- building up a lump sum (but watch out for low surrender values if you cash in the policy in the first few years). If for your heirs, see p. 261
- paying off a mortgage.

unit-linked bonds
- taking 5 per cent a year tax-free from your investment – see p. 256

unit-linked bonds and growth bonds
- deferring income until you pay lower rate of income tax

income bonds
- providing an income.

Broadly speaking, a life insurance policy is a qualifying policy if you pay regular premiums on it (e.g. monthly or yearly). There are other conditions about the length of the policy and how much the premiums can vary from year to year, but the insurance company will normally take care of these to make the policy qualify. Note that all policies taken out on or before 19 March 1968 are qualifying policies, whether they are regular-premium policies or not – as long as they haven't been altered since that date.
ICTA 1988 s266, s539, Sch 14–15

Non-qualifying policies

You may have to pay higher-rate tax on the proceeds of a non-qualifying policy when it matures. The gain you make counts as a taxable gain – see below for how to work out the gain and how it is taxed.

Tax the company pays

Though *you* get a tax-free return from a qualifying policy (or a return which is free of basic-rate tax from a non-qualifying policy), the insurance company has to pay tax on its profits, capital gains and income from investments. The company's tax bill is seen by the Inland Revenue as taking care of the basic-rate tax on what you get from the policy.

Note that some of the business done by friendly societies is *tax-exempt*. So they don't have to pay corporation tax, or tax on investment income or capital gains which come from this business.

Working out the gain on a non-qualifying policy

When a policy comes to an end, the gain is normally the amount you get *less* the total premiums paid (but see p. 256 if you've cashed in part of your policy earlier). If the gain arises because the person dies, the gain is the cash-in value of the policy immediately before death (if this is less than the sum insured) *less* the premiums paid.

How the proceeds are taxed
The gain (as calculated above) is added to your investment income for the year in which the policy comes to an end. You're liable for higher-rate income tax on the gain (but *not*

basic-rate tax). So if you pay tax at the higher rate of 40 per cent, as the basic rate is 25 per cent you'd have to pay tax at 40 − 25 = 15 per cent on the policy gain – see the example below. But if adding the gain to your income means that you'd be paying tax at a higher rate than you would otherwise have done – because it pushes part of your income over the higher-rate threshold – the Revenue should apply *top-slicing relief* to reduce your tax bill.

The gain counts as investment income. So before the introduction of independent taxation of husband and wife on 6 April 1990 (see p. 70), a gain made by a wife or married couple was added to the husband's income. A gain made on or after 6 April 1990 is added to the income of whoever made it.

Top-slicing relief

Top-slicing relief, in effect, spreads the gain you make over the years that the policy has run. To work out your tax bill with top-slicing relief, first work out your *average yearly gain* by dividing the total gain by the number of *complete* years for which the policy ran. Then add this average yearly gain to your income for the tax year, and work out the higher-rate tax on the average yearly gain. To get your tax bill on the whole gain, multiply the tax bill on your average yearly gain by the number of complete years you have spread the gain over. See Example 1 below.

But note that cashing in *part* of a non-qualifying policy could create a *chargeable event* – see p. 257. If there has been a chargeable event before the policy came to an end, top-slicing relief uses only the number of years since the chargeable event.

ICTA 1988 s266, s539, Sch 15 (qualifying policies); ICTA 1988 s540, s541, s547, s550 (tax on proceeds)

EXAMPLE 1

Harris Granby bought a £20,000 single-premium bond in February 1988. He cashed it in for £30,000 in June 1992, making a gain of £10,000. He already has taxable income for the 1992–3 tax year of £22,000. If his tax bill were worked out in the normal way he would have to pay tax on his gain as shown overleaf.

253

rate of tax	income on which Harris pays this rate of tax	gain on bond	amount of tax
20 per cent	£2,000		£400
25 per cent	£20,000		£5,000
25 per cent		£1,700	£425
40 per cent *		£8,300	£3,320
total gain on bond		£10,000	
basic and higher rate			
tax on gain			£3,745
subtract tax at basic rate on gain (25 per cent of £10,000)			£2,500
total tax bill on gain			**£1,245**

* Higher-rate tax paid on taxable income over £23,700 in the 1992–3 tax year

But Harris gets top-slicing relief. With this, the *average yearly gain* of £2,500 (i.e. the £10,000 total gain divided by the four complete years the policy ran for) is added to his investment income for the year. His total tax bill on the gain is the higher-rate tax he'd pay on this average yearly gain, times the number of complete years he held the bond. Top-slicing relief saves Harris £1,245 − £480 = £765.

rate of tax	income on which Harris pays this rate of tax	gain on bond	amount of basic and higher rate tax
20 per cent	£2,000		£400
25 per cent	£20,000		£5,000
25 per cent		£1,700	£425
40 per cent		£800	£320
total gain on bond		£2,500	
total tax on average yearly gain			£745
subtract tax at basic rate on average yearly gain (25 per cent of £2,500)			£625

so tax bill on average yearly gain is	£120
total tax bill on gain (£120 × 4)	**£480**

The introduction of the 20 per cent lower-rate band has no effect on the calculation.

Age-related allowances

Although when you cash in all or part of a non-qualifying policy any gain is free of basic-rate tax, the whole gain (i.e. without top-slicing relief) is counted as part of your income for the year. For most people this has no effect on their allowances. But if you're aged 65 or over during the tax year, increasing your income can reduce the *age-related allowances* (see p. 94) you get.

Age-related allowances are reduced by half of the amount by which a person's 'total income' exceeds a certain limit – £14,200 for the 1992–3 tax year. So if the gain from an insurance policy (or the excess if you cash in part of a policy) means a reduction in your age-related allowances, you'll effectively pay more income tax, whether or not you're liable for higher-rate tax.
ICTA 1988 s257

Cashing in a policy early

Life insurance policies with an investment element have some value – the *surrender value* – even before the policy comes to an end. How much tax you have to pay (if any) depends on whether or not the policy is a qualifying one.

Cashing in a qualifying policy
If you've been paying regular premiums for at least three-quarters of the term of the policy, or 10 years, whichever is less, the gain you make remains tax-free. So with a 25-year term, there'd be no tax to pay if you surrendered after 10 years; with a 10-year term, there'd be no tax after 7½ years. But if you cash in the policy before this, you'll be taxed on the gain in the same way as when a non-qualifying policy pays out. So you'll be liable for higher-rate tax if it applies to you and will get top-slicing relief if this would cut your

tax bill. You pay tax on the difference between the surrender value and the *gross* premiums paid (i.e. the premiums you've paid *plus* any premium subsidy – see p. 259).

Cashing in a non-qualifying policy
If you cash in a non-qualifying policy before the end of its term you pay tax on the surrender value in the same way as if it had run for its full term – see p. 252. So you may have to pay higher-rate tax (but not basic-rate tax) on the amount by which the cash-in value exceeds the premiums you've paid. You'll get top-slicing relief if this would reduce your tax bill.
ICTA 1988 s540

EXAMPLE 2

Ernest Strident has a 10-year unit-linked savings plan for which the premium is £50 a month. After five years he decides to cash in the policy. The total premiums to date are £3,000 and the surrender value is £3,500, so he's made a gain of £500. As he is a higher-rate taxpayer, he has to pay tax at $40 - 25 = 15$ per cent on the £500 gain, i.e. £75 in all.

Cashing in part of a policy

You may want to cash in part of your policy, rather than the whole of it. Or, if bonuses are added, you could surrender a bonus. This is treated in the same way as cashing in part of your policy.

Cashing in part of a qualifying policy
If you cash in part of a qualifying policy after 10 years (or after three-quarters of its term if this is less), the gains you make are tax-free. But if you cash in part of the policy before this, you'll be taxed in the same way as for non-qualifying policies – see below.

Cashing in part of a non-qualifying policy
If you cash in part of a policy rather than the whole of it, you may be able to avoid paying tax straight away. What happens is that you get a tax-free allowance for each *complete* year that the policy has to run. So long as the

allowance you're due is more than the total amount you get from the policy, there's no tax to pay at the time. But when the term of the policy finally comes to an end or you cash the rest of the policy in, there may be tax to pay (see overleaf).

For each of the first 20 years of the term of a policy the allowance is $\frac{1}{20}$ (i.e. five per cent) of the premiums paid so far. For each year after the 20th year the allowance is $\frac{1}{20}$ of the premium paid in that year and the previous 19 years. So, if you pay £1,000 a year in premiums, your allowance after the first year will be £50, after the second £100, after the third £150, and so on. Allowances not used each year are carried forward. Complete years are calculated from the date the policy is taken out – but you don't get an allowance until the first complete year starting after 13 March 1975.

If you exceed your total allowances, this creates a *chargeable event*. The difference between your total allowances and what you've had from the policy (the *excess*) is counted as a gain. This gain is treated in the same way as if you cash in a whole policy, so is subject to higher-rate tax, but not basic-rate tax. You'll get top-slicing relief if this reduces your tax bill, with the gain spread over the number of years you've had the policy, or the number of years since the last chargeable event, if there's been one already. When an excess is added to your income, the allowances you've taken into account are cancelled, and you start building up allowances again.
ICTA 1988 s546

EXAMPLE 3

Harvey Redbridge pays tax at the higher rate of 40 per cent. He has bought a single-premium bond for £10,000 and wants to withdraw as much as he can without paying tax at the moment. For each of the first 20 years Harvey gets an allowance of $\frac{1}{20}$ of the total premiums paid so far – i.e. $\frac{1}{20}$ of £10,000 = £500. He can cash in £500 each year without paying tax in that year. For the 21st year onwards his allowance is $\frac{1}{20}$ of the premiums paid in that year and the previous 19 years – zero in Harvey's case as he paid for the policy all at once in the first year. So if he uses up his allowances in the first 20 years he won't be able to cash in any more of his policy without paying tax at the time (unless he's a basic-rate taxpayer by then).

257

Paid-up policies

Making a policy paid-up means that you stop paying the premiums but don't take your money out. Making part of a policy paid-up means you can reduce your premiums.

If you make a policy paid-up the same rules apply as if you were to cash it in. However, you won't have to pay any tax until the policy finally pays out.
ICTA 1988 s540

When the policy comes to an end

If you've cashed in part of a policy before it finally comes to an end, the total gain on which you may have to pay tax is:

- the amount you get at the end *plus* any amounts you've had in the past, *less*
- the total premiums paid, any excesses you've already had (see p. 257) and any pre-14 March 1975 gains on the policy which the Revenue was told about (either by you or the insurance company).

If after making these deductions you're left with a negative figure, you can subtract this from your 'total income' to reduce your higher-rate tax bill. But you can't subtract more than the total of the excesses you've made from partial surrenders and pre-14 March 1975 gains.
ICTA 1988 s540, s541, s547, s549

EXAMPLE 4

When Harvey's single-premium bond comes to an end (see Example 3), he's still paying tax at 40 per cent and so he'll have to pay tax on his gain. If Harvey used up his £500 allowance for each of the first 20 years, he'd have had $20 \times £500 = £10,000$ from the policy. If he got another £10,000, say, when the policy ended, his total gain would be £20,000 *minus* the £10,000 premium = £10,000, which would be added to his income for the year. Harvey would pay higher-rate (but no basic-rate) tax on the proceeds, i.e. $40 - 25 = 15$ per cent $\times £10,000 = £1,500$.

Capital gains and unit-linked policies

With a unit-linked policy, the insurance company invests your premiums in units in one or more investment funds.

However, you don't own the units – the insurance company does. And so while you can get a tax-free return, the company has to pay tax on its investment income and on the capital gains it makes. In practice, the company doesn't have to sell units every time a policy is cashed in. So, in effect, the rate at which it pays any tax on capital gains can be lower than the full percentage – say, 10–20 per cent. This is either deducted from the investment fund or from the proceeds of the policy when you cash it in. So if you see that a deduction has been made for tax on capital gains, it's not tax on *your* gains but on the company's. You can't claim it back as being part of your £5,800 capital gains tax exemption or by setting losses against it. (If you're not likely to pay capital gains tax, you might consider investing in unit trusts rather than unit-linked life insurance.)

Cluster policies

With some policies, instead of your premiums buying just one insurance policy, they can be used to buy several policies. For example, if your premium was £50 a month you might get a cluster of 10 policies, each with a premium of £5 a month. The advantage of cluster policies is that you don't have to treat all the policies in the same way. If you're a higher-rate taxpayer and you cash in part of a non-qualifying policy, you will be taxed on any *excess* that arises (see p. 257). You could end up paying less tax at the time if you have a cluster of policies, and cash in one (or more) of them. (But if you're paying tax at the same rate when you finally cash in the rest of the proceeds, you'll pay the same amount of tax in the long run.)

Tax relief on premiums

If you took out a qualifying policy before 14 March 1984, you are almost certainly getting a 12½ per cent subsidy on the premiums (whether you pay tax or not). You get the subsidy by paying lower premiums: if your premium is £100 a year (*gross*) you hand over £87.50 (*net*); the insurance company claims the extra £12.50 from the Inland Revenue. But there's a limit on the amount of premiums you can get the subsidy on: the maximum is £1,500 a year of *gross* premiums or one-sixth of your 'total income', whichever is greater. In general, your 'total income' is your before-tax income (including the taxable gains from insurance policies) *minus* your outgoings – see p. 28.

This means that if your 'total income' is £9,000 or less, the subsidy stops when your *net* premiums reach £1,312.50 (£1,500 *less* the 12½ per cent subsidy). Premiums for a deferred annuity (see opposite) also count towards this limit. With the introduction of independent taxation on 6 April 1990 (see p. 70), a husband and wife can each have premiums up to the limit (before 6 April 1990, the limit applied to their combined 'total income'). A divorced couple go on getting the subsidy on premiums for policies on each other's lives provided the policy was taken out before the divorce and after 5 April 1979.
ICTA 1988 s266, s274, Sch 14

Hanging on to your subsidy

The subsidy continues for policies taken out before 14 March 1984. But if you vary the terms of such a policy and the benefits are increased or the term extended (whether or not this is by exercising an option already in the policy) you'll lose all your subsidy. However, benefits which increase automatically as part of the original contract will not affect the subsidy.

If you're thinking of changing a policy which gets the premium subsidy, check with the insurance company to see if your planned change would affect the subsidy.

Life insurance with a personal pension

If you're self-employed or an employee not in an employer's pension scheme, you may be able to get tax relief at your highest rate of tax on premiums for special term insurance sold with personal pension plans. You can claim full tax relief on premiums of up to five per cent of your *net relevant earnings* – i.e. your taxable profits from being self-employed or your earnings from a job where you're not in the employer's pension scheme. But what you pay in such premiums reduces the maximum amount you can pay in to a personal pension.

ICTA 1988 s637, s640

Death and superannuation benefits

You can still get tax relief on certain combined sickness and life insurance policies issued by friendly societies. You'll get tax relief on the life part of your premium, at half your top rate of tax – so if you're paying tax at 40 per cent, you'll get tax relief at 20 per cent.

You can get tax relief at the same rate for the part of a trade union subscription which is for superannuation (i.e. pension), funeral or life insurance benefits.
ICTA 1988 s266

Premium subsidy for deferred annuities

You get a 12½ per cent subsidy on premiums used to buy a *deferred annuity*. You get this on gross premiums of up to £100 (i.e. premiums you pay of up to £87.50). There's also tax relief at the basic rate (25 per cent for 1991–2) on premiums for deferred annuities which will pay an income to your dependants after your death, providing you *have* to pay the premiums either under an Act of Parliament or under the rules of your job.
ICTA 1988 s266, s273, s274

Dealing with the proceeds

A life insurance policy will usually pay out to your estate, if you die. But you may want the proceeds to go to someone else. You could do this on your death by simply leaving the money in your will. But in that case, the proceeds of the policy will be added to your estate, and there might be an inheritance tax to pay – see p. 318. You could instead *assign* the policy to someone else during your lifetime. You can do this by completing a *deed of assignment* and sending a *notice* to the life insurance company (ask the company or a solicitor for details). You may want to assign the policy for a number of reasons:

- to make a gift
- to avoid inheritance tax by writing the policy in trust
- to raise cash
- to get a loan.

Assignment and subsidy

If you get the premium subsidy and assign your policy, you can still get the subsidy while you continue to pay the premiums. But if the premiums are paid for by someone else (other than your husband or wife) they won't qualify for the subsidy.

Gifts

If you give a policy away (by assigning it to somebody else) it counts as a gift for inheritance tax purposes. The value the Revenue puts on the gift is either the market value of the policy *plus* any amounts paid out earlier, or the total amount paid in premiums up to the time you give the policy away, whichever is higher. The market value will often be close to the cash-in value. But, for example, the market value of a policy on someone close to death will be almost as high as the amount the policy would pay out on death. If you continue to pay the premiums after you've given the policy away, the amount you pay also counts as a gift. But there shouldn't be any inheritance tax to pay as the payments will normally come into one of the tax-free categories – see p. 326. If you die, the proceeds won't form part of your estate.

If you've been given somebody else's life insurance policy, you are liable for any tax that's due when the policy pays out or is cashed in – see p. 256 for how much (if any) tax you'll have to pay.

ICTA 1988 s540; IHTA 1984 s167

Trusts

By getting the policy *written in trust*, you may be able to avoid inheritance tax as the proceeds are not added to your estate. The proceeds can then also be paid to the beneficiaries without waiting for probate.

If you want the policy to pay out to your wife (or husband) or children, the simplest way of setting it up in trust is to get a policy worded according to the *Married Women's Property Act 1882*. Otherwise, you'll have to get a declaration of trust written on the policy – ask the insurance company about this. As a gift, the proceeds of policies written in trust will not form part of your estate, but the premiums may count as gifts for inheritance tax purposes unless they come into one of the tax-free categories – see p. 326. If the policy pays out while you're still alive (e.g. a growth bond), you'll have to pay any income tax that's due – though you will be able to claim it back from the trustees. For more about trusts, see p. 339.

ICTA 1988 s547, s551

Selling your policy

If you sell a non-qualifying policy, it's treated in the same way as though you had cashed it in – see p. 255. You may have to pay higher-rate tax on the amount that you sold the policy for *less* the premiums you've paid.

If you sell a qualifying policy you'll be taxed as above if you do so in the first 10 years or within three-quarters of its term if this is shorter (this also applies if you made it paid-up in this period and then sold it later on). If you buy a policy, there may be capital gains tax to pay if you eventually make a gain on it (as with other assets – see Chapter 14 p. 264).

Note that you can't avoid paying the income tax that's due by selling your policy and buying it back – in the hope that you'd be liable for capital gains tax instead. If you've had your own policy reassigned to you, you'll have to pay income tax on the gain, not capital gains tax.
ICTA 1988 s540, s544

Security for a loan

You may be able to use your insurance policy as security for a loan either from the life insurance company or from somewhere else, e.g. a bank. A loan from the insurance company is treated as a partial surrender (for the amount of the loan) if the policy was taken out before 26 March 1974 and is non-qualifying, or if it's qualifying and the money is lent at less than a commercial rate of interest. Any repayment (other than interest) of the loan you make to the life insurance company is treated as a premium when working out the tax bill at the end. If you're still alive when the policy pays out, you'll be liable for any extra tax that's due.

Note that it won't be treated as a surrender if the loan is to a person over 64 borrowing the money to buy an annuity, nor if the loan is from somewhere else, e.g. a bank or building society, rather than the insurance company.
ICTA 1988 s540

14 CAPITAL GAINS TAX

The simplest example of making a capital gain is *selling something you own at a profit*. For example, you buy a Victorian etching for £10,000, and sell it a couple of years later for £12,000. Your capital gain (ignoring any allowance for inflation) is £2,000, or a bit less if you can claim some expenses of buying and selling.

But you can make a capital gain even though no buying or selling is involved, e.g. if you give something away. So here are the basic rules:

- you can make a capital gain (or loss) whenever you *dispose of an asset*, no matter how you come to own it
- broadly, anything you own (whether in the UK or not) counts as an asset, e.g. houses, jewellery, shares, antiques
- you dispose of an asset not only if you sell it, but also if you give it away, exchange it or lose it. You also dispose of an asset if you sell rights to it, e.g. grant a lease, or if it is destroyed or becomes worthless, or if you get compensation for damage to it, e.g. insurance money, and don't spend all the money on restoring it
- not every gain you make will be taxable, nor will every loss be recognised by the Revenue
- there is no capital gains tax to pay when you die
- special rules apply to gifts between husband and wife (see p. 278), and can apply if you dispose of a business (see p. 280)
- for some gifts and business assets, you can avoid an immediate tax bill (see pp. 275 and 279).
  TCGA 1992 s1, s2, s15, s21–s24

> Note: nearly all statutory references are to the Taxation of Chargeable Gains Act 1992. We haven't, in all cases, given the full reference – so *s222 = TCGA 1992 s222*. Other statutes are mentioned individually.

Overseas

If you are domiciled in the UK (see p. 164), capital gains tax applies to gains you make anywhere in the world – i.e. overseas as well as in the UK (*s1*). If the gains cannot be remitted to the UK (because of exchange or currency controls operated by the country the gain is made in), you can ask the Inland Revenue to defer bringing them into the tax net until they can be remitted (*s13*).

If you are living abroad, capital gains tax still applies to you for any tax year in which you are *resident* or *ordinarily resident* in the UK (see p. 163) – even if only for part of that tax year (*s2*). But if you are not domiciled in the UK (see p. 164), gains made abroad are liable to capital gains tax only if remitted to the UK (*s12, s16*).

A person who goes abroad for longer periods of time may cease to be resident and ordinarily resident. If you cease to be both, you won't be liable for UK capital gains tax on disposals from the day after you leave the UK until 5 April before you come back. If you've been away for more than three years, this exemption continues until the day before you return. You could take advantage of this to dispose of assets which would produce chargeable gains (if you still want to hold the assets, you could buy them back the next day, establishing a higher initial price for when you return to the UK).

Tax-free gains

Gains on some assets are free from capital gains tax (CGT). (The other side of the coin is that *losses* on these assets can't normally be used to reduce your taxable gains for tax purposes.)

The main assets on which gains are tax-free are:

- your only or main home – see p. 207 (*s222*)
- private motor cars. This rule normally favours the Revenue since you usually sell your car for a loss. But if you sell a vintage or classic car at a gain, that will be tax-free unless you make a habit of doing this, in which case you could be taxed as though you were trading in cars (*s263*)
- National Savings Certificates, Yearly Plan, Premium Bonds, Capital Bonds and SAYE deposits (*s121*)
- British money including post-1837 gold sovereigns (*s21*)
- currency for personal use abroad. Normally, foreign currency is an asset for CGT purposes. But gains on

currency for the use of your family and yourself abroad, e.g. on holiday or to maintain a home abroad, are tax-free (*s269*)

- betting winnings (*s51*)
- British Government stocks (or options in them), though income tax might be due on any accrued interest. This exemption now extends to many types of corporate bond, as long as you acquired them after 13 March 1984 (*s115, s117; FA 1984 s64*)
- shares, unit trusts and investment trusts held in a PEP – see p. 242 (*s151; ICTA 1988 s333*)
- shares issued after 18 March 1986 under the Business Expansion Scheme (see p. 238) sold more than five years after you bought them – on their first disposal only (*s150*)
- life insurance policies. The proceeds – whether on maturity, surrender or sale – are free of CGT provided you didn't buy the policy from a previous holder, but note the insurance company will have paid CGT on gains before you get the proceeds (*s210*)
- damages for any wrong or injury suffered by you in your private or professional life, e.g. damages for assault or defamation (*s51*)
- settled property. If you have been given an interest under a UK settlement (but not the underlying property), the proceeds if you sell it are tax-free (*s76*)
- timber. A gain on the disposal of timber – whether growing or felled – is tax-free provided that you're not taxed as carrying on a forestry trade (in which case the disposal will be liable for income tax as a trading transaction). The exemption does not apply to the land on which the timber was growing (*s250*)
- decorations for valour. A gain on the disposal of an award for valour or gallant conduct is tax-free, e.g. your father's VC or George Cross, provided that you did not buy the award (*s268*)
- gifts to charities or certain national institutions (*s257*)
- a gift of *heritage property* is tax-free if it satisfies certain conditions (for what *heritage property* is, see p. 327) (*s258*)
- any chattel which had a predictable useful life of no more than 50 years when you first acquired it, e.g. electronic equipment, yachts and race-horses, provided that you have not used the asset in your business so that it qualified for capital allowances (*s45*)
- for chattels with a predictable life of more than 50 years,

gains may be partly tax-free – broadly speaking, the rules are as follows:

If the *disposal proceeds* are less than £6,000, any gain is tax-free. So if you buy a watercolour for £1,500 and sell it for £5,750 the gain is tax-free.

If the *disposal proceeds* are more than £6,000, your taxable gain is *either* your actual gain *or* ⅗ of the excess over £6,000, whichever is the lower.

If the disposal proceeds are less than £6,000, and you've made a loss, you're assumed to have received £6,000. So if you buy a picture for £7,000 and sell it for £5,000, your loss, for tax purposes, is £1,000.

If you sell a set of articles, e.g. a set of matching chairs, separately, but in effect to the same person, the Revenue is likely to treat the sales as a single sale. So if you sold six chairs for £2,000 each, you'd be taxed as though you'd made a single sale of £12,000, not six sales of £2,000 (*TCGA 1992 s262*).

Working out your gains or losses

To work out your chargeable gain (or loss) on assets which aren't tax-free, this is what you do:

Step one   Take the *final value* of the asset. This will be:

- the *disposal proceeds* if you sold it
- its *market value* if you gave it away
- the *insurance proceeds* if it is destroyed. For damaged assets, see p. 294.

Step two   Subtract the *initial value* of the asset to get the *gross capital gain* (or loss). The initial value is:

- *what you paid for it* if you bought it
- its *market value at the time of the gift* if you were given it (though see p. 275 for special rules about gifts)
- its *probate value* if you inherited it.

If you acquired the asset before 31 March 1982, use the market value on that date as the initial value (but there is an alternative – see p. 268).

Step three   Deduct any *allowable expenses* which you incurred in acquiring or disposing of the asset, or in increasing its value – this gives you the net capital gain (or loss). You can include:

- legal fees, stamp duty, commission, advertising
- the legal cost of defending your title to the asset
- money spent on the asset which has increased its value (but not maintenance or normal repairs).

TCGA 1992 s38

With assets acquired before 31 March 1982, don't include any expenses incurred before that date at this stage (but see below).

A gain can be reduced, eliminated or turned into a loss by *indexation* which is explained fully on p. 270. This increases the amount of your initial value and allowable expenses in line with the Retail Prices Index (RPI) since March 1982 and prevents you being taxed on gains made purely because of inflation. Gains after indexation are called *chargeable gains*; losses after indexation are called *chargeable losses*.

EXAMPLE 1

Larry Beaulieu bought a second home in January 1987 for £55,000. He paid legal fees of £450 and stamp duty of £550. In July 1988, he added an extension costing £10,000. In the 1992–3 tax year he sells the home for £100,000, with agents' fees of £2,070 and legal fees of £300.

Larry works out his capital gain (before any indexation allowance):

	£
sale proceeds	100,000
less **purchase price**	55,000
less **allowable expenses:**	
costs of acquisition	1,000
costs of improvement	10,000
expenses of disposal	2,370
net capital gain	**31,630**

Assets acquired before 31 March 1982

Indexation began in March 1982, so gains before that date are not indexed. This could mean paying tax on gains which were made purely from inflation. In 1988, the Chancellor decided to wipe the slate clean and ignore all gains made before 31 March 1982. Only gains made since that date are chargeable, and indexation takes account of inflation since that date.

So when working out the gain on an asset bought before 31 March 1982, you now use its market value on that date, not the cost when you originally acquired it. You also ignore any expenses incurred before 31 March 1982 in working out the net gain (or loss). Indexation allowance applies to the market value on 31 March 1982 and to any expenses incurred since that date.

For most people, these new rules 'rebasing' to 1982 will mean less capital gains tax to pay. But in some cases, the new rules could mean a bigger tax bill, as the following example shows.

EXAMPLE 2

Roger Wiley bought shares in XYZ Telephones plc in January 1980, at a cost of £10,000. By March 1982, their value had fallen to £5,000, though they then recovered – Roger sold them for £15,000 in June 1992. Ignoring indexation allowance, Roger had made a net gain of £15,000 − £10,000 = £5,000 on the shares.

But the gain is much bigger if Roger uses the new rules for assets acquired before 31 March 1982:

	£
sale proceeds	15,000
less **value on 31 March 1982**	5,000
net capital gain	10,000

Where you've owned something before 31 March 1982 which fell in value up to that date and has risen since, using the new rebasing rules will artificially inflate your gain. The opposite is true if you bought something before 31 March 1982 which rose in price up to that date and has since fallen in value – the loss you make is artificially inflated.

Where either of these things would happen, the gain or loss will be worked out using the old rules – rebasing will not apply. This means that the initial value is what you paid for the asset; and you can claim expenses incurred before 31 March 1982. In this case, both initial value and pre-31 March 1982 expenses are indexed from 31 March 1982.

With two sets of rules, it is quite possible that you will make a loss using one set and a gain using the other. If, in Example 2, Roger had sold the shares in 1992–3 for £8,000, then using the new rules there would have been an unindexed gain of £8,000 − £5,000 = £3,000; under the old rules, there would have been an unindexed loss of £10,000 − £8,000 = £2,000. If you make a gain under one set of rules and a loss under the other, it will be treated as though you had made neither a gain nor a loss on disposal. *TCGA 1992 s35*

All seems too complicated?

Having two sets of rules means keeping paperwork for pre-March 1982 acquisitions to check on which set of rules applies. To simplify matters (or if your paperwork from before 31 March 1982 is in a mess), you can elect for all your assets to come under the new rules. Assets acquired before 31 March 1982 will be treated as if you'd acquired them on that date, and only expenses incurred since that date can be deducted from their gains.

You must make the election within two years of the end of the first tax year after 5 April 1988 in which you dispose of an asset bought before 31 March 1982. Once you make this election, you can't change your mind. You'll be no worse off making the election if all or most of your assets were worth more on 31 March 1982 than when you acquired them.
TCGA 1992 s35(5)

Indexation allowance

Indexation allowance gives some protection against being taxed on paper profits. It works like this: your initial value and allowable expenses are linked to the Retail Prices Index (RPI) and increased in line with the index. The effect is that your taxable gain is reduced (or your chargeable loss increased). See p. 353 for a list of the RPI figures since March 1982 when indexation started.
TCGA 1992 s53–s55

How to work out the indexation allowance

First work out your net gain or loss in the normal way, taking no account of the indexation rules: take the asset's *final value* and subtract the *initial value* and *allowable expenses* (see p. 267).

Then, for the initial value and each allowable expense, you must work out the indexation allowance. Multiply the initial value or expense by the following (worked out to three decimal places):

$$\frac{RD - RI}{RI}$$

where RD = the RPI for the month in which the asset is disposed of, and RI = the RPI for the month in which the initial value or expense became 'due and payable'.

So if, for example, you buy something for £5,000, and the RPI for the month in which you buy it is 105, and the RPI for the month in which you sell it is 120, your indexation allowance for the initial value is worked out like this:

$$£5,000 \times \frac{120 - 105}{105}$$

$$= £5,000 \times 0.143$$
$$= £715$$

EXAMPLE 3

Larry Beaulieu works out the indexation allowance due on the gain he made selling his holiday home in the 1992–3 tax year (see Example 1 on p. 268).

The relevant RPI figures are as follows:

January 1987 (when he bought the home)	100.0
July 1988 (when he built the extension)	106.7
RPI when he sells the home	139.0

(Note: the selling RPI has been estimated for the purposes of this calculation – see p. 353 for details of where to find actual figures.)

He can work out the indexation allowance on the initial value (£55,000) and costs of acquisition (£1,000) together, since they were incurred in the same month of January 1987. The indexation allowance on these January 1987 costs of £55,000 + £1,000 = £56,000 is as follows:

$$£56,000 \times \frac{139.0 - 100.0}{100.0} = £56,000 \times \frac{39.0}{100.0}$$
$$= £56,000 \times 0.390$$
$$= £21,840$$

271

The indexation allowance on the cost of the extension is:

$$£10,000 \times \frac{139.0 - 106.7}{106.7} = £10,000 \times \frac{32.3}{106.7}$$
$$= £10,000 \times 0.303$$
$$= £3,030$$

$$\text{Total indexation allowance} = £21,840 + £3,030$$
$$= £24,870$$

$$\text{Net chargeable gain on sale of home} = £31,630 - £24,870$$
$$= £6,760$$

Working out the tax bill

The first step in calculating your capital gains tax bill is to add together all your *chargeable gains* for the tax year and deduct your *chargeable losses* for the year. The result is your *net chargeable gains* for the tax year. But you won't have to pay tax on the whole of your net chargeable gains: the first slice of chargeable gains is tax-free. And you may be able to set off losses from earlier years against your gains this year.

If your chargeable losses exceed your chargeable gains, you will have made a *net chargeable loss*. This can be used to reduce your capital gains tax bill in future years.
TCGA 1992 s2

The tax-free slice

The first slice of net chargeable gains in any tax year is free of capital gains tax. The size of this tax-free slice is set each year and should rise year-by-year in line with inflation, unless Parliament decides otherwise. In recent years Parliament has decided otherwise – the tax-free slice was actually reduced in 1988.

For the 1992–3 tax year, the tax-free slice is £5,800. A husband and wife get a £5,800 tax-free slice each, which they can set against only their own net gains.

If your net chargeable gains are less than the amount of the tax-free slice, there will be no capital gains tax to pay.

But you can't carry any unused part of the tax-free slice forward to future years.
TCGA 1992 s3, Sch 1

EXAMPLE 4

Nerys Peacock has made a chargeable gain on her holiday flat of £15,000 in the 1992–3 tax year. In the same year, she sold shares, with a chargeable loss of £12,475.

Nerys has a net chargeable gain for the tax year of £15,000 − £12,475 = £2,525. The tax-free slice for the year of £5,800 will wipe out this net chargeable gain, and there will be no capital gains tax to pay.

However, it's worth noting that Nerys has 'wasted' losses of £3,275, because her net chargeable gains were less than the tax-free slice. She needed only £9,200 of losses to reduce her net chargeable gains to the level of the tax-free slice, and the extra £3,275 which brought the total below £5,800 can't be carried over to another year.

Losses from previous years
If your net chargeable gains come to more than the tax-free slice, any losses you have left from previous years can be deducted from the total. Until the introduction of independent taxation of husband and wife, the losses of one partner could be set against the gains of the other – this no longer applies.

Note that losses from previous years are deducted after the tax-free slice, so they aren't wasted by reducing your net chargeable gains below £5,800. If you don't use all the losses carried over from previous years, they can be carried forward to future years.
TCGA 1992 s2, s3

EXAMPLE 5

In the 1991–2 tax year, Gregor Knight lost £6,000 on some shares he had sold. He had no gains in that tax year to set the loss off against, so the loss was carried forward for future years.

In the 1992–3 tax year, Gregor made a net chargeable gain of £9,750 on selling a picture (and no other gains or losses). His tax-free slice for 1992–3 was £5,800, so he would pay capital gains tax on £9,750 − £5,800 = £3,950. However, he can set off some of the £6,000 loss carried forward from the previous year to reduce this taxable gain to zero.

This leaves £6,000 − £3,950 = £2,050 in losses to be carried forward to future years.

How much tax

If there's anything left of your net chargeable gains after you have deducted the tax-free slice and losses carried over from previous years, there will be capital gains tax to pay. The remaining total is added to your taxable income and taxed as if it were income.

For the 1992–3 tax year, the first £2,000 of taxable income is taxed at 20 per cent, the next £21,700 at 25 per cent and anything over £23,700 is taxed at 40 per cent. If your taxable income plus the capital gains add up to less than £2,000, the gain will be taxed at 20 per cent. If they add up to an amount between £2,000 and £23,700, part or all of the gain will be taxed at 25 per cent. If the total is over £23,700, part or all of the capital gain will be taxed at the higher rate of 40 per cent.
FA 1988 s98

EXAMPLE 6

Linford Brooke made a net chargeable gain in 1992–3 of £11,500. He has no losses to carry forward from previous years. His taxable income for 1992–3 is £21,200.

The first £5,800 of Linford's net gain is tax-free, so tax is due on £11,500 − £5,800 = £5,700. For the 1992–3 tax year, Linford already has taxable income of £21,200, so that leaves £23,700 − £21,200 = £2,500 of the gain to be taxed at the basic rate of 25 per cent. The remainder of the gain (£5,700 − £2,500 = £3,200) is taxed at the higher rate of 40 per cent.

The tax bill on the £11,500 gain is as follows:

£5,800 (the tax-free slice) at 0 per cent	£0
£2,500 at the basic rate of 25 per cent	£625
£3,200 at the higher rate of 40 per cent	£1,280
Total CGT	**£1,905**

Gifts

When you give something away, you're usually treated as disposing of it for what it is worth, even though you get nothing for it. So if you buy a picture for £20,000 and give it away a few months later when it's worth £25,000, you'll make a gain (ignoring indexation) of £5,000.

The person who receives the gift is treated as having paid what the property is worth. So, with the gift of the picture, if the person receiving the picture sells it later for £28,000, the gain (ignoring indexation) is £28,000 minus £25,000 = £3,000.

If the asset is one which is exempt from CGT – see list starting on p. 265 – there is no tax liability if you give it away.

TCGA 1992 s17

Hold-over relief

For gifts made before 14 March 1989, the giver can pass the chargeable gain on to the recipient. The recipient, who must be resident or ordinarily resident in the UK, has to agree to holding over the gain. Capital gains tax is put off until the recipient disposes of the gift (when the tax bill could be higher).

From 14 March 1989 onwards, hold-over relief is restricted to gifts of business assets (see p. 279) and heritage property, and gifts to political parties. You can also claim hold-over relief on gifts which count as chargeable transfers for inheritance tax purposes (mainly to companies and certain trusts – see p. 319).

If hold-over relief is claimed, the recipient's initial value is the market value of the gift at the time of the gift, less the chargeable gain the giver made on it. This has the same effect as if the recipient had owned the gift ever since the giver acquired it, and incurred the same expenses.

Other points to note:

- indexation: the recipient's initial value (see above) is linked to the RPI from the month of the gift
- hold-over relief can be claimed again on a subsequent gift (from 14 March 1989 only on the restricted list of gifts eligible for hold-over relief)
- if the ultimate recipient keeps the gift until death, there will be no CGT to pay, since there is no CGT charge on death (see p. 278)

- it's pointless to claim hold-over relief if (without claiming the relief) your net taxable gains for the year are no more than £5,800. You won't pay tax either way, and the recipient could pay more
- hold-over relief can be claimed on gifts into (and out of) a trust. For gifts into trust, the relief can be claimed by the giver alone
- if you part with something for less than its full worth, you can still claim hold-over relief. But if the amount you actually get for it is higher than your allowable expenses, you will have to pay capital gains tax on the sum received less expenses at the time (assuming that it is more than the tax-free slice) and only the gain that is left after that can be held over.

To claim hold-over relief, both the giver and the recipient must tell the Inland Revenue within six years of the tax year in which the gift is made. If the recipient emigrates within this time limit and still owns the gift, the capital gains tax will have to be paid on the held-over gain (and it will be collected from the giver if the recipient won't pay).
FA 1980 s79; FA 1982 s82; TCGA 1992 s67, s165

EXAMPLE 7

David Charter sold a painting in February 1989, with a chargeable gain of £6,720. Suppose that instead of selling it, he had given it to his daughter Avril. Since this was before 14 March 1989, they could still claim hold-over relief on the gift – so no tax is due at the time of the gift.

For capital gains tax purposes, Avril is now assumed to have acquired the painting in February 1989 at an initial value equal to its market value at the time of the gift less David's chargeable gain. This is £19,500 − £6,720 = £12,780.

> **Gifts: think about inheritance tax**
>
> If you make a gift of property and pay CGT on the gift your CGT liability will neither increase nor reduce the inheritance tax, if any, on the gift.
>
> If the recipient pays the CGT for you, that will reduce any inheritance tax there may be – not surprising since you will have given them less.
>
> If you make a gift and hold-over relief is claimed, any inheritance tax on the gift will reduce the CGT when the recipient comes to dispose of the property.

CGT *and the family*

If you dispose of an asset to a *connected person,* you are treated by the Revenue as disposing of the asset for its market value at the time of the gift. A *connected person* includes your wife or husband *and:*

- a relative. *Relative* means brother, sister, parents, grandparents and other ancestors or lineal descendant (but not uncle, aunt, cousin, nephew or niece)
- the wife or husband of a relative
- your wife or husband's relative
- the trustees of a settlement which you have set up
- a company which you control
- a person with whom you are in partnership or their wife or husband or relative.

So if you don't sell for the proper commercial price, you'll be taxed as if you had, even if you didn't intend to make a gift. You may, however, be able to claim hold-over relief – see p. 275.

More important still is that if you make a loss on a disposal to a connected person, you can set that loss off only against a gain from another disposal by you to that person. This is the case even though your loss is a proper commercial one – i.e. based on the market value. So if you sell shares at a loss to your son, the loss cannot be used to reduce your general taxable gains for the year.
TCGA 1992 s18, s286

Gifts between husband and wife

The following applies to gifts between a husband and wife who are not separated.

- Whether or not any money changes hands, there is no tax to pay at the time of the disposal, and there is no gain or loss for tax purposes.
- The recipient gets the benefit of the giver's initial value plus the giver's allowable expenses, plus any indexation allowances up to the time of the gift – the same as the rules for hold-over relief.
- The recipient's initial value is linked to the RPI from the month of acquisition.
  TCGA 1992 s58

Death

There is no CGT to pay on death. This has profound implications on whether you should make gifts in your lifetime, or wait until you die. This is because:

- rates of *inheritance tax* (IHT) for gifts made on death are higher than for gifts made more than three years prior to death – see p. 325
- for *capital gains tax* there is often a tax liability on gifts made during life. Even if hold-over relief can be claimed, the eventual tax bills for the recipient can be substantial.

There is, therefore, often a 'trade-off' between the two taxes. If your estate is likely to be liable for a lot of inheritance tax on death, it may be worth giving now – paying capital gains tax on any gains you realise and cutting down inheritance tax on your death. The alternative is to hang on, avoiding capital gains tax altogether, but risking a higher inheritance tax bill.

- In general, the less well-off you are, the better it is to hang on to things until you die.
- Remember that you can pass property gradually from your estate without tax, by making use of the £5,800 tax-free slice of CGT, and by using the exemptions for IHT.
- If you can claim a large indexation allowance, and lots of allowable expenses (and, in the case of homes, various periods where the gain is ignored – see p. 208), the CGT bill may be little or nothing, so then it may be worth

giving something away before you die.
TCGA 1992 s62

Capital gains tax and executors

On death, your estate passes to your personal represent-atives. The Revenue regards them as acquiring the property at its *market value at the date of your death*. The effect is that the value of everything you own is given a 'free uplift' to its value at the date of death. The beneficiaries of your estate acquire the assets at the market value as from the date of death (this is the probate value). Indexation applies from the date of death.

Allowable losses in the tax year of your death (made before your death) are set off first against your taxable gains for that period. (Until 6 April 1990, any losses left over could be set off against taxable gains of your widow or widower for the whole year, unless the survivor elected against this.) If there are still losses left over they can be set against your taxable gains for the three tax years before the tax year of death, taking later years first (but the losses are needed only to reduce the chargeable gains to the level of the tax-free slice – see Example 5 on p. 273). This is the only time when allowable losses can be carried back.
TCGA 1992, s62

CGT and business

Replacing business assets

If you dispose of a *qualifying business asset* and invest an amount equal to the disposal proceeds in another qualifying business asset during the period of one year *before* the disposal or within three years *after* the disposal, you can claim *roll-over relief* on your taxable gain on the disposal of the old asset.

Qualifying assets are:

* land and buildings occupied and used for the purpose of your trade
* plant or machinery which is fixed but which does not actually form part of a building, e.g. heavy engineering equipment bolted to the floor of the workshop
* ships, aircraft and hovercraft – but not vehicles
* goodwill.
  TCGA 1992 s152–s159

How it works

The gain is usually rolled over by reducing (for tax purposes) your acquisition cost for the new asset by the amount of the chargeable gain. So when you dispose of the new asset, its initial value (in working out your gain) is reduced. You can roll over your tax liability again by investing in another qualifying asset.

If you reinvest in a *wasting asset*, i.e. in an asset with a predictable life not exceeding 50 years when you acquire it, or in an asset which will become a wasting asset in the next 10 years, your gain is deferred until the earliest of the following:

- you cease to use the new asset for the purposes of the trade
- the tenth anniversary of your acquisition of the new asset
- you dispose of the new asset without reinvesting the proceeds in a new qualifying asset. If you *do* reinvest (in a non-wasting asset), the original gain is rolled over into the new asset, and the deferred gain is cancelled.

Other points

- Any indexation allowance available on the old asset is taken into account in determining the size of the gain rolled over.
- If you have more than one business, the reinvestment need not be in the same business as the one in which the old asset was used.
- If the asset you disposed of was used for private purposes as well as business purposes, or if you do not spend an amount equal to the whole of the disposal proceeds on the new asset, only a proportionate part of your taxable gain is deferred.
- You may even be able to claim roll-over relief if you dispose of an asset which you own personally but which is used for the purposes of the trade carried on by your 'family company' (see opposite) if you then purchase a new qualifying asset which is used for the purposes of the trade carried on by the same family company. Roll-over relief is available in this situation even if you charge the company a full market rent for the asset.

Retirement relief

If you are aged 55 or over or have to retire before then due to ill-health, and you dispose of a business (or shares in it), part or all of your gain may be tax-free. This relief is available for any kind of disposal including sale, gift and selling off assets after the business has ceased. You don't actually have to retire to get the relief. You will be able to claim the relief if:

- you are 55 or over, *or*
- you are retiring due to ill-health. In this case, you'll need to satisfy the Revenue that you are incapable of carrying on your work and that your incapacity is likely to be permanent.

The disposal requirements are:

- you must be disposing of the whole or part of a business which you have owned for at least one year, *or*
- you must be disposing of shares which you have owned for at least one year in a family trading company or a holding company for the business you worked in. To satisfy this condition, you must be entitled to at least 25 per cent of the voting rights (or at least 5 per cent if you and your family have more than 50 per cent of the voting rights) *and* you must be a *full-time* working director in the company or a subsidiary. 'Full-time' generally means that you spend substantially the whole of your working hours in the directorship.

Relief is also available where trustees dispose of shares or assets in which you have an interest (though not if your interest is only for a fixed period of time).
TCGA 1992 s163, s164, Sch 6

How much tax relief?
You get the maximum retirement relief if you have owned the business for 10 years:

- the first £150,000 of capital gains is free of capital gains tax altogether
- half the gain between £150,000 and £600,000 is taxable.

If the gain is more than £600,000, then £150,000 plus half of £600,000 − £150,000 = £450,000 is tax-free. This is a maximum tax-free gain of £150,000 plus £225,000 = £375,000.

If you have owned the business for less than 10 years, you get 10 per cent of the maximum relief for every complete year of ownership. So if you have owned the business for just one year, gains up to 10 per cent of

281

£150,000 are tax-free (i.e. gains of up to £15,000). And 10 per cent of half the gain betweeen £150,000 and £600,000 is tax-free (a maximum of 10 per cent of £225,000, or £22,500). You must have at least one complete year of ownership – for the period of ownership after that, you're entitled to relief in proportion to the period. So if you have owned the business for 8 years and 3 months, your relief is 82.5 per cent.

The relief applies to the permanent capital assets of the business – it doesn't apply to the value of trading stock. Similarly, if you dispose of shares, the relief will apply only to the value of the shares that represents chargeable business assets. You don't have to have owned every asset for the whole time that you have owned the business – you can still get the full relief on assets owned for less than 10 years if you have owned the business for more than 10 years.

You get only one lot of retirement relief, but you need not use it on one disposal – you can claim it bit by bit as you divest yourself of the business.

TCGA 1992 s163, s164, Sch 6

EXAMPLE 8

Bill Whitsock bought a newsagent's shop in March 1987 when he took early retirement. In July 1992, he sold the shop as a going concern at the age of 65 – his chargeable gain was £45,000.

Bill had owned the business for five years four months, so is entitled to 5.3×10 per cent = 53 per cent of the maximum retirement relief. This means that 53 per cent of the first £150,000 of gain can be tax-free – a total of £79,500 tax-free. So Bill's whole gain is tax-free.

Gifts of business assets

If you give business assets (or sell them at an undervalue) to an individual or trust you can claim hold-over relief (see p. 275) as long as the recipient isn't resident overseas.

There is a special hold-over relief for a gift of business assets by an individual to a company resident in the UK. The relief applies to the disposal of a business asset which you have used in your business for the period you have owned it. It also applies to shares in your family trading company.

If you claim the relief, the gain you make on the disposal is held over and deducted from the acquisition cost of the asset for the company. If you charged the company a special low price for the asset but still made some gain, that gain is chargeable. But the rest of the gain is held over.
TCGA 1992 s165

Retirement relief or hold-over relief?

Ideally, you should go for retirement relief, rather than for hold-over relief, because hold-over is only a deferral of tax, not exemption from tax.

If retirement relief is not available, or is insufficient, the general hold-over relief for gifts or the special relief for gifts of business assets can be very useful in passing on your business in your lifetime. But holding over your gain is likely to reduce the other person's acquisition cost and increase his or her gain.

Shares and unit trusts

Special rules for shares are necessary because of their uniform nature. One share of a particular class in a given company is just the same as another share of the same class in that company, e.g. one ordinary share of £1 in ICI is worth just as much as any other £1 ordinary share in ICI.

Rules are straightforward if all the shares you own of a particular type were acquired by you at the same time, and disposed of all together. In this case, you calculate CGT in the same way as for any other asset – see Example 9 below.

Problems begin if you have acquired shares of the same description at different times. When you come to dispose of the shares, special rules decide *how much the shares cost you; which shares you've disposed of;* and *what your indexation allowance is* (if any). The rules are explained on the following pages.

Investment trusts and unit trusts

The same rules apply to shares in an investment trust as for quoted shares in any other type of company. The rules for shares also apply to units in a unit trust.

283

EXAMPLE 9

Don has a holding of 2,500 £1 ordinary shares and 500 seven per cent £1 preference shares in European Plastics PLC. He acquired the ordinary shares for £2,100 in August 1982 and he acquired the preference shares for £250 in May 1973.

In the 1992–3 tax year he disposes of all the ordinary shares for £5,250 and all the preference shares for £360. The gross gain on each disposal, ignoring incidental costs, is:

ordinary shares	£	**preference shares**	£
proceeds	5,250	proceeds	360
less cost	2,100	less cost	250
gross gain	3,150	gross gain	110

In each case, Don is entitled to an indexation allowance:
RPI for month of disposal (for this example) 139.0
RPI for March 1982 is 79.44
RPI for August 1982 is 81.90

The indexation allowance is:

ordinary shares
$$\frac{139.0 - 81.90}{81.90} \times £3,150$$

$$= 0.697 \times £2,100 = £1,464$$

preference shares
$$\frac{139.0 - 79.44}{79.44} \times £110$$

$$= 0.750 \times £250 = £188$$

The chargeable gain on the ordinary shares =
£3,150 − £1,464 = £1,686

The chargeable gain on the preference shares =
£110 − £188 = (£78)

If Don had sold only half of his holding of ordinary shares and only half of his holding of preference shares, his allowable costs for each disposal would have been half the allowable costs shown in the example.

Which shares do you sell?

If you have acquired shares of *the same class in the same company* at different times, the Revenue has special rules for deciding which shares you've disposed of. These rules decide:

- the price you paid for the shares (or their *initial value* if you didn't buy them)
- when you acquired the shares
- how much indexation allowance you're entitled to, if any.

Example 10, on p. 287, shows how the rules work in practice.

Shares listed on The Stock Exchange or dealt in on the Unlisted Securities Market (USM) are valued at the *lower* of:

- the lower of the two quoted closing prices shown in The Stock Exchange Daily Official List for that day, plus *one-quarter* of the difference between the lower and the higher closing price
- half-way between the highest and lowest recorded prices for the day of valuation.

If you dispose of shares in stages, the Revenue looks at an earlier disposal before a later disposal in seeing which shares you have disposed of.

The Revenue will say that you have disposed of the shares in the following order:

Batch one: shares acquired on the same day as disposal

If you acquire and dispose of (or vice versa) shares of the same type on the same day, the disposal will be matched to the acquisition made on that day.
TCGA 1992 s105

Batch two: shares acquired within 10 days of the disposal

Next, the Revenue looks at all the shares of the same type which you acquired at any time within 10 days before the disposal. There is no indexation allowance for shares owned for 10 days or less. This is to prevent you buying shares at the end of one month and selling them at the beginning of the next to get one month's indexation allowance.
TCGA 1992 s107(3), (4), (5)

Batch three: shares acquired after 5 April 1982

Shares (except those disposed of on the same day or within 10 days) are pooled. The cost of each share is the average cost of acquiring the shares in the pool. So if you bought 2,000 shares for £5,000, 2,000 for £6,000, 2,000 for £7,000, the average is £18,000 ÷ 6,000 = £3 a share. You have a separate pool for each type of share you hold in a company. Any more shares of that type which you acquire are added to the pool, unless disposed of on the same day or within 10 days. The total acquisition costs of pooled shares are treated as expenditure on a single asset.
TCGA 1992 s107(8), (9), s108

Batch four: shares acquired before 6 April 1982

If you bought several lots of the same share at different times they are put into the 1982 pool. The cost of each share is its market value on 31 March 1982 (or the original cost if this is to your advantage and you have not made the rebasing election – see p. 268). Indexation runs from March 1982.
TCGA 1992 s109

Batch five: shares acquired on or before 6 April 1965

The Revenue will match the shares you dispose of with shares bought later rather than earlier – see p. 293 for how they are valued. However, you can elect for all such shares to be treated as if they had been acquired on 6 April 1965 and pooled with your Batch four shares instead. In most cases, this will not only greatly simplify the calculations, but will also mean you pay less capital gains tax – tell your Tax Inspector within two years of the end of the first tax year after 5 April 1985 in which you dispose of such shares.
TCGA 1992 s35, Sch 2

Rights and bonus issues

Shares you get under a rights or bonus issue belong to the same batch as the original shares to which they relate.

Rights issues give you the right to buy new shares in proportion to your existing shareholding. When you come to sell shares, you take the cost of the original shareholding *plus* the cost of the rights issue, apply the index-linking rules to them separately, divide by the number of shares in the whole shareholding and multiply by the number of shares you've sold. This is your acquisition cost for the shares you've sold.

Bonus issues give you free shares to tack on to existing shares. Your acquisition cost (or your pool cost) will be affected – e.g. if you buy 2,500 shares for £5,000, and get a bonus of 1,500 shares, your cost per share falls from £2 to £1.25. This adjusted cost is indexed from the same day as the original shareholding was indexed.
TCGA 1992 s126–s128, s131, s132

EXAMPLE 10

Sue Shearson built up a holding of Worldwide Pharmaceuticals 50p ordinary shares over 25 years :

1 August 1962	1,500 shares for £1,250
1 May 1964	500 shares for £375
1 May 1968	2,000 shares for £1,600
4 September 1972	1,000 shares for £850
13 June 1979	1,500 shares for £1,300
26 November 1982	2,500 shares for £2,350
1 April 1985	1,250 shares for £1,800
16 July 1985	2,000 shares for £3,200

She has begun to sell parcels of shares since 1985, as follows:

25 June 1987	2,000 shares for £4,500
19 March 1992	5,000 shares for £12,400

Notes
1. The market value of the shares on 31 March 1982 was 92p.
2. The relevant RPI figures are as follows: March 1982 – 79.44; November 1982 – 82.66; April 1985 – 94.78; July 1985 – 95.23; June 1987 – 101.9; March 1992 – 136.7.

The 1987 sale The first lot of shares that Sue sold were the 2,000 in June 1987. Sue hadn't bought any shares in Worldwide Pharmaceuticals that day or during the previous 10 days, so these shares are taken to come from her pool of shares bought since 5 April 1982. The shares in this pool were acquired in three lots:

2,500 at £2,350 in November 1982
1,250 at £1,800 in April 1985
2,000 at £3,200 in July 1985
Total: 5,750 at £7,350

The first step is to work out the value of the pool at the time the shares were sold, incorporating indexation. This means working out the indexation allowance at the time shares were bought compared to when there was a previous addition to the pool:

April 1985: indexation allowance on November 1982 shares
$$= £2,350 \times \frac{94.78 - 82.66}{82.66}$$
$$= £345$$

So the value of the pool including the indexation allowance in April 1985 was the new shares at £1,800 + £2,350 + £345 = £4,495

July 1985: indexation allowance on existing pool
$$= £4,495 \times \frac{95.23 - 94.78}{94.78}$$
$$= £21$$

So the value of the pool including the next indexation allowance in July 1985 was the new shares at £3,200 + £4,495 + £21 = £7,716

In June 1987 when the first sale takes place: indexation allowance on existing pool
$$= £7,716 \times \frac{101.9 - 95.23}{95.23}$$
$$= £540$$

So the 'indexed value' of the pool in June 1987 is
£7,716 + £540 = £8,256.

If Sue sold all 5,750 of her post-April 1982 shares on 25 June 1987, she could have subtracted from the proceeds the indexed value of the pool i.e. £8,256. But she sold only 2,000 of the shares, so she can deduct from the £4,500 proceeds:

$$\frac{2,000}{5,750} \times £8,256 = £2,872$$

So the chargeable gain on the June 1987 sale is:

£4,500 − £2,872 = £1,628

The value of the remaining 5,750 − 2,000 = 3,750 shares in the pool on 25 June 1987 is:

$$\frac{3,750}{5,750} \times £8,256 = £5,384$$

This figure can now be used as the initial cost of calculating the gain on subsequent disposals from the pool, indexed to June 1987.

The March 1992 sale   Sue sold 5,000 shares in March 1992 for £12,400. Of these shares, 3,750 are the remainder of the post-April 1982 shares and 5,000 − 3,750 = 1,250 come from the pre-April 1982 shares.

   The gain on the 3,750 post-1982 shares can be worked out using their value at the June 1987 sale, worked out above (£5,384). The sale proceeds are:

$$\frac{3,750}{5,000} \times £12,400 = £9,300$$

The net gain is £9,300 − £5,384 = £3,916.

Indexation allowance on this net gain runs from June 1987 (RPI = 101.9) to March 1992 (RPI = 136.7):

$$£5,384 \times \frac{136.7 − 101.9}{101.9} = £1,839$$

Chargeable gain on 3,750 post-April 1982 shares

= £3,916 − £1,839 = £2,077

The remaining 1,250 shares sold in March 1992 brought in £12,400 − £9,300 = £3,100. These shares come from the 1982 pool, which is made up of shares bought before 6 April 1982 and after 5 April 1965 as follows:

2,000 at £1,600 in May 1968
1,000 at £850 in September 1972
1,500 at £1,300 in June 1979
Total: 4,500 at £3,750

The initial value of this pool is taken as £3,750 if the actual cost is used. But there is a choice between using the actual cost and the market value on 31 March 1982 of 92p. 4,500 shares at 92p is £4,140, so Sue decides to go for rebasing to 31 March 1982 – this higher initial value means a lower capital gain. The initial value of the 4,500 shares becomes £4,140, with indexation allowance running from March 1982.

The indexation allowance on this pool if all the shares had been sold in March 1992 would be:

$$£4,140 \times \frac{136.7 - 79.44}{79.44} = £4,140 \times 0.721$$
$$= £2,985$$

So if Sue had sold all 4,500 of the 1982 pool shares in March 1992, she could have subtracted from the proceeds the initial cost of £4,140 and indexation allowance of £2,985 – a total of £7,125. But she has sold only 1,250 of these shares, so she can deduct from the £3,100 proceeds:

$$\frac{1,250}{4,500} \times £7,125 = £1,979$$

Chargeable gain on the 1982 pool shares = £3,100 − £1,979
$$= £1,121$$

Total chargeable gains on shares sold in March 1992
= £2,075 + £1,121
= £3,196

For Sue's records, she still has 4,500 − 1,250 = 3,250 shares in her 1982 pool. Their value at March 1992 is:

$$\frac{3,250}{4,500} \times £7,125 = £5,146$$

This figure can be used when calculating the cost of subsequent disposals from this pool, indexed to March 1992.

Finally, there are also 2,000 shares from before 6 April 1965. These will not be touched until all the shares in the 1982 pool have gone. When, finally, Sue starts to dispose of the pre-1965 shares, it will be 'last in, first out' (the May 1964 purchase will go before the August 1962 shares) unless she opts to add them to her 1982 pool. Putting them into the 1982 pool would give them an initial value of 92p a share (their market value at 31 March 1982).

Since this is higher than the 75p–83p they actually cost, Sue would be well advised to go for this option.

Regular savings plans

With unit trust or investment trust monthly savings plans, working out your gains and losses could be very complicated. You would have to work out the gain and indexation allowance for each instalment when making a disposal from the pool.

If you want to avoid the detailed calculations, you can opt for a simplified way of working out the initial costs and indexation allowances. This assumes that all 12 monthly instalments are made in the seventh month of the year (the year is the accounting year of the fund). If you have made small one-off investments or reinvested the income, the amounts are added to the total of monthly instalments. On the other hand, small withdrawals are subtracted from the total.

Special rules will apply if:

• you add a one-off lump sum of more than twice the monthly instalment in any month (this is treated as a separate investment)
• you increase the monthly instalments after the seventh month (the extra is added to next year's fund)
• you withdraw more than a quarter of the amount invested in the year by regular instalments (you will have to calculate the gain and indexation allowance on each investment).

To opt for this simplified method, you must write to your tax office within two years of the end of the first tax year after 6 April 1988 in which you dispose of the units or shares *and* any of the following applies:

• you face a capital gains tax bill
• the disposal proceeds are more than twice the amount of the tax-free slice for the year (£5,800 for 1992–3)
• your other disposals in the year create net losses.
SP 3/89

EXAMPLE 11

Hugh Jacks invests £100 a month in a unit trust regular savings plan. The distributions are reinvested. Hugh opts for the simplified method of calculating the initial costs and indexation allowance for the investment.

The unit trust's accounting year runs from 1 January to 31 December. In the 1992 accounting year, distributions to the value of £100 were reinvested. Using the simplified method, Hugh is taken to have invested the 12 instalments of £100 plus the £100 reinvested distributions, i.e.:

$$£100 \times 12 + £100 = £1,200 + £100$$
$$= £1,300$$

This investment will be indexed from the seventh month of the accounting year, i.e. July 1992.

Payment by instalments

Newly issued shares are often paid for by instalments. With a privatisation issue, indexation allowance on the total paid runs from the date you acquire the shares. With other share issues, indexation allowance depends on when the instalments are paid:

- if paid within 12 months of when the shares were acquired, indexation allowance on the instalments runs from when the shares were acquired
- if paid more than 12 months after the shares were acquired, indexation allowance runs from when the payments were made.
  TCGA 1992 s113

Takeovers, mergers and reconstructions

If you exchange your existing shares for new shares on a takeover or merger, or if the company is being reconstructed, the exchange will not normally give rise to a disposal. As far as *time of acquisition* and *cost* are concerned, the new shares will be in the position of the old.

But if you exchange your old shares for new shares and cash, you are taken to have disposed of a proportion of

your old shares. The gain or loss which you make on the disposal is a proportion of the gain or loss you would have made if you had disposed of the shares entirely for cash. That proportion is the percentage of the exchange represented by cash. So if the exchange is ¼ cash, ¾ new shares, your gain or loss will be ¼ what it would have been if you had taken all cash.
TCGA 1992 s126–s138

Quoted shares acquired before 6 April 1965

The Revenue assumes that these shares were disposed of by you on 6 April 1965 and immediately re-acquired by you for what they were worth on that date. The normal rule for calculating the market value of quoted shares (see p. 285) is *not* used. Instead, the Revenue makes a calculation which is more favourable to you, using the greater of:

- the lower of the two quoted prices shown in The Stock Exchange Official Daily List for that day, plus half the difference between them
- the price half-way between the highest and lowest prices at which bargains were recorded on that day, excluding bargains at special prices.

These shares are *not* pooled with shares of the same type which you acquired after 5 April 1965 unless you have chosen this option. Instead, your chargeable gain (or loss) on a disposal of the shares is the difference between market value at 6 April 1965 and the disposal proceeds (less any indexation allowance).

This calculation is then compared with the 'truth' – i.e. the Revenue sees whether you would have made a gain, or a loss, using the initial value of the shares when you first acquired them (in most cases, what you actually paid for them).

If the first calculation would have the effect of increasing a real loss (or gain), the Revenue takes the actual loss (or gain) instead.

If one calculation shows a gain, and the other shows a loss, you are treated as having made neither a gain nor a loss for tax purposes.
TCGA 1992 s35, Sch 2 paras 1–7

Bed-and-breakfasting

You 'bed-and-breakfast' shares by selling them, and then buying them back the following day. The purpose is as follows:

- if you have made a gain on the shares, and your net chargeable gains for the year are below the £5,800 tax-free slice, you could sell enough shares to bring your gains for the year up to, but not beyond, the tax-free slice. This would create a higher acquisition cost for the shares, so your taxable gain on a later disposal would be reduced
- if your chargeable gains for the year look like being more than the tax-free slice, and you own shares which are standing at a loss, you could sell enough shares to bring your gains for the year down to the tax-free slice.

Insurance proceeds

If you receive insurance proceeds for damage to, or the loss of, an asset, you may have to pay capital gains tax, unless the proceeds of disposal of that asset are tax-free. So if you receive insurance money in compensation for theft of your jewellery, you may have a tax liability – but not if you get insurance money when your main home burns down.

However, there's no liability on the proceeds if you spend them in restoring or (generally within one year of the loss) replacing the asset. The rules work like this. For restorations:

- the proceeds are deducted from your allowable costs for the asset
- if you spend the money on restoring or replacing the asset, and if this is an allowable expense for CGT (it normally is), the figures balance – i.e. what you spend is added back to your allowable expenses.

For replacements:

- the proceeds are deemed to be equal to your allowable costs for the original asset including any indexation allowance
- any excess of the proceeds (plus any remaining value in the original asset) is deducted from the allowable cost of the replacement asset.

There may be difficulty where insurance proceeds are spent restoring a damaged item which was badly in need of repair at the time of the damage, since part of the expense will be for repair (not allowable) rather than for restoration (allowable). You also have to be a little careful about what constitutes replacement: if you 'replace' your stolen necklace with a watercolour, the Revenue is unlikely to be co-operative.
TCGA 1992 s23

Paying CGT

If, in the tax year ending 5 April 1993, all the points listed below apply, enter *gains not exceeding £5,800, disposals not exceeding £11,600* in the *Chargeable assets disposed of* section of the 11P Tax Return (for form P1 leave the capital gains section blank):

- you made chargeable gains of no more than £5,800
- the total value of the assets liable to CGT which you disposed of was no more than £11,600.

In any other case – or if, overall, you made a loss for the year – enter a description of all the chargeable assets disposed of in the year, and figures for chargeable gains and allowable losses. Include gains and losses on all homes, even though a gain on your main home is normally tax-free. When entering a loss, don't forget to write *loss*. Attach details of how you worked out your gains and losses.

If you disagree with the assessment of tax which the Revenue makes, you must make a written appeal to your tax office within 30 days of the issue of the assessment. If you don't appeal, the tax is due either on 1 December after the end of the tax year in which the taxable gains were made, or 30 days after the assessment is issued if that gives a later date for payment.
TCGA 1992 s3(6)

15 *STAMP DUTY*

Stamp duty – brought in nearly 300 years ago – is a tax on *documents* required for the change of ownership of property. What is taxed is not, for example, the actual sale of a house or shares, nor the person doing the buying or selling, but the document associated with that transaction. If there's no document, there's no tax – and all quite legal, too. This feature of the tax is one that, in theory at least, gives great scope for tax-avoiders. But in practice it's usually impossible to avoid documents: the ownership of houses, for example, has to be transferred by a written document.

There are two main types of stamp duty:

- *ad valorem duties*, which are charged as a percentage of the price of the house, shares or whatever – the higher the price, the higher the duty
- *fixed duties*, where the duty is fixed – often in pennies rather than pounds – and not related to the value of the transaction.

Transfers of houses and land

Sales or exchanges of houses, land and other property are liable for ad valorem duty of one per cent, with the exception that transfers up to £30,000 pay no tax. On 20 December 1991, this threshold was increased to £250,000 – to revert to £30,000 on 19 August 1992. Although there is nothing in the legislation to say who should pay the tax, it is normally the buyer.

Once the price of a house goes over £30,000, stamp duty becomes payable on the *whole* price. To take an extreme, if unlikely, case, the tax on a purchase price of £30,000 is nil, but on a price of £30,001 the tax would be £301.

> If you're buying a home priced at a little more than £30,000,
> it's going to pay you handsomely if you can get the price down
> to £30,000. If bargaining won't do the trick, and if you are
> buying carpets, curtains and other fittings, try to get agreement
> to pay for these separately – duty is charged only on the price
> of the house. This could well save you some £300 in tax.

It is not possible to avoid stamp duty by splitting up the
purchase of a house or land into two or more parts, each
part for £30,000 or less. To qualify for exemption from tax,
the solicitor or you (if doing-it-yourself) have to submit a
certificate which says: '*It is hereby certified that the transaction
hereby effected does not form part of a larger transaction or of a
series of transactions in respect of which the amount or value of the
consideration exceeds £30,000.*'

Tenants buying their houses at a discounted price under
the Right to Buy Scheme pay stamp duty on the discounted
price.

Exchanges of property

These are not quite so uncommon any more since
developers will sometimes buy a would-be purchaser's old
house. With an exchange, there is no tax if no money
passes hands; where there is a balancing payment, tax is
charged on that balancing payment. For example, if Mr
and Mrs A buy Developer B's spanking new estate house
for £88,000, and if Developer B buys Mr and Mrs A's old
house for £71,000, Mr and Mrs A would owe a balance of
£17,000. This £17,000 is what is taxed – and since it's well
below the tax-free limit of £30,000, no stamp duty would be
payable.

Leases

What you pay for an *existing* lease on a flat or house is
taxed in exactly the same way as transfers of houses and
land (including the £30,000 tax-free exemption).

But *new* leases – such as a long lease on a new or
refurbished flat – are treated differently, and often taxed
twice over. The premium on a long lease (that is, the lump
sum you are paying for the lease) is taxed in the same way
as a transfer of a freehold house (except that you do not
benefit from the £30,000 exemption if the yearly ground
rent is over £300). But the yearly payments you have to

make under the lease (excluding the service charges) are also taxed. The amount of tax depends on the length of the lease and the average amount of the yearly payments. To give one example, for new leases over 35 but not over 100 years, the once-and-for-all stamp duty on yearly payments between £100 and £150 would be £18.

Transfer of shares

Transfers of shares are currently liable for ad valorem duty of ½ per cent. This is rounded up to the nearest 50p. The stockbroker adds the tax to the cost of the shares, and it's the buyer of the shares who normally pays the tax. There is no tax-free amount – i.e. all of the transaction, whatever the amount, is liable for tax.

In October 1986, stamp duty reserve was introduced. Under this, some purchases of shares which had previously escaped stamp duty, e.g. shares bought and resold in the same Stock Exchange account, became subject to stamp duty reserve tax. It's charged at the same rate as stamp duty.

Abolition of stamp duty on share transfers

Both stamp duty on share transfers and stamp duty reserve tax are due to be abolished. The Stock Exchange is introducing a 'paperless' share trading system using computers to record sales. No document, no tax – and rather than extend these taxes to paperless transactions, the government has decided to abolish them both. The abolition will happen when the Stock Exchange introduces its new system, planned for mid-1993 as we went to press.

16 *BUILDING UP A PENSION*

During your working life, you will probably be building up an income from various sources for your retirement. You may well build up rights to a state pension through your National Insurance contributions. And you may get pensions from the state, from employers' pension schemes you've belonged to and from your own personal pension plans. You may also have some income from savings and investments, or perhaps you'll have created some ready cash by moving to a smaller home or selling a business.

Although a state retirement pension provides a basic income which is currently kept in line with inflation, few people would want to have no other income. The real advantage of employers' pension schemes and personal pension plans over other forms of savings is the tax concessions. You get full tax relief on the contributions you make into the scheme up to certain limits. No tax is charged on investment income or capital gains made by a pension fund. And you can normally swap part of your pension for a tax-free lump sum. Details of how income from pensions is taxed are given in Chapter 5. In this chapter we'll look at the tax implications of your pension choices, and the limits on contributions and benefits available in each case. At the end of the chapter we'll look at how to make use of unused tax relief from past years.

The state pension scheme
Basic retirement pension

You qualify for a basic state retirement pension by paying (or being credited with) enough National Insurance contributions of certain types during your working life. The contributions which count are:

- Class 1 contributions – paid by people who work for an employer, although reduced-rate contributions paid by

some married women and widows don't count towards a pension
- Class 2 contributions – paid by the self-employed
- Class 3 contributions – voluntary payments to make up gaps in your contribution record
- flat-rate contributions made before 6 April 1975 – the predecessors of Class 1 and Class 2 contributions.

Class 4 contributions paid by the self-employed don't carry any entitlement to a pension.

Additional pension (SERPS)

Since 1975, during periods spent working for an employer, you have been able to build up the right to the additional state pension or State Earnings Related Pension Scheme (SERPS). Like the basic state pension, your SERPS pension will be increased each year in line with the Retail Prices Index, but will be related to your average pay between certain limits (adjusted for increases in average earnings) and the number of years you have been credited with National Insurance payments into the scheme.

Many employers' pension schemes are 'contracted-out' of SERPS. This means you pay less National Insurance, but you don't build up any SERPS pension. Instead, if your employer's pension scheme is based on your *final pay*, it has to guarantee that your pension is broadly equivalent to (or better than) the SERPS pension you would have earned during the same period. If your employer's scheme is based on the value of your share of the investments in the pension fund (a *money purchase* scheme), it must guarantee to make certain payments to the fund, and you get *protected rights* (see below).

You can also provide an alternative to SERPS by taking out an *appropriate* pension plan. You won't get a guarantee that it will give you a better pension than SERPS, but you will get some protected rights, including a widow's or widower's pension. Appropriate plans are often referred to as *protected rights* plans and *rebate* plans. If you take out one of these, some of the National Insurance contributions paid by you and your employer will be rebated to the plan provider (a life insurance company, friendly society, unit trust, bank or other authorised provider) together with a basic-rate tax rebate on your National Insurance rebate. The government will also make an extra contribution to the plan as an added incentive until 1993, if you qualify. If you are young and not in an employer's scheme (or in an employer's scheme which is not contracted out), it might be worth considering contracting out through a personal plan in the hope of getting a better pension than SERPS would give you; but if you're already in a contracted-out employer's scheme it's probably not worth leaving it just to be able to contract out through a personal plan.

Graduated pension

Graduated pensions are a relic of the state scheme which existed from 1961 to 1975. They were built up by people who earned more than £9 a week. The Department of Social Security keeps records of the pension each person has earned, and you'll get a small pension at retirement.

National Insurance for the state pension

National Insurance contributions are worked out on your weekly or monthly earnings *before* deducting payments to an employer's pension scheme or personal pension plan. You don't pay contributions on fringe benefits or expense payments that you get.

Class 1 contributions for employees (1992–3)
- You pay two per cent of your pay on the first £54 each week – the lower earnings limit (but nothing if you earn less than this).
- You pay nine per cent of your pay between £54 and £405 each week – the upper earnings limit – or seven per cent if you are contracted out through your employer's scheme.
- You don't pay any National Insurance on pay over the upper earnings limit.

Class 2 contributions for the self-employed (1992–3)
- You pay £5.35 a week if your earnings are more than £2,900 in the tax year.

Employers' pension schemes

An employer's pension scheme is an effective way of saving for your retirement. The employer normally pays most or all of the cost – a valuable tax-free fringe benefit. If the scheme is contributory, you get tax relief at your highest rate of tax on your own contributions, so the cost to you is less than the amount invested in the fund. Each time you're paid, your employer subtracts the amount of your pension contributions (including any additional voluntary contributions you make – see p. 307) from your gross pay and uses the PAYE system to work out the tax that's due on the pay that's left.

In addition, the pension fund doesn't have to pay any tax on its investment income or capital gains, so the return on its investments is likely to be higher than with other ways of saving. At retirement, you are allowed to receive a substantial tax-free lump sum. The pension you get is taxed as earned income, not investment income.

To qualify for these tax concessions a pension scheme must either be set up under an Act of Parliament (as many schemes for public employees are), or be *exempt approved* by the Inland Revenue. Approval is automatic if the scheme meets all the statutory conditions, but the Inland Revenue has the power to approve schemes which don't entirely conform.

Your employer doesn't have to offer membership of a pension scheme and can't make you join one.

Benefits from employers' pension schemes

The benefits you get will vary from scheme to scheme, but common benefits are:

- a pension payable to you on retirement
- the right to swap some of your pension for a tax-free lump sum
- a pension for your widow, widower or dependants
- a pension if you choose to retire early, or have to do so because of ill health
- life insurance.

The maximum benefit you can get is restricted by the Inland Revenue and by the rules of the scheme, which may not be as generous as the Inland Revenue allow. It can depend on when the scheme was set up and when you joined the scheme.

If you joined your employer's scheme after 17 March 1987, your pension can build up to one-thirtieth of your final salary for every year of service, up to a maximum of two-thirds of final pay after 20 years. If you joined a scheme set up after 13 March 1989, or joined any scheme after 1 June 1989, there is an *earnings cap* which puts a limit on your final salary for pension purposes. In the year 1992–3 the earnings cap is £75,000, meaning that the maximum pension you can get is £50,000 ($2/3 \times$ £75,000 after 20 years' service).

If you joined your pension scheme before 17 March 1987, the following limits apply:

years of service before retirement age	proportion of 'final salary'
1 to 5	$1/60$ for each year
6	$8/60$
7	$16/60$
8	$24/60$
9	$32/60$
10 or more	$40/60$

These proportions are *before* you exchange any pension for a lump sum. But if you're entitled to other pensions from previous jobs or from personal pension plans, these will be taken into account in working out the maximum you can get.

The scheme can define 'final salary' in any way it chooses, as long as it's not more favourable than either:

- your pay in any of the five years before normal retirement date, or
- your average pay for any three or more consecutive years in the 13 years before normal retirement date.

Note that a controlling director's 'final salary' must not be more than would be allowed by the second definition.

'Pay' can mean your salary plus bonuses, commission, director's fees and the taxable value of any fringe benefits. If the first definition is used, payments apart from salary must be averaged over at least three years. If the pension is based on the amount you earned in years before the final one, the scheme is allowed to increase the figure in line with any increase in the cost of living from the end of that earlier year until your retirement (known as *dynamisation*). You may want to check the precise rules of your scheme to find out what your pension might be; there are many variations on a theme within the limits allowed by the Inland Revenue.

These rules apply to your pension in the first year of retirement, but the scheme can provide for your pension to be increased (within limits) each year to compensate for inflation. Indeed, final salary pensions earned by pension contributions after a certain date will have to be increased by five per cent a year (or the rate of inflation if lower).

Your lump sum

Scheme rules may allow part of the maximum pension to be exchanged for a tax-free lump sum. The maximum lump sum allowed depends on the number of years you've worked for the employer before normal retirement age, and your 'final salary'.

If you joined your employer's scheme before 17 March 1987, the following limits apply:

years of service before retirement age	proportion of 'final salary'
1 to 8	$3/80$ for each year
9	$30/80$
10	$36/80$
11	$42/80$
12	$48/80$
13	$54/80$
14	$63/80$
15	$72/80$
16	$81/80$
17	$90/80$
18	$99/80$
19	$108/80$
20 or more	$120/80$

If you joined on or after 17 March 1987, your lump sum cannot normally grow faster than three-eightieths for each year of service. (But note: if you joined between 17 March 1987 and 13 March 1989, you cannot take more than the smaller of £150,000 or 1½ times your final salary as a lump sum.) If you joined the scheme after 31 May 1989, or the scheme was set up after 13 March 1989, your lump sum can't be more than 1½ times your final pay up to the earnings cap – see p. 303 or 2¼ times your initial annual pension, including dependants' benefits and benefits gained by additional voluntary contributions.

Widow's and widower's pension
If you die, your widow's or widower's pension is restricted to two-thirds of your final pension, but most schemes offer less than this. Some schemes enable you to take a lower pension when you retire, and leave a higher pension for your surviving partner, but you won't be allowed to leave a pension greater than the one you took when you retired.

Death-in-service benefits
Some employers give death in service benefits to all employees, others restrict it to pension scheme members. Your dependants can get a tax-free lump sum of up to four times your final salary to share and each can get a pension. The total pension payable to any individual cannot be more than two-thirds of the maximum pension you could have got had you continued working until retirement on your present salary. The total of all the pensions paid cannot be greater than the maximum pension. In practice, few schemes are this generous.

Early retirement
Employers' schemes set a normal retirement age, e.g. 65 for a man and 60 for a woman, although much lower ages are possible. Whether or not early retirement will affect your pension will depend on when you joined the scheme.

If you joined a pension scheme set up after 13 March 1989, or joined any pension scheme after 31 May 1989, the *tax* rules allow you to take your pension at 50 and there's no requirement for the pension to be reduced (but your scheme's rules may not allow this).

If your present employer's scheme was set up before 14 March 1989, you can receive your pension at 50 if you're a

305

man or 45 if you're a woman within 10 years of retirement. Unfortunately, your benefits must be reduced if you take early retirement. Your pension will be the greater of:

$\frac{1}{60}$ of your final pay × number of years' service

or

$\frac{\text{number of years with employer}}{\text{total possible years with employer (up to 40)}}$ × the maximum pension you could have got

Your maximum lump sum will be worked out in a similar way, and will be the best of:

$\frac{3}{80}$ of your final pay × number of years' service

or

$\frac{\text{number of years with employer}}{\text{total possible years with employer (up to 40)}}$ × the maximum lump sum you could have got

Many employers' schemes pay less than the maximum and may not allow early retirement, and these limits apply to the sum of all the pensions you may be entitled to, not the individual schemes themselves.

You can choose to be bound by the new rules and get a full pension if you want and if your scheme allows it, but then the earnings cap of £75,000 will also apply if you do.

Early retirement due to ill health

The definitions of ill health relevant to early retirement vary widely among schemes. You won't be allowed to get a pension of more than you would have got if you had retired at the normal time with your present salary, but most schemes will give you less than the maximum.

How much can you pay in?

The employer must contribute more than a token amount to the pension scheme. There is no set limit on an employer's contributions, as long as they are reasonable compared with the benefits provided. An employer can also make special payments to provide additional benefits for selected members (e.g. an employee who joined the company late in life and hasn't earned much pension entitlement).

Basically, it's the employer who decides whether to pay the full cost of the scheme or whether the scheme is to be contributory. If it's contributory, your employer decides how much you will pay, but to satisfy Inland Revenue rules it can't normally be more than 15 per cent of your before-tax earnings. If your scheme was set up after 31 May 1989, or you joined your present scheme after 1 June 1989, there is also a cash limit on contributions – £11,250 in the 1992–3 tax year.

Additional voluntary contributions (AVCs)

In addition to any regular contributions, an employee may make additional voluntary contributions (AVCs) to the scheme, or to a Free-Standing Additional Voluntary Contribution plan (FSAVC) from an authorised pension provider (the same people who sell personal pension plans). This is particularly useful in the years before retirement if the total benefits you'll get from your employer's pension scheme fall short of the maximum allowed by the Inland Revenue. You get full tax relief on these contributions, and there is no tax charged on income or capital gains your money earns from being invested, so AVCs are a very tax-efficient investment.

At retirement, you can normally decide which of the possible retirement benefits you want your AVCs to top up, e.g. your pension (or increases to it to compensate for inflation), your dependants' pensions, or a combination of these. (Note: if you started making AVCs after 8 April 1987, you can't use them to boost your tax-free lump sum.) You must keep within the individual limit for each benefit. Consult your pensions manager if you want to make AVCs. Things you'll need to consider are:

- what benefits the scheme would provide in return for your AVCs. There is no point in paying contributions which would earn you more pension or other benefits than the maximum you're allowed
- you're not allowed to pay more than 15 per cent of your earnings in any tax year in pension contributions *including* any AVCs.

EXAMPLE 1

John Friar is 62 and due to retire when he's 65. Because he's changed jobs several times in his working life, his total pension will be a lot less than the maximum allowed. So he arranges to pay £100 a month in additional voluntary contributions. As he's a basic-rate taxpayer, he gets tax relief of £25 on each £100 he pays in – so the true cost to him is only £75 a month. The money is paid into a special AVC account currently paying 12 per cent interest tax-free.

Leaving a scheme

When you leave a job, the money or pension rights that have built up for you may be *preserved*, so that you get a pension when you retire. In a money purchase scheme, the money already invested will simply grow as before. In a final pay scheme preserved pensions must be increased by five per cent, or the rise in the Retail Prices Index if lower, if you leave a scheme after 1 January 1991. Alternatively, pension rights from both money purchase and final salary schemes can be *transferred* to your new employer's scheme if the new scheme agrees to accept them, or you can buy an insurance policy (known as a section 32 policy) which will provide retirement benefits. You may also be able to transfer your pension rights into a personal pension plan.

If you have been a member of a contributory scheme for less than two years you may be able to withdraw your contributions (but not your employer's contributions) if the scheme allows it – most schemes do allow a refund. They can also allow you to withdraw any contributions you made before 6 April 1975.

But note:

- normally, 20 per cent tax will be deducted by the trustees from contributions you withdraw, but there's no further tax to pay
- if the scheme is *contracted out*, there will almost always be a deduction from your refund to buy you back into the state scheme
- getting a refund means that you forfeit the right to a preserved pension from the scheme – something you might regret later in life.

Personal pension plans

The National Insurance paid by self-employed people (including partners in a partnership) qualifies them for the basic state pension but not a SERPS pension. If you are self-employed, you'll almost certainly need to make additional provision for retirement. A personal pension plan makes this possible, with full tax relief on your contributions (up to certain limits) and with the money invested in a tax-free fund.

If you are in a job but not a member of the employer's scheme (either because there isn't one, you aren't eligible, or you've chosen not to join), you can take advantage of a personal pension plan to top up your basic and additional state pensions. The basic rule is that you can't belong to an employer's scheme (even if it's a non-contributory scheme) and have a personal pension at the same time. But you can belong to an employers scheme and pay into a personal plan if:

- the personal plan is used only for contracting out of SERPS, and you are not already contracted out through your employer's scheme, or
- you pay for the personal plan with non-pensionable earnings, e.g. from freelance earnings, or
- you take out an FSAVC plan; in fact, an FSAVC plan is *not* technically a personal plan, and the rules on contributions and benefits are very different (see p. 307).

You're not disqualified just because your employer provides you with some life insurance cover which will pay out a lump sum if you die, or provides a pension only for your spouse or dependants. You'll still be entitled to take out a personal pension as well.

Planning with personal pension plans

Personal pension plans provide benefits for you by investing your contributions to build up a fund. When you retire, part of your fund can be taken as a tax-free lump sum, but the remainder must be used to buy an annuity, which will give you your pension, widow's or widower's pension and other benefits. It is impossible to predict how well your investments will do, or the price of annuities when you retire, so you won't know what your pension will be until you actually retire.

The tax limits which apply to your contributions and benefits depend on when you took out your plan. If you took out a plan before 1 July 1988, it is an old-style plan (also called a *section 226A plan*, *section 620 plan* or *retirement annuity contract*). New-style plans are those taken out on or after 1 July 1988. You cannot take out an old-style plan now, but you can continue paying into an existing old-style plan.

How much can you pay in?

The rules about how much you can pay into personal pension plans each year are complicated and depend partly on how much you have paid in previous years. Companies may refuse to accept premiums which are above the Inland Revenue limits. If you do pay too much into an old-style plan, you won't get tax relief on the excess.

If you pay too much into one of the new personal pension plans your contributions must be refunded – you won't be allowed to leave them invested.
ICTA 1988 s619, s626 (Retirement annuity policies), s639, s640 (Personal pension policies)

Net relevant earnings
The maximum you can pay into personal pension plans in a tax year depends on your *net relevant earnings* for the tax year. A husband and wife each have their own net relevant earnings. If you're self-employed, these are your *taxable profits* being assessed for the tax year. This will normally mean your business takings (including money owed to you) for your accounting year ending in the previous tax year, less allowable business expenses, capital allowances, stock relief and any losses from earlier years of the business which haven't been set off against other income. If you're in a job, your net relevant earnings for the tax year are your salary, plus the taxable value of fringe benefits, less any allowable expenses. For freelance work, net relevant earnings are the fees you've received less any allowable expenses. Earnings above the earnings cap (£75,000 in the tax year 1992–3) don't count towards net relevant earnings. The earnings cap is raised in line with the Retail Prices Index each year. The table overleaf gives more details.
ICTA 1988 s646

	Income taxed on	Net relevant earnings for 1992–3 tax year
If you're in a job	current-year basis	pay from that job in 1992–3 tax year
If you have freelance earnings	current-year basis [1]	taxable profits in 1992–3 tax year
If you're self-employed	preceding-year basis [2]	taxable profits [3] in accounting year ending in 1991–2 tax year

[1] If a substantial part of your income comes from freelance work, you may be taxed on a preceding-year basis as if you were self-employed

[2] In the first two and last three years of business, there are special rules about what income your tax bill is based on – see pp. 173 and 177.

[3] If your business makes certain payments (patent royalties, covenant payments, annuities), they must be deducted from your taxable profits when working out your net relevant earnings

EXAMPLE 2

Harry Hook has been self-employed for some years, and in his accounting year which ended on 31 December 1991 (i.e. in the 1991–2 tax year) his taxable profits were £14,500. Harry also has a part-time lecturing job. There's no pension from this job, and in the 1992–3 tax year he earns £2,700. Harry's net relevant earnings for 1992–3 are £14,500 + £2,700 = £17,200.

Limits on your contributions
The amount you can pay in will depend on your age and the type of plan you are contributing to.

Maximum percentage of net relevant earnings

Age	old-style plan %	new-style plan %
up to 35	17.5	17.5
36 to 45	17.5	20
46 to 50	17.5	25
51 to 55	20	30
56 to 60	22.5	35
61 to 74	27.5	40
over 74	You cannot make further contributions	

ICTA 1988 s640(2) (Personal pension policies); s619(2), s626 (Retirement annuity policies)

The contribution limits are based on your income, even if your employer makes some or all of the contributions. Your contributions can be spread over as many different plans as you like. If you have a mixture of old-style and new-style plans, the overall limit is that for the new-style plans, but you won't be able to put more into an old-style plan than the limit for the old-style plan.

How much tax relief?

You get tax relief at your highest rate of tax on personal pension premiums up to your contribution limit each year. Husband and wife each have their own limit worked out on their own net relevant earnings. Tax relief on associated life insurance policies is limited to premiums of not more than five per cent of net relevant earnings. This limit is part of the overall limit, not additional to it.

If you're an employee taking out one of the new personal plans and decide to contract out, the minimum contribution paid by the DSS (and the government's incentive, if you qualify) will not count towards the overall limit.

If you're self-employed, premiums you pay in, say, the 1992–3 tax year will normally reduce your tax bill for that year, even if you're using up unused relief from earlier years (see p. 315). But if you backdate a premium, you reduce the tax bill for the year it's backdated to – so you get a tax rebate if you have already paid tax for that year.

If you are an employee taking out a new-style plan you pay your premium for the current year with basic-rate tax deducted – so for every £100 you wished to invest, you would hand over only £75. The Inland Revenue pays the balance directly to your plan. Higher-rate taxpayers should claim the higher-rate tax relief from the Inland Revenue.

EXAMPLE 3

David Lloyd is an employee who wants to build a large pension but doesn't have an employer's scheme to which he can contribute. His net relevant earnings for the 1992–3 tax year are £32,000. He is aged 50, so he can get tax relief on up to 25 per cent of £32,000, that is £8,000.

David has both an old-style plan and a new-style plan, and wants to use the maximum £8,000 of his contribution limit. He could put it all in his new-style plan, but he could not put it all in his old-style plan as this would exceed the 17.5 per cent limit on old-style plans. He decides to put the maximum of £5,600 (17.5 per cent of £32,000) into his old-style plan, and contribute the remaining £2,400 into his new-style plan.

He will pay his contributions to the new-style plan net of basic-rate tax, so he will only pay £1,800. His plan provider will claim the tax rebate of £600 and pay it into the plan. Contributions to the old-style plan will be made without deducting tax, so he will have to hand over the full £5,600 but he will claim his tax relief through PAYE.

Benefits from personal pension plans

Your pension
Neither old-style plans nor new-style plans have upper limits on the pension you can get. There is no minimum pension either – so you could lose out if your investments do badly.

Your lump sum
If you took out your old-style plan before 17 March 1987, your lump sum can't be more than three times your remaining pension, but subsequent rules have been less generous. If you took our your plan between 17 March 1987 and 30 June 1989, there is an additional cash limit of £150,000.

If you started your new-style plan before 27 July 1989, you are allowed to take a quarter of your fund after you have provided for dependants' pensions – subject to the cash limit of £150,000. If you started your plan on or after 27 July 1989, you can take a quarter of the fund remaining after any *protected rights* or *contracted out* pension has been provided, for plans which have been partly used to contract-out of SERPS; the £150,000 cash limit doesn't apply.

Widow's and widower's pension
A contracted-out pension plan will pay a widow's or widower's pension as part of your protected rights. But with other pension plans a surviving spouse or any other dependant is not automatically entitled to a pension if you die after retirement.

Any provision you make will be made at retirement when you purchase annuities with your accumulated fund. In

313

addition to your initial pension, you can buy a guarantee that the pension will continue for up to 10 years – even if you die before then – and you can buy a dependant's pension to be paid after you die. All these provisions will reduce your initial pension.

There is no upper limit for any dependants' pensions, but their sum cannot be greater than the pension you are getting when you died.

If you die before you draw the pension
A plan used to contract out of SERPS will be used to provide dependants' pensions if you die before retirement. Other plans will make a lump sum of returned contributions, and possibly interest as well. You can include dependants' pensions and a lump sum as part of your pension plan, but this will count towards your contribution limit and reduce the size of your pension if you don't die. With an old-style plan there is no overall limit on dependants' pensions, but you won't be able to leave dependants' pensions totalling more than the pension you would have got if you retired on the day of your death.

You can use up to five per cent of your net relevant earnings to provide a lump sum in the event of your death by linking your plan to a term life insurance policy.

Early retirement by choice
The Inland Revenue does not impose an upper limit on a pension taken early from a personal plan, but your accumulated fund will be less than it would have been if you had contributed to the fund for longer. And your annuity will be less (for the same amount of money) if you retire early because it will be paid for more years. With old-style plans, the earliest age at which you can withdraw your pension is usually 60; with new-style plans, it is 50.

Many plan providers charge penalties if you stop contributions before normal retirement or the retirement date agreed when the plan was taken out.

Early retirement due to ill health
You can receive your pension as soon as you are too sick to continue working, but it could be worth little if you have not paid contributions for very long, or your fund has not had time to accumulate.

Many pension plan providers will let you buy a *waiver of premium* benefit, which allows the fund to accumulate as though you were still paying premiums. Plan providers are also allowed to offer *permanent disability insurance*, which guarantees you a minimum income if you become incapable of working for health reasons. Up to 25 per cent of your contributions can be used to provide these sickness benefits, but these premiums will reduce the amount invested for your main pension benefit.

Unused relief from the last six years

You can get tax relief on premiums above your allowance (up to the whole of your net relevant earnings for the year) if you didn't pay the maximum premiums allowed in any of the previous six tax years. You have to use up the earliest unused relief first.

With new-style plans you would get tax relief for a previous year only if you were not a member of an occupational pension scheme in that year.

To work out if you've got any unused relief you have to use the limits that applied in the relevant tax year. To claim *carry forward relief* you will need to complete **form PP42**, available from your tax office.
ICTA 1988 s642

Backdating contributions

You can ask in any tax year to have all or part of the premiums you pay in that year treated for tax purposes as if you'd paid them in the previous tax year (as long as you have sufficient unused relief for that year). And if you didn't have any net relevant earnings in the previous tax year, you'll be able to get the premiums treated as if you'd paid them in the year before that.

This means that if you can't afford to make payments this year to use up all the tax relief available to you (including any unused relief from previous years) you may be able to catch up next year. It also means that if your top rate of tax was higher last year, it will be worthwhile asking for some of the premiums you have paid this year to be treated as if you'd paid them in the previous year. That way you'll get more tax relief (and you'll get part of your tax relief sooner).

Lloyd's underwriters can ask for a premium they have paid in the tax year to be treated as though it were paid up to three tax years before, as long as in that year they have sufficient unused relief resulting from Lloyd's underwriting activities.

To elect to carry back contributions, get **form PP43** from your tax office.
ICTA 1988 s641

Making the most of available relief

Backdating premiums and using up unused relief from past tax years can be combined to give even greater benefit. If, say, you have £1,000 of unused relief from seven years ago, you can ask to have £1,000 of the premiums you pay this year treated as though you'd paid them last year. As long as you've used all last year's available relief, the premiums can then use the relief from six years earlier.

If you had no net relevant earnings last year, you can backdate part of this year's premium to the year before and use up unused relief from six years before that – i.e. eight years ago.

The two facilities can also be usefully combined for someone approaching retirement (or even after retirement as long as he or she is under 75) who has had non-pensionable earnings for a number of years. It can be very worthwhile withdrawing other savings in order to pay the maximum contributions into a personal pension plan in order to use up all the available relief.

If you are near retirement and not making any pension contributions, but you have other savings for your retirement (say, in a building society account), it *may* be sensible to transfer some or all of your money to a pension plan. You would do this by claiming unused tax relief from the past six or seven years. You would then get a tax rebate at your highest rate on all your contributions – but you won't be able to get all your capital back, as only part can be taken as a lump sum (see p. 313).

EXAMPLE 4

Arnold Chippendale is a self-employed cabinet-maker. He took out an old-style plan in 1980, paying £15 a month (£180 a year). He has never increased his premiums and has savings of £30,000 in his building society account. With a little over 10 years to go before retirement, he wonders if it's worth putting some of his savings into his pension plan.

Arnold will be able to use all his unused tax relief for the last six years, but if he backdates some of his premiums to last year he can reclaim relief from seven years ago.

Year	Net relevant earnings £	Maximum contribution £	Premium paid £	Unused tax relief £
1985–6	10,000	1,750 (17.5%)	180	1,570
1986–7	10,000	1,750 (17.5%)	180	1,570
1987–8	11,000	1,925 (17.5%)	180	1,745
1988–9	12,000	2,400 (20%)	180	2,220
1989–90	17,000	3,400 (20%)	180	3,220
1990–1	18,000	3,600 (20%)	180	3,420
1991–2	20,000	4,000 (20%)	180	3,820
1992–3	20,000	4,000 (20%)	180	3,820
		22,825	1,440	21,385

Arnold decides to put £21,385 into his pension plan, i.e. the maximum contribution of £22,825 less the premiums already paid of £1,440. This is the full amount of his available unused tax relief since 1985–6 for an old-style plan. In order to get the unused relief for 1985–6 he asks the Revenue to treat part of this payment (£10,000) as though it were paid in 1991–2. Arnold gets a tax rebate of about £5,346. He decides to put this back into his building society account which, along with the remaining £8,615, still leaves him £13,961.

Unused tax relief from longer ago
If an assessment becomes final for a tax year more than six years ago and means that there's some unused tax relief, you can use it as long as you pay the premiums within six months of the assessment becoming final, *and* pay the maximum amount allowable for the current tax year.
ICTA 1988 s625, s642

317

17 *INHERITANCE TAX*

When you come to pass your money on – whether as a gift in your lifetime or as a legacy when you die – there could well be a bill for inheritance tax (IHT). And this can be true even if you don't think of yourself as being rich. This chapter explains the basic rules, and tells you how to work out an inheritance tax bill. It explains the straightforward ways of saving tax and gives an introduction to more complex schemes, including the use of trusts.

A voluntary tax?

Don't be misled. Careful planning can greatly reduce – or even wipe out – any liability to IHT. No planning at all can mean a heavy bill. But remember that if you don't plan, you yourself will be no worse off. It just means that there's less for your heirs. So don't gamble with your own financial security just to save tax for others.

Domicile

We're assuming that everyone who reads this is domiciled in the UK. Your domicile is, broadly, the country where you've chosen to end your days. It can be quite different from the country where you're living – though if you've been resident in the UK for 17 out of the last 20 tax years you'll have UK domicile (so far as IHT is concerned) whether you like it or not. If you're not domiciled in the UK, rules are different. For example, if you *are* domiciled in the UK, gifts to a non-UK-domiciled husband or wife are exempt only up to £55,000.
IHTA 1984 s267, s18(2)

Inheritance tax is a tax on what you leave on death (your estate). But it may also cover gifts you make in your lifetime, especially if you die within seven years of making them.

Gifts in your lifetime

For inheritance tax purposes there are three types of gifts you can make during your lifetime:

- **tax-free gifts** (also known as *exempt transfers*) This includes gifts between husband and wife, gifts to charity and small gifts of up to £250 a year to anyone else – see p. 326 for a full list of tax-free gifts
- **Potentially Exempt Transfers** (PETs) Taxable only if you die within seven years of making them – the tax is collected after your death (see p. 321). PETs include all gifts to people which aren't tax-free (such as gifts to children) and gifts to some types of trust
- **chargeable transfers** Gifts which aren't tax-free and don't count as PETs – and tax may be due at the time of the gift. Chargeable transfers are largely gifts to companies and certain types of discretionary trust.

It's only with a very narrow range of gifts that you might have to pay inheritance tax in your lifetime. If you're not involved with trusts or companies, you can miss out the next section and go straight to *What happens when you die* on p. 321.
IHTA 1984 s2, s3A; FA 1986 s101

Tax on chargeable transfers
If you make a gift which is liable to inheritance tax in your lifetime, you begin to clock up a *running total* of chargeable transfers. The inheritance tax bill depends on the amount of your running total of chargeable transfers so far. The rates for the 1992–3 tax year are as follows:

Running total	Rate of inheritance tax
£0–£150,000	nil per cent
over £150,000	20 per cent of the excess over £150,000

When you make your first chargeable transfer, there will be no inheritance tax to pay if it falls in the nil-rate band. If it is more than the amount of the nil-rate band, then inheritance tax is due on the excess at 20 per cent. When you make your next chargeable transfer, it is added to the first, and if the running total is more than the nil-rate band, tax is due.

Further chargeable transfers will be added to your running total to see if tax is due on them. But any chargeable transfer made more than seven years before drops off the running total.

Note that if you had a running total of gifts made before 18 March 1986 under capital transfer tax (which was replaced by inheritance tax in the 1986 Budget), this is included in your running total for inheritance tax until the seven years are up.
IHTA 1984 s7

How large is the gift?

Inheritance tax is charged on the *loss to the giver,* not on the gain to the getter. With chargeable transfers, it's normally the giver who pays the inheritance tax at the time of the gift, so the tax paid is part of the gift. This means that the tax bill is worked out on the *grossed-up* value: the amount which after deduction of inheritance tax would leave you with the amount you actually hand over.

Suppose, for example, you gave £80,000 in a chargeable transfer, and your running total means that the whole gift was liable to tax at 20 per cent. The tax bill is *not* 20 per cent of £80,000 (£16,000), but £20,000. This is because, to have £80,000 after deduction of 20 per cent inheritance tax, you'd have to give a grossed-up gift of £100,000 – making a tax bill of £20,000 (20 per cent of the £100,000 grossed-up value).

If the getter agrees to pay the tax, then the gift does not have to be grossed up.
IHTA 1984, s3

EXAMPLE 1

Marion Jones gave £100,000 to a discretionary trust in March 1989, with a further £60,000 in June 1992. The gifts were not tax-free and count as chargeable transfers (the trustees agreed to pay the inheritance tax, so there is no need to gross-up the value of the gifts). Marion had made no previous chargeable transfers in the seven years before March 1989.

Until the March 1989 gift, Marion's running total was nil: the £100,000 gift in March 1989 gave her a running total of £100,000. However, this was within the nil-rate band for inheritance tax, so no tax was due on this gift.

When Marion made the second gift of £60,000 in June 1992, that took her running total to £100,000 + £60,000 = £160,000. This is over the top of the nil-rate band for the 1992–3 tax year of £150,000, so inheritance tax is paid on the excess:

$$£160,000 - £150,000 = £10,000$$
$$\text{tax at 20 per cent of } £10,000 = £2,000$$

Any further gifts Marion made to the trust in the next few years would be added to the £160,000 running total, and taxed at the rates in force at the time of the gift. Seven years after the March 1989 gift – in March 1996 – the £100,000 would drop out of the running total.

What happens when you die

On your death, the whole of your estate – roughly speaking, what you own when you die – is liable to inheritance tax, as are any gifts made in the previous seven years (PETs and chargeable transfers).

For inheritance tax purposes, your estate comprises:

- all property you owned at the time of death
- the proceeds of any insurance policies paid into your estate (unless *in trust* directly to your dependants – see p. 262)
- the value of any PETs made in the seven years before death (they become chargeable transfers on death)
- the value of any chargeable transfers made in the seven years before death
  less
- debts (e.g. an outstanding mortgage), though the amount deducted may be restricted if the debts arise from gifts you made previously
- reasonable funeral expenses (including the cost of a headstone).

IHTA 1984 s4, s5, s172; SP7/87

Tax on death

Some of the bequests in your will may be tax-free, e.g. those to your spouse or to charity (see p. 326 for a list). If there is no will, what you have left will be distributed according to the rules of intestacy, and again some of the resulting transfers may be tax-free.

The value of the tax-free gifts is deducted from your estate to give its taxable value. The inheritance tax depends on the total taxable value – the rates for the 1992–3 tax year are as follows:

Running total	Rate of inheritance tax
£0–£150,000	nil per cent
over £150,000	40 per cent of the excess over £150,000

So if the total value of the estate is less than the amount of the nil-rate band (£150,000 for 1992–3), there is no inheritance tax to pay. If the total is more than the nil-rate band, inheritance tax is due at 40 per cent of the excess only.

IHTA 1984 s7

EXAMPLE 2

Gerald Finch dies leaving an estate worth £160,000. His will donates £5,000 to charity, makes bequests of £5,000 each to his son and daughter, and leaves the rest to his wife. He has made no chargeable transfers or PETs in his life.

Bequests to charity and spouses are tax-free gifts. Only the two gifts to his children are taxable, and at £10,000 they are well within the nil-rate band. No inheritance tax is due on his estate.

EXAMPLE 3

When widow Susan Bailey died, she left £10,000 to charity and the remaining £180,000 of her estate to be divided between her two children. She had made no chargeable transfers or PETs in the previous seven years.

The £10,000 bequest to charity is tax-free, but the £180,000 left to her children is liable to inheritance tax:

- the first £150,000 isn't taxed
- that leaves £180,000 − £150,000 = £30,000 to be taxed at 40 per cent: 40 per cent of £30,000 = £12,000. The £12,000 is deducted from the £180,000 to give £168,000, and this is divided equally between the two children, who get £84,000 each.

EXAMPLE 4

Roger Ferguson gave his son John £80,000 in June 1989, his daughter Margaret £80,000 in July 1989 and his youngest child Brian £80,000 in March 1990. He died in May 1992, leaving £160,000 to be divided between the three children.

The three gifts made in 1989 and 1990 are PETs, and since Roger has died within seven years of making them, they must be added to what he has left, to find the value of his estate for inheritance tax purposes. Roger has already used up his £3,000 annual exemption for gifts (see p. 329). That means the total value of his estate for inheritance tax is £160,000 + £80,000 + £80,000 + £80,000 = £400,000. The total tax bill is as follows:

- the first £150,000 isn't taxed
- that leaves £400,000 − £150,000 = £250,000 to be taxed at 40 per cent: 40 per cent of £250,000 = £100,000.

Some of this tax bill comes from the estate and some from Roger's children – see Example 5 overleaf.

Who pays the tax?
Any tax due on lifetime gifts made in the previous seven years is paid by the person who received the gift. To work out how much is due from each person, you must work out the tax on each gift as it is added to the running total, using the tax rates at the time of death. Tax already paid on chargeable transfers is deducted from the recipient's bill (but there is no refund if it is more than the final bill). The tax due on what's left on death comes out of the estate.
IHTA 1984 s199–s201

EXAMPLE 5

The total tax bill for the Fergusons in Example 4 is £100,000 – but not all of that comes from Roger's estate. To see where the tax comes from, we must consider the various gifts in the order they were made.

1   The first gift was £80,000 to John. Since there were no previous PETs or chargeable transfers, this creates a running total of £80,000. This is within the nil-rate band, so no tax is due.

2   The next gift was £80,000 to Margaret. This is added to the running total of £80,000 to give a new cumulative total of £160,000. This is over the nil-rate band, so tax will be due:

- the first £150,000 isn't taxed
- tax on the next £160,000 − £150,000 = £10,000 is at 40 per cent: 40 per cent of £10,000 = £4,000. So Margaret will have to pay £4,000 in inheritance tax.

3   The next gift was £80,000 to Brian. This is added to the running total of £160,000 to give a cumulative total of £240,000. The tax due on this running total is worked out as follows:

- the first £150,000 isn't taxed
- tax on the next £240,000 − £150,000 = £90,000 is at 40 per cent: 40 per cent of £90,000 = £36,000. This £36,000 is the total tax paid so far: Margaret is already responsible for paying £4,000 of this total, so Brian has to pay £36,000 − £4,000 = £32,000 of inheritance tax.

4   The final 'gift' is what Roger left on death: £160,000. This brings the running total to £240,000 + £160,000 = £400,000, on which tax is due of £100,000. £36,000 of this has already been paid by Margaret and Brian, leaving £100,000 − £36,000 = £64,000 to come from the estate.

After paying the tax, the estate is worth £160,000 − £64,000 = £96,000. This is divided between the three children, who each get ⅓ of £96,000 = £32,000.

Note that if Roger had intended to give equal benefit to all three of his children, he failed: the gifts of £80,000 to each of the three children end up being worth very different amounts:

- John paid no inheritance tax on his, so it's worth the full £80,000
- Margaret paid £4,000 on hers, so it ends up worth £80,000 − £4,000 = £76,000

- Brian faced a tax bill of £32,000, so his gift is worth just £80,000 − £32,000 = £48,000.

The children could have covered themselves against this eventuality by taking out a special life insurance policy which would pay out enough to cover the inheritance tax if Roger died within seven years of making the gifts to them. Alternatively, Roger could have made provision in his will for any inheritance tax on the lifetime gifts to come from his estate.

Gifts more than three years before death

The inheritance tax on gifts made more than three years before death is reduced on the sliding scale below:

Years between gift and death	Percentage of the 40 per cent rate payable	Bill for each taxable £1,000
Up to 3 years	100	£400
More than 3 but not more than 4	80	£320
More than 4 but not more than 5	60	£240
More than 5 but not more than 6	40	£160
More than 6 but not more than 7	20	£80
More than 7	tax-free	tax-free

IHTA 1984 s7

EXAMPLE 6

Harry Patel gave his son Sammy a gift of £160,000 four and a half years before he died. Harry left all of his estate to his wife Sonia, so there was no tax to pay on it. But the gift to Sammy was a PET, and Harry had died within seven years of making it.

The tax on the gift was (at 1992–3 rates) worked out as follows:

- the first £150,000 isn't taxed
- that leaves £160,000 − £150,000 = £10,000 to be taxed at 40 per cent: 40 per cent of £10,000 = £4,000.

However, the gift was made more than three years before Harry died, so Sammy's tax bill of £4,000 is reduced on the sliding scale. Only 60 per cent of the tax is payable, as the gift was made more than four but not more than than five years before Harry's death. So Sammy must find 60 per cent of £4,000 = £2,400 in inheritance tax.

When a gift is made

It's usually easy to decide when a gift is made. For example, if you give your son £100,000 by cheque, it will be the date on which the cheque is cleared by your bank and your account is debited.

If you make a gift with some strings attached (known as a *gift with reservation*) the gift will not be made, for IHT purposes, until it becomes a completely free gift (i.e. the benefit ceases to be reserved). For example, if you gave your home to your son, but continued to live there, this would be treated as a gift with *reservation of benefit*. If you were still living there on your death the house would be counted as part of your estate, even though it would actually belong to your son. You could avoid the problem if you paid your son a full market rent for the property, but this would not normally be sensible as your son might have to pay tax on the rent.

The rules for gifts with reservation of benefit apply only for gifts made after 17 March 1986, so a gift made before then is unaffected. The rules are complicated: if you are considering a gift with a possible reservation of benefit, get professional advice.

FA 1986 s102, Sch 20

Tax-free gifts

Tax-free gifts are ignored by the Revenue. If a gift is tax-free:

- there's no tax to pay on it, by you or by anyone else
- the gift isn't added to your running total, so it doesn't eat up your nil-rate band.

If you're going to make gifts, it's clearly sensible to use the opportunities you have to make gifts tax-free. Tax-free gifts fall into three categories:

- gifts which are tax-free whenever they are made – i.e. regardless of whether they're made during life or on death
- gifts which are tax-free only if made on death
- gifts which are tax-free only if made during life.

Gifts tax-free whenever they are made

- Gifts between husband and wife of any amount. These

can be in cash, property, or anything else. There's no limit at all – even if you're separated. (For divorce, see p. 86.) If the person who receives the gift isn't domiciled in the UK but the donor is, gifts above a total of £55,000 will count as a PET.

- Gifts to UK charities of any amount. Special anti-avoidance rules can apply if you give part of a property (e.g. a share in land or a business) to a charity and keep the rest yourself.
- Gifts of any amount to British political parties. (But before 15 March 1988, if a gift is made on, or in the year before death, only the first £100,000 is tax-free.)
- Gifts of any amount to certain public institutions, e.g. the National Gallery, the British Museum, the Victoria and Albert Museum, local authorities and universities.
- Gifts of heritage property to a non-profit-making body, provided treasury approval is obtained. *Heritage property* is outstanding land or buildings, and books, manuscripts or works of art of special interest.
- Gifts of land in the UK made to registered housing associations after 13 March 1989.
- Gifts of shares or securities to a trust for the benefit of all or most of the employees of a company provided that the trustees hold more than half of the ordinary shares in the company and having voting control.
IHTA 1984 s18, s23–s26, s28

Gifts tax-free on death only

- The estate of a person whose death was caused or hastened by active military service in war or of a warlike nature. This would include the estates of servicemen killed in Northern Ireland. It can also include people wounded in earlier conflicts who die earlier than they otherwise would have done.
- A lump sum paid under an employer's pension scheme to your dependants if you die before reaching retirement age, provided the trustees have discretion as to who gets the money (they usually do). Because they have discretion, the lump sum never forms part of your estate, so there's no gift for tax purposes. Within set limits you can say who you want to get the money, and your wishes will normally be respected. The total lump sum can be up to four times your salary at the time of your death together with a return of your contributions to the scheme.

- A lump sum paid to your dependants on your death at the discretion of the trustees of your personal pension plan.
  IHTA 1984 s151, s152, s154, SP10/86

Gifts tax-free in life only

The following gifts are tax-free in your life-time. But if you exceed the limits (e.g. give more as a wedding gift than the tax-free limit – see below), that doesn't mean you have to pay any tax when you make the gift. Unless the gift is a chargeable transfer (see p. 319), it will be a PET – taxable only if you die within seven years.

- Wedding gifts. Each parent of the bride or groom can give up to £5,000 tax-free (it doesn't have to be to their own child). A gift by either the bride or the groom to the other in anticipation of the marriage is tax-free up to £2,500, though once they are married they can normally make tax-free gifts of any amount to each other. A grandparent or more distant ancestor can give up to £2,500 tax-free. Anyone else can give up to £1,000. Gifts don't need to be in cash. Strictly speaking, wedding gifts have to be made *in consideration of the marriage,* and *conditionally on the marriage taking place.*
- Gifts made as normal expenditure out of income. This allows you to give money away year after year without an IHT liability. The gifts must be part of a pattern, though not necessarily to the same person each time. If your giving has just begun, the first gift will be covered by the exemption if it's clear a pattern of gifts will follow, e.g. you start to pay regular premiums on a life insurance policy for someone's benefit. Gifts must come out of income, so anything other than cash won't usually be covered. Your gifts must leave you with sufficient income to maintain your normal standard of living. If you resort to capital, e.g. sell shares, in order to live in your usual way, you will lose the exemption unless you make up the lost capital out of income in a later year.
- After divorce, transfers of property to an ex-husband (or ex-wife) will usually be exempt from tax. This is because there won't usually be any *donative intent* – i.e. any intention to make a gift. In other words, the transfer is made as part of the divorce settlement.
- Gifts for the maintenance of your family. A gift for the maintenance of your spouse or ex-spouse is tax-free. So

is a gift for the maintenance of a child of one or both of you (including an adopted child) if the child is under 18 or is still in full-time education or training. The exemption also covers gifts for the maintenance of a child you have been taking care of for some time in place of either of his parents.

- Gifts to meet the regular needs of a relative of either you or your spouse are tax-free if the relative is unable to support himself or herself owing to age or infirmity. Gifts to your mother or mother-in-law are covered even if she is able to support herself, provided she is widowed, separated or divorced.

- Small gifts. You can give an unlimited number of people gifts of up to £250 (each) a year. You won't need to use this exemption if the gift is tax-free for another reason. If you give more than £250 to anyone, the exemption (for that person) is lost *even for the first £250*.

- Any gifts of up to £3,000 in a single tax year which aren't tax-free for any other reason. These gifts don't have to be in cash. If you don't use up the exemption in one year, you can use the rest of it in the following year, provided you've used up that year's exemption first. Any part of the £3,000 still unused at the end of the following year is lost – i.e. it can't be carried forward.

IHTA 1984 s10, s11, s19–s22

EXAMPLE 7

In the 1991–2 tax year, Simon Patel used up £1,000 of his £3,000 exemption. In the 1992–3 tax year, he makes gifts of £4,500 which aren't tax-free for any other reason. The Revenue will say that the first £3,000 (of the £4,500) came out of the 1992–3 allowance. The other £1,500 of the gift comes out of the unused 1991–2 allowance. But the remaining £500 unused allowance from 1991–2 can't be carried forward to 1993–4.

Valuing a gift

The next few pages deal with how to value (for IHT purposes) something which is given away. This is the first step in working out the tax on a gift. Remember that, if it's a PET, it's the value of the gift at the date it's made on which tax will be charged if you do not survive seven years. If you are going to make a gift of land, antiques, paintings, a business, or unquoted shares or securities, get a professional valuation first:

- it's useful evidence when you're negotiating a value with the Revenue
- you're less likely to get an unexpectedly high tax bill.

If property counts as *business property* or *agricultural property* there are special rules for valuing it which can reduce the tax – see pp. 334 and 335.

'Market value'

In the normal case, *value* equals *open market value*. This means that the value of an asset is taken to be the price which it would fetch if it were sold in the open market at the time of the gift.

For gifts of money, there's no problem. The value of the asset is the amount of money. For a gift of a car or furniture, the value is what you could expect to have sold it for. (So when you're valuing an estate on death, you should use the *second-hand* value of furniture, fridges, etc.)

The rest of this section deals with exceptions to the normal rule.

IHTA 1984 s160

Value of property on death

The Revenue assumes that any piece of property, e.g. land, or a holding of shares, is sold in one lump. So it won't speculate as to whether your property could have been broken up for sale in parts to get a higher or a lower price, unless the division would have been a natural and easy thing to do.

No account is taken of the difficulty (or impossibility) of putting the property on the market at one time. The Revenue will assume that there's a ready market, and that the sale itself won't affect the market value. This can cause severe probems where shares in a private company are involved: the value, for tax purposes, can be higher than the price you could get.

IHTA 1984 s160

Joint interest in land

If you have a joint interest in land, e.g. you're a co-owner of a house, the starting point is to take the open market value of the land as a whole, and allocate to you your share of that value. Your share is then discounted (i.e. reduced in value for IHT valuation purposes – by 10 per cent, say).

Life insurance policies

For how these are valued, see p. 263.

Unit trusts
Units in a unit trust scheme authorised by the Department of Trade and Industry are valued at the manager's buying ('bid') price on the day concerned, or the most recent day before that on which prices were published.

Quoted shares and securities
The market value of shares and securities quoted on the Stock Exchange and the Unlisted Securities Market (USM) is the lower of *either:*

- the lower closing price on the day of the gift plus a quarter of the difference between the lower and higher closing prices for those shares for the day (known as the *quarter up* rule), *or*
- half-way between the highest and lowest recorded bargains in those shares for the day.

EXAMPLE 8

You hold £1 ordinary shares in XYZ PLC whose ordinary shares are listed on the Stock Exchange. You need to know their market value on 1 June 1992. The Stock Exchange Official Daily List which is published after that day but which records prices on that day shows that a £1 ordinary share in XYZ PLC was quoted at 175–181 with bargains marked at 176, 176½ and 179. The quarter up valuation gives 176½ and the mid-way valuation gives 177½. So the market value is taken to be 176½ a share.

Unquoted shares and securities
Valuing these can get you into murky waters. It's very much a matter for negotiation with the Revenue. Some clues are:

- bargains in shares on the Third Market are shown in the Stock Exchange List, but the Revenue won't accept the price of these bargains as final
- if the Revenue has recently decided for someone else what your particular type of shares are worth, that value will probably apply to your holding
- the fictional 'purchaser' of the shares will be assumed to possess information about the company confidential to the directors at the time of the gift. This could put the value up or down
- the Revenue will probably try to compare your unquoted shares with quoted shares in a company of equivalent size in the same line of business (if there is one)
- if you own 75 per cent of the ordinary shares you will usually have the power to put the company into liquidation. This could mean your holding is worth 75 per cent of the underlying assets of the company
- if you have a bare majority of the ordinary shares, you will be able to decide what dividends are paid, so the after-tax earnings of the company must be a better guide to the value of your shares. The value of the assets will probably still be the starting-point – *less* a discount, because you can't put the company into liquidation
- if you are a minority shareholder (and not a director), the dividends paid will be a good guide to the value of your shares
- for securities other than shares, e.g. loan stock, the rate of interest and the likelihood of its being paid are important. If you have a right to repayment of your principal at any time and the company is in a position to repay you, the value of your securities should be increased.

IHTA 1984 s168

Life interests and reversions

If you give someone, e.g. your widow, the right for life to all the income from particular property or the exclusive right to occupy or enjoy certain property, for IHT you will put her in the same position as if she owned the property – see p. 340. So there is no tax advantage in giving your widow just a life interest. However, from a practical point of view, you may wish to give a person no more than a life interest so that you can be sure that your capital will find its way to your children or grandchildren, for example, once the *life tenant* has died.

But make sure that your trustees have a wide power to apply capital for the benefit of the life tenant in case of emergencies.

Because the person with the life interest is treated as owning the whole property, a gift of the reversion (i.e. rights to the property when the life interest ends) is normally valued at *nil* – provided it's never been bought or sold.

IHTA 1984 s4, s5, s48, s49

Related property

Property is *related*, for tax purposes, if it is owned by your spouse (either directly or through trustees), or if it is now, or has been in the previous five years, owned by a charity to which you or your spouse gave it.

Where property is related to other property, and its value as part of the combined properties is greater than its value on its own, the higher value may be taken as the actual value.

IHTA 1984 s161

EXAMPLE 9

Suppose you own 55 per cent of the ordinary shares in ABC Ltd and your wife owns 45 per cent. The value of your holding on its own is £70,000 and the value of your spouse's is £40,000. Suppose the value of a 100 per cent holding is £160,000. The value of your holding for IHT is 55 per cent of £160,000, i.e. £88,000 – and not £70,000.

Related property disposed of after your death

Suppose that on your death you own 45 per cent of the ordinary shares of a family company, your wife owns 35 per cent and your son 20 per cent. Your 45 per cent will be valued as $^{45}/_{80}$ of an 80 per cent holding (i.e. your share of your and your spouse's combined holding). However, if your executors make an actual sale of your 45 per cent and your spouse does not sell at the same time, and if the sale is to a complete outsider – at a price which is less than the holding's related value – within three years of your death, your executors can claim that the valuation on your death should be readjusted to a valuation on an unrelated basis.

IHTA 1984 s176

Other sales after death: quoted shares or securities; interests in land

- If quoted shares or securities, or units in an authorised unit trust, are part of your estate on death and the person who is liable to pay the IHT on them sells them within a year of your death for less than their value immediately before your death, the later (lower) value may be substituted to re-calculate the tax liability.
- If your estate on death includes an interest in land which is later sold – by the person liable to pay the IHT on the property – within three years of your death, and the sale price is less than the value at the date of your death (*less* by at least five per cent or £1,000), that later value may be substituted for the value on your death and the tax re-calculated.

IHTA 1984 s178–s198

Business property

If certain conditions are met, business property is valued at less than its market value for IHT purposes. This *business property relief* cuts the tax bill on a gift or bequest:

- an unincorporated business (e.g. a solicitor's practice or a corner shop) is reduced by 100 per cent, i.e. to nil
- shares or loan stock with a controlling interest (i.e. the majority of the general voting rights) are also halved in value
- unquoted shares or loan stock where you haven't got a controlling interest have their value reduced by 50 per cent (if you own more than 25 per cent, the value can be reduced by 100 per cent if you have owned at least 25 per cent for two years or more). Shares dealt on the Unlisted Securities Market are treated as unquoted
- land, buildings or equipment you own which is mainly or wholly used by a business you control or a partnership of which you are a member (the rules are complicated) has its value reduced by 50 per cent.

In all these cases, to get the relief, you must have owned the property for at least two years immediately before the gift or your death. If you've owned it for less than this, you may still qualify if the property replaces other property which you acquired more than two years before.

You won't, in any case, get the discount if the business consists wholly, or mainly, of:

- dealing in securities, stocks or shares, land or buildings
- the making or holding of investments.

Property for personal use doesn't qualify for the discount. So if, for example, you control a company which owns cars used mainly for private purposes, the relief won't apply to the cars.
IHTA 1984 s103–s114

Agricultural property

If you own agricultural land or buildings, they can be valued at less than their market value for inheritance tax if certain conditions are met. You can get *agricultural property relief* at:

- 100 per cent if you have vacant possession or can get it within 12 months
- 50 per cent if the land is tenanted and you haven't the right to vacant possession within a year.

You need to have either owned the land for seven years while someone else has used it for agriculture, or to have farmed it yourself for two years.
IHTA 1984 s115–s124B

Basic tax planning

There are no universal rules of inheritance tax planning which dictate what everyone should do and should not do. It all depends on your personal circumstances. Inheritance tax is not just a tax on the rich. On the other hand, many people who are no more than comfortably off – worth up to £160,000, for example — worry too much.

If you don't plan for inheritance tax, it's no skin off your nose. It simply means that there's less for your heirs. So don't dive into complicated schemes just to give your children slightly more than they would otherwise get. Above all, don't risk your own – or your spouse's – financial security by giving away more than you can afford while you're still alive.

All that apart, it does of course make a lot of sense to take account of the tax rules when you're planning your gifts. You may not necessarily go for the biggest tax-saving: IHT planning is a mixture of knowing the rules and applying common sense. Overleaf we tell you how.

First principles

- Make use of your exemptions – in particular, the annual exemption of £3,000 and the *normal expenditure out of income* exemption.
- Watch out for capital gains tax on lifetime gifts. Gifts of cash and certain other assets are not liable to capital gains tax, but gifts of things like shares, holiday homes and valuables to anyone other than your spouse may mean a capital gains tax bill – see p. 264.
- If you can afford to make substantial gifts – more than the nil-rate band – make them sooner rather than later. If you survive for three years after making the gift, the tax is reduced on a sliding scale (see p. 325), and if you survive seven years there is no tax at all.
- If you have a stable marriage, make gifts to your spouse so that he or she can make tax-free gifts to other people. (The gifts to your spouse must be genuine. If he or she *must* hand it on, the husband and wife exemption won't apply and the whole gift may be treated as a PET.)

Estate spreading

Estate spreading means giving away wealth now. The idea is to reduce the amount you're worth, so that there will be less tax to pay when you die. Estate spreading can make sense if:

- it doesn't destroy your financial independence *and*
- inheritance tax on death would be substantial, *or*
- the person receiving the gift needs it now.

For a married couple the first step in estate spreading is often said to be the equalisation of their estates – i.e. their total wealth is divided equally between them. Because gifts between husband and wife are normally exempt, this can usually be done tax-free.

This can have a number of advantages, particularly if one spouse had little personal wealth before. For example, both may be able to make use of the annual exemption, the small gifts exemption, and gifts made as normal expenditure out of income (see p. 328), whereas, if the family wealth had remained largely in the hands of one spouse it would have been possible for only that spouse alone to make use of these exemptions. If the joint wealth is fairly substantial it may be possible for each spouse to make gifts of more than the exemptions available. These will count as PETs and will be totally tax-free after seven years.

The other major advantage is in the amount of inheritance tax payable on death. As each spouse now has wealth in his or her own right, each can leave part at least of their estate to the children or grandchildren. Without equalisation, there might be no tax at all to pay on the first death, but a very high bill on the second.

IHTA 1984 s18

Estate freezing

Estate freezing uses various techniques for 'freezing' the value of some of your wealth now and allowing the increase in value which would otherwise come to you (and increase the value of your estate) to go to someone else. There are various ways of doing this for a family business, for example, so that future growth goes to your children – you should take professional advice if you think you could benefit.

One common way of freezing your estate is to put investments into trust for your children or grandchildren. This reduces the value of your estate, though it may involve an inheritance tax bill at the time of the gift – see p. 319. But the gift can be set up to take advantage of the nil-rate band (i.e. up to £150,000 in 1992–3). And any growth in the investments accumulates in the trust and is no longer part of your estate. There's more about trusts on p. 339.

A simple way of setting up a trust for your children or grandchildren is to use life insurance policies. Provided the premiums can be paid out of your *normal expenditure,* they will be tax-free gifts (see p. 328). But you must make sure that the proceeds don't form part of your estate – see p. 262.

Unit trusts can also be put into trust for your children or grandchildren in this way, using a regular savings plan. Some unit trust managers can help set up the trust.

The family home

This is most people's largest single asset, and can, on its own, push you over the nil-rate band. You can't give it away and continue to live in it to save inheritance tax – it will count as a *gift with reservation* (see p. 326). Only if whoever you give it to lives in the property with you and pays a fair share of the expenses could you hope to save inheritance tax.

A couple may be able to save some inheritance tax if they jointly own the home, depending on the form of ownership (in England and Wales):

- *joint tenants* share ownership of the home. If one dies, their share automatically goes to the other, and can't be given to anyone else. But it still forms part of the estate for inheritance tax purposes, so there could be tax to pay if the other joint tenant is not your wife or husband. If the joint tenants are married, there'll be no inheritance tax on the first death, but the whole value of the house would be in the estate when the second partner died

- with a *tenancy in common*, each owns a completely separate share of the home which can be left to whoever they wish. So you could leave your share to your children rather than your spouse: there would be a possible inheritance tax liability on the value of your share, but the size of your partner's estate would be reduced.

If it's important to you to pass on the family home intact, take professional advice on the best way to organise it.

Make a will

Your will can be a very important step in planning to reduce your inheritance tax (though it is currently possible to rearrange things after your death to reduce the bill – see p. 343). Drawing up your will may also alert you to steps you need to take to minimise your tax bill, e.g. by making lifetime gifts.

Apart from any tax-saving, a will is also the best way to make sure that your worldly goods end up where you want after your death. If you don't leave a valid will, the intestacy rules distribute them in ways that might not be what you intended. For example, if you live with someone without being married to him or her, he or she might get nothing.

Here are some points to bear in mind:

- if you're married, make sure that you leave your spouse enough to live on. Remember that old age can be expensive and prolonged – so, if you can, leave a large safety margin. It's only when you've done this that you should look at ways of cutting the inheritance tax bill

- consider making enough taxable gifts on death to use up your nil-rate band. You can do this by making gifts direct to your children or grandchildren
- unless you say that gifts are *subject to tax,* the tax on them will normally come out of the residue of your estate. If you've left the residue to your spouse, much (or all) of it could be swallowed up in paying the tax on other gifts – with after-tax gifts, the getter pays the tax
- if you are uncertain about what to do with the whole or part of your estate, you can set up a discretionary trust (see p. 341) in your will, giving the trustees two years to give away the property. You can discuss your wishes with the trustees so that they know what sorts of priorities you would set; and if they make the gifts within the two years, the tax is the same as if you had made the gifts yourself.

If there's a large asset you're hoping to pass on, such as a family home, business or farm, take professional advice about drawing up the will – there are various subtle tax points to be watched.

Trusts

Trusts are not only for the rich. Even if you're no more than comfortably off, one type of trust – the *accumulation and maintenance trust* – can be worth considering for your children, grandchildren or other younger people for whom you've got a soft spot. And many people who are not rich at all set up trusts in their wills. Before looking in detail at how trusts work, there are three sorts of characters to be defined for nearly all trusts:

- **a settlor**   The person who sets up the trust, and puts money (or property) into it
- **trustees**   The people who 'own' the trust property. But unlike a normal owner, they can't do what they like with it. They have to follow the instructions of the *instrument* – often a deed or a will – which sets up the trust. There are also legal rules about what they must (and must not) do
- **beneficiaries**   The lucky people who will – or, in some cases, may – be given money, or property, or the use of property, from the trust. See Example 10.

EXAMPLE 10

Ned Settlor sets up a trust in his will. He wants his wife Gladys to have all his money, but he wants the house to go to the children after her death. So he leaves the money direct to Gladys, but he leaves the house to trustees 'in trust for my wife Gladys for her life and afterwards to my children in equal shares'. Gladys and the children are the beneficiaries.

Note: Ned is careful to take competent legal advice. As a result, the trust is worded so that:

- if Gladys is short of money, the trustees can 'advance' money to her – i.e. they can raise capital on the security of the house, and give it to Gladys. (If they do advance money in this way, the children will get less)
- if Gladys wants to move, she can sell the house and buy another.

Trusts with an interest in possession

The simplest type of trust is one with a life interest, e.g. a gift 'to Gladys for life, and then to my children in equal shares'. Gladys has an *interest in possession*, while the children have a *reversionary interest*, i.e. they are entitled to the trust property when the interest in possession comes to an end.

Gifts to an interest in possession trust made on or after 17 March 1987 are treated as PETs – there is no inheritance tax unless you die within seven years of making the gift (see p. 319). If you make the gift on death, the property forms part of your estate.

The property covered by the interest in possession is treated as being owned by the person who has the interest. If he or she dies or gives it away, inheritance tax is charged as if it were his or her own property:

- if the person dies, the value is added to his or her estate
- if the person gives it away, it is a PET (and tax is due only if he or she dies within seven years of the gift).

The only difference between an interest in possession and ordinary property is that the inheritance tax is paid by the trustees, not the person with the interest in possession.

If you have an interest in possession and the property becomes yours, you become 'absolutely entitled' to it – there is no inheritance tax at this stage. There will, of course, be inheritance tax when you die or give it away. There's also no inheritance tax if the property goes back to the settlor (or to the settlor's wife or husband if she or he has not been dead for longer than two years).
IHTA 1984 s49–s54

Discretionary trusts

These are trusts where the trustees can decide who gets the money. For example, you could set up a trust under which the trustees could pay income (or capital) 'in such proportions as they in their absolute discretion shall decide, to all or any of my children, David, Maureen, Alison, any of their children, grandchildren or remoter issue, with any income or capital remaining on 1 August 2072 to be given to charitable purposes'.

Gifts to discretionary trusts on death, e.g. if you set one up in your will, count as part of your estate. In your lifetime, they count as chargeable transfers (see p. 319). But gifts to the following types of discretionary trusts are treated as PETs (with no inheritance tax unless you die within seven years of the gift):

- a trust for disabled people
- an accumulation and maintenance trust (see below).

Gifts from a discretionary trust of its capital are liable to inheritance tax at a rate which depends on the amount given away. And the money or property in the trust may be liable to inheritance tax even if it is not given to anyone else. Once every 10 years, there will be a *periodic charge* on the trust which has the effect of collecting about the same amount of inheritance tax as if the trust's property belonged to an individual and were passed on at death once every 30 years.
IHTA 1984, s58–s69

Accumulation and maintenance trusts

This is a special type of discretionary trust. If you stick to the rules, there is no inheritance tax to pay when the capital from the trust is paid to the beneficiaries, and there is no periodic charge.

341

Accumulation and maintenance trusts are commonly used to put money into trust for children:

- while your children are still young, you set up the trust and put some capital in it
- income made by the trust is accumulated (i.e. kept in the trust). Any income which isn't accumulated must be used for the 'maintenance, education or benefit' of your children
- some time after your children reach 18, and by the time they reach 25, the trust may come to an end and the property may be shared among them. If you don't want the trust to hand out the capital, you can give the children the right to the income instead. You can give the capital later (see Rule 2 below).

If you set up a trust for your children, you'll be taxed at your top rate of tax on any income paid out for them while they're under 18 (unless they're married) – see box opposite for rules. The money will count as *your* income, not your children's.

If the trust *isn't* for your children, or they're over 18 or married, income paid out for them will count as *their* income. Any child, no matter how young, is entitled to the full single person's allowance of £3,445. So if, say, a child has no other income, and is paid income of £3,000 (gross), the trustees deduct tax at 35 per cent (£1,050), and hand over £1,950. The child can claim back the £1,050.

The rules in detail
Rule 1 At least one of the beneficiaries must be alive when the trust is set up. So a trust 'for my son Alan's children' is no good unless Alan already has a child. Any children of Alan's born later are added to the list of beneficiaries. If all the beneficiaries die, but others could be born, the trust still keeps going.

Rule 2 At least one of the beneficiaries must get an *interest in possession* in at least part of the trust property by the time he or she reaches the age of 25. A right to the income of part (or all) of the property is an interest in possession. So is the right to a share of the trust capital.

Rule 3 There can be no entitlement to trust property until a beneficiary has acquired an interest in possession.

(This doesn't contradict rule 2: to get an interest in possession you must have a *right* to income or capital. If trustees merely decide to hand out income or capital to you there's no right to it, and no interest in possession.)

Rule 4   The trust must come to an end within 25 years, unless rule 5 applies.

Rule 5   The trust can last for more than 25 years if all the beneficiaries have one grandparent in common. Illegitimate and adopted children count in the same way as legitimate children. If one of the beneficiaries dies before getting an interest in possession, his or her share can go (if the trust deed says so) to his or her widow, widower, or children.
IHTA 1984 s71, Trustee Act 1925 s31, s32

Income paid to your children

Income paid from a trust set up by you to children of yours who are under 18 and unmarried is taxed as your income (and at your top rate of tax). You get a tax credit equal to the tax which the trustees have to deduct before they pay out the income.

   Normally, the trustees have to deduct tax at the 25 per cent basic rate, *plus* an additional rate of 10 per cent – making 35 per cent in all. If you pay tax at the basic rate of 25 per cent only, you can claim the extra 10 per cent back from the Revenue – but you must pay this to the trustees or your child.

   If you have to pay tax at the higher rate of 40 per cent on the income, you will have to hand over an extra $40 - 35 = 5$ per cent to the Revenue. You can claim back this extra tax from the trustees (or – though you probably wouldn't want to – from the child who receives the income).
ICTA 1988 s663, s667

After you've gone

Re-arrangement of your estate by agreement – the basics

After your death the gifts you made on death can currently be re-arranged – the revised gifts take effect for inheritance tax just as if they had actually been made by you. (The same is true of arrangements made between your relatives if you die without leaving a will.) Various rules apply:

- the new arrangements must take effect within two years of your death
- the arrangements must have the consent of all beneficiaries under your will who are affected by them
- the parties to the arrangement must give their consent in return for what they get under the arrangements (or for no return at all) – not in return for anything else.

To reclaim any IHT paid, you must do so generally within six months of re-arrangement. The relief can be claimed even if:

- the effect is to make someone a beneficiary of your estate who was not one under your will
- the people concerned have already received their gifts.

If someone refuses a gift (or disclaims it within two years) your estate is taxed as if the gift to that person was never made. No claim needs to be made in this case.
IHTA 1984 s142

Re-arrangement – is it worth it?

A re-arrangement of your gifts is a good idea if you haven't left enough for your surviving spouse and have given more than enough to other members of your family. They can re-direct their gifts without a further inheritance tax charge. (Such a re-arrangement could mean a *refund* of tax because more of the revised gift would be tax-free.)

Alternatively, if your surviving spouse has far more than will be needed, he or she can direct gifts to other members of your family. And if, for example, you have given property to your wife for life and after her death to your son, they could (if your son is over 18) agree to split the property between them now. This might reduce the tax when your wife dies. However:

- the arrangements can't alter retrospectively the income tax position. Someone who has been entitled to receive income from a gift which is subsequently given up is taxed on the income he or she was entitled to receive
- if a parent redirects an income-producing legacy to his or her unmarried child under 18, the parent will be taxed on that income until the child reaches 18 or marries
- there is a similar rule for capital gains tax. Variations and disclaimers within two years of your death can be

treated as if you had made the revised gifts yourself and as if the original gifts had not been made. The CGT relief does not have to be claimed just because the inheritance tax relief is.

CGTA 1979 s49

Paying inheritance tax

Who has to pay

The Revenue looks first to the giver for tax on a chargeable transfer. So if you want the other person to pay the tax, get a promise that he or she will pay. If you don't pay the tax, the Revenue can get it from the other person anyway. If the person receiving the gift has given it away to someone else, the Revenue can recover the tax from that person.

If you die within seven years of making a PET, the tax, if any, is due from the person you made the gift to. The same is true if you die within seven years of making a chargeable transfer on which further tax becomes due.

For tax on your death, your personal representatives – or the trustees of settled property if you died having an *interest in possession* in settled property – are liable for the tax. So are the beneficiaries if they have received the property.

IHTA 1984 s199–s205

When to tell the Revenue

When you make a chargeable gift you have to tell the Revenue if:

- your total of taxable gifts for the current tax year exceeds £10,000, or if
- your running total, including the current gift, exceeds £40,000.

You tell the Revenue about lifetime gifts on **form C–5** which you get from the Capital Taxes Office (address on p. 362).

Always keep accurate records of the gifts you've made, and the tax, if any, you've paid on them.

For inheritance tax on your death, your personal representatives must prepare an *Inland Revenue account* and submit it to the Probate Registry as part of seeking probate. This lists the value of every asset in your estate (shares, homes, valuables, etc.), including those which are jointly owned. They'll also have to give details of:

- gifts made in the seven years before death which aren't tax-free, including transfers of value (e.g. where you sold something for less than its market value)
- interests you had in trusts.

When to pay the tax

Tax on lifetime gifts is normally due six months after the end of the month in which you make the gift. But if you make the gift after 5 April and before 1 October, tax is due on 30 April in the following year.

Tax on your death is payable six months after the end of the month in which you die but your personal representatives will usually want to get probate (or letters of administration) before then. To do so they will have to deliver the accounts and pay the tax first.

Interest is charged on unpaid tax from the time it was payable. The rate for inheritance tax was 8 per cent when we went to press.
IHTA 1984 s226, s233

Payment by instalments

Sometimes IHT can be paid in instalments and in some cases the instalments do not attract interest. The instalment option is available for lifetime gifts (if the other person pays the tax) and for gifts on death of:

- land and buildings, wherever situated
- a business or an interest in a business
- timber, where a lifetime gift has triggered IHT deferred from a previous owner's death
- a controlling holding of shares or securities – whether quoted or unquoted – in a company
- a non-controlling holding of unquoted shares or securities in a company, if certain conditions are specified.

If you want to pay by instalments you should tell the Revenue by the normal due date for paying tax (see above). The tax has to be paid in 10 equal yearly instalments. The first instalment is due on the normal due date for paying the tax. Normally interest is due on the outstanding tax.

But in the following cases, interest is due only if instalments are not paid on time for:

- agricultural land
- a business, or an interest in a business
- many holdings of unquoted shares or securities.

IHTA 1984 s227–s229, s234

Quick succession relief

If you die within five years of receiving a gift on which inheritance tax has been paid, some of that tax can be subtracted from the tax due on your estate. The amount subtracted is worked out by two simple calculations:

- divide the net value of the gift to you by the gross value of the gift, and multiply the result by the tax paid on the gift
- deduct 20 per cent of the answer for each *complete* year since the gift.

You get this tax credit whether or not you still own the gift at your death.

There is a similar relief for inheritance tax on the termination of your interest in settled property, whether or not the termination takes place on your death.

IHTA 1984 s141

EXAMPLE 11

Joe Brown left Bruce White £30,000 free of tax on January 1988. Joe's estate paid the inheritance tax which came to £8,000. Bruce died 18 months later. His estate is given an inheritance tax credit of:

$$\frac{(30,000)}{(38,000)} \times £8,000 \times 80 \text{ per cent} = £5,052.63$$

Life insurance

Life insurance policies provide a way of paying inheritance tax (in addition to offering a simple way of setting up trusts – see p. 262):

- *term* insurance can provide money to pay inheritance tax if you die within seven years of making a PET (this would have helped Margaret and Brian Ferguson pay the tax on their gifts in Example 5 on p. 324)

- *whole life* insurance can pay out to cover the inheritance tax when you die on an asset you don't want to sell, such as a family home or business.

For how to keep the proceeds out of your estate (and avoid paying inheritance tax on them), see p. 262.

18 *TAX FACTS*

You can query your tax liability for up to six tax years before the current tax year – i.e. go back to the 1986–7 tax year if you claim before 6 April 1993. This chapter gives the income tax rates, allowances and taxable values for company cars and car fuel benefit for earlier years. We give capital gains tax rates and the RPI figures you'll need. And we give rates of inheritance tax/capital transfer tax. There's a list of useful Inland Revenue leaflets; and we take you through the Inland Revenue concessions.

Tax calendar
Dates when tax for the 1992–3 tax year is due

Types of income or gain	Date tax due
Wages or salary. Most pensions from employers	Deducted when you get the income (e.g. monthly, weekly) under PAYE
Investment income already taxed. Share dividends and unit trust distributions. Bank and building society interest. Interest on most local authority loans.	Tax at basic rate deducted (or deemed to have been deducted) before you get the income. Any higher-rate tax is due on 1 December 1993 [1]
Investment income not taxed before you get it [2]	1 January 1993 [1]
Rents which count as investment income [3]	1 January 1993 [1]
Profits from being self-employed [4]	Normally two equal lump sums: 1 January 1993 and 1 July 1993 [1]
Capital gains	1 December 1993 [1]

[1] Or 30 days after date on the Notice of Assessment, if this is later
[2] Tax normally based on income received in 1991–2 tax year. But for special rules for opening and closing years, see p. 232
[3] For how rents from property are taxed, see p. 217
[4] Tax normally based on profits for accounting year ending in 1991–2 tax year (see p. 174). Special rules for opening and closing years

Note: If most of your income comes from employment or an employer's pension, any tax due on income from other sources – provided it doesn't vary much from year to year – may in practice be deducted under PAYE so you will not be paying tax at dates shown in *Date tax due* column.

Allowances for the last six tax years

With the introduction of independent taxation in April 1990, there were some changes to allowances. Everyone is now entitled to a personal allowance, on top of which a married man can claim the married couples allowance. These allowances are increased if you are over 65. For the amounts of allowances for the 1992-3 tax year, see p. 93).

		1991–2	1990–1
Personal allowance	£	3,295	3,005
Higher personal allowance 64+ [1]	£	up to 4,020	up to 3,670
Higher personal allowance 74+ [1] [2]	£	up to 4,180	up to 3,820
Married couple's allowance [3]	£	1,720	1,720
Higher married couple's allowance 64+ [1][3]	£	up to 2,355	up to 2,145
Higher married couple's allowance 74 + [1][2][3]	£	up to 2,395	up to 2,185
Additional personal allowance	£	1,720	1,720
Blind person's allowance	£	1,080	1,080
Widow's bereavement allowance	£	1,720	1,720
Wife's earned income allowance	£	–	–
Housekeeper or person looking after children allowance	£	–	–
Dependent relative allowance Single woman claiming Other	£	– –	– –
Son or daughter's services allowance	£	–	–

[1] Your age at the start of the tax year (6 April) – husband or wife in the case of the married couple's allowance
[2] Prior to 1989–90 the age for this higher allowance was 79+
[3] The amounts given here were the married man's allowance prior to 1991–2

1989–90	1988–9	1987–8	1986–7
2,785	2,605	2,425	2,335
up to 3,400	up to 3,180	up to 2,960	up to 2,850
up to 3,540	up to 3,310	up to 3,070	–
4,375	4,095	3,795	3,655
up to 5,385	up to 5,035	up to 4,675	up to 4,505
up to 5,565	up to 5,205	up to 4,845	–
1,590	1,490	1,370	1,320
540	540	540	360
1,590	1,490	1,370	1,320
up to 2,785	up to 2,605	up to 2,425	up to 2,335
–	–	100	100
–	–	145	145
–	–	100	100
–	–	55	55

Rates of tax charged on each slice of taxable income over the last seven tax years

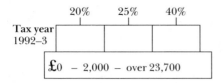

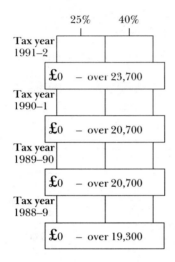

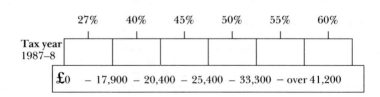

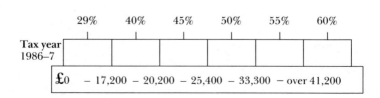

Retail Prices Index (RPI) to work out your indexation allowances for capital gains tax

The RPI was rebased in January 1987 – in other words, it went back to 100. We've reworked the index figures for months before January 1987. Index figures for months after this book goes to press are published in the Department of Employment's Monthly Gazette (try your local reference library).

	1982	1983	1984	1985	1986	1987	1988	1989	1990	1991	1992
Jan	n/a	82.61	86.84	91.20	96.25	100.0	103.3	111.0	119.5	130.2	135.6
Feb	n/a	82.97	87.20	91.94	96.60	100.4	103.7	111.8	120.2	130.9	136.3
Mar	79.44	83.12	87.48	92.80	96.73	100.6	104.1	112.3	121.4	131.4	136.7
Apr	81.04	84.28	88.64	94.78	97.67	101.8	105.8	114.3	125.1	133.1	138.8
May	81.62	84.64	88.97	95.21	97.85	101.9	106.2	115.0	126.2	133.5	139.3
Jun	81.85	84.84	89.20	95.41	97.79	101.9	106.6	115.4	126.7	134.1	139.3
Jul	81.88	85.30	89.10	95.23	97.52	101.8	106.7	115.5	126.8	133.8	
Aug	81.90	85.68	89.94	95.49	97.82	102.1	107.9	115.8	128.1	134.1	
Sept	81.85	86.06	90.11	95.44	98.30	102.4	108.4	116.6	129.3	134.6	
Oct	82.26	86.36	90.67	95.59	98.45	102.9	109.5	117.5	130.3	135.1	
Nov	82.66	86.67	90.95	95.92	99.29	103.4	110.0	118.5	130.0	135.6	
Dec	82.51	86.89	90.87	96.05	99.62	103.3	110.3	118.8	129.9	135.7	

Capital gains tax rates for the last seven years

Tax year	tax-free slice	rate of tax on rest
1986–7	£6,300	30%
1987–8	£6,600	30%
1988–9	£5,000	25% or 40%
1989–90	£5,000	25% or 40%
1990–1	£5,000	25% or 40%
1991–2	£5,500	25% or 40%
1992–3	£5,800	20% or 25% or 40%

353

Inheritance tax rates

The top set of figures gives rates of tax for gifts chargeable during life. The bottom set of figures gives the tax rates for gifts chargeable on death (or within three years of death). The tax on gifts made between three and seven years of death is reduced on a sliding scale (see p. 325).

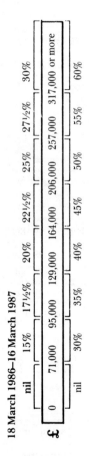

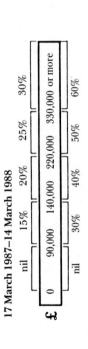

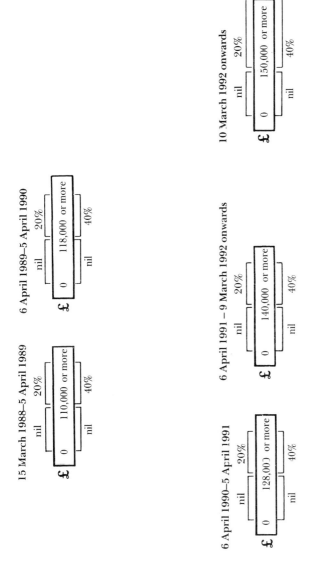

15 March 1988–5 April 1989

£ 0   nil   110,000 or more   20% / nil / 40%

6 April 1989–5 April 1990

£ 0   nil   118,000 or more   20% / nil / 40%

6 April 1990–5 April 1991

£ 0   nil   128,000 or more   20% / nil / 40%

6 April 1991 – 9 March 1992 onwards

£ 0   nil   140,000 or more   20% / nil / 40%

10 March 1992 onwards

£ 0   nil   150,000 or more   20% / nil / 40%

Taxable value of company cars

These figures apply if you count as earning £8,500 (see pp. 145 and 153) and do average business mileage, i.e. 2,501–17,999 miles. If you travel more than this, the value is halved; if less, multiply by 1.5.

*Market value of car when new

Tax year from 6 April in one year to 5 April in the next	Size of engine	
1992–3		
	up to 1,400cc 1,401cc–2,000cc 2,000cc+	
1991–2		
	up to 1,400cc 1,401cc–2,000cc 2,000cc+	
1990–1		
	up to 1,400cc 1,401cc–2,000cc 2,000cc+	
1989–90		
	up to 1,400cc 1,401cc–2,000cc 2,000cc+	
1988–9		
	up to 1,400cc 1,401cc–2,000cc 2,000cc+	
1987–8		
	up to 1,400cc 1,401cc–2,000cc 2,000cc+	
1986–7		
	up to 1,300cc 1,301cc–1,800cc 1,800cc+	

Age of car at the end of the tax year					
Under 4 years	4 years or more	Under 4 years	4 years or more	Under 4 years	4 years or more
*up to £19,250		*£19,251–£29,000		*more than £29,000	
£2,140	£1,460	£5,750	£3,870	£9,300	£6,170
£2,770	£1,880				
£4,440	£2,980				
*up to £19,250		*£19,251–£29,000		*more than £29,000	
£2,050	£1,400	£5,500	£3,700	£8,900	£5,900
£2,650	£1,800				
£4,250	£2,850				
*up to £19,250		*£19,251–£29,000		*more than £29,000	
£1,700	£1,150	£4,600	£3,100	£7,400	£4,900
£2,200	£1,500				
£3,550	£2,350				
*up to £19,250		*£19,251–£29,000		*more than £29,000	
£1,400	£950	£3,850	£2,600	£6,150	£4,100
£1,850	£1,250				
£2,950	£1,950				
*up to £19,250		*£19,251–£29,000		*more than £29,000	
£1,050	£700	£2,900	£1,940	£4,600	£3,060
£1,400	£940				
£2,200	£1,450				
*up to £19,250		*£19,251–£29,000		*more than £29,000	
£525	£350	£1,450	£970	£2,300	£1,530
£700	£470				
£1,100	£725				
*up to £19,250		*£19,251–£29,000		*more than £29,000	
£450	£300	£1,320	£875	£2,100	£1,400
£575	£380				
£900	£600				

Car fuel benefit

This table shows the taxable value for free petrol if you count as earning £8,500. The £8,500 limit has remained unchanged since 6 April 1979.

size of engine	1992–3	1991–2	1990–1	1989–90	1988–9
up to 1,400cc	£500	£480	£480	£480	£480
1,401–2,000cc	£630	£600	£600	£600	£600
2,000cc +	£940	£900	£900	£900	£900

size of engine	1987–8	1986–7
up to 1300cc	£480	£450
1301–1800cc	£600	£575
1800cc +	£900	£900

The taxable values for diesel fuel for 1992–3 are as follows:

size of engine	1992–3
up to 2,000cc	£460
2,000cc +	£590

The tables above give the taxable values for car fuel benefit for average or low business mileage, i.e. up to 17,999 miles. For mileage of 18,000 and over, the values are halved.

Tax forms you might come across

In this section, we list and explain briefly the more common Inland Revenue forms:

Tax Returns

P1	For people with fairly simple tax affairs
11P	For people who earn at a rate of £8,500 or more a year and who work for an employer
11	Mainly for the self-employed
1	For partnerships, trustees, executors and personal representatives

Reclaiming tax

P50	If you're out of work for more than 4 weeks and are not claiming unemployment benefit or income support, use this form to claim back tax you've overpaid
R40	If you're a non-taxpayer, but tax has been deducted from any income you receive from certain investments, or alimony or maintenance payments, use this form to claim back tax
R185 (AP)	Use this form to claim tax back on covenant payments you've received (for pre-15 March 1988 covenants)
R232	Use this form to claim back tax for your child (or for an incapacitated person)

Employment

P45	Your employer will give you this when you leave a job
P46	Your employer will give you this to fill in when you start your first job
P15	Coding claim – you should fill this form in at the same time as P46 and send it to the Revenue immediately to get your PAYE code
P38(s)	For students who get holiday jobs, if their total income doesn't exceed the personal allowance (£3,445 in the 1992–3 tax year)
P60	Your employer gives you this (or an equivalent certificate) at the end of the tax year – it tells you how much you've earned during that year and how much tax has been deducted

P11D   Your employer uses this form to declare to the Revenue how much you've been paid during the tax year in the way of expenses, fringe benefits, etc.

Payments you make

R185   Use this form to certify that you've deducted tax from a payment you're making

43   Use this form if you need to provide the Revenue with details of personal pension payments

C–5   Use this form if you need to tell the Revenue about any chargeable transfers for inheritance tax purposes

Income

P2(T)   This is the **Notice of Coding** the Revenue will send you to tell you what your PAYE code is

Notices of Assessment

300   **Schedule A or D Notice of Assessment**
              You'll get this form if you let property or are self-employed

P70(T)   **Schedule E Notice of Assessment**
              You may be sent this form if most if your income comes from a job

900   Notice of Assessment for higher-rate taxpayers

CG4   Capital gains tax assessment

Inland Revenue leaflets

Here we list the main explanatory leaflets available from the Inland Revenue. You can get them from your local tax office or Tax Enquiry Centre (unless otherwise stated). Some leaflets are updated very regularly, so make sure you've got the newest edition.

IR1   Extra-statutory concessions
IR6   Double taxation relief
IR9   The tax treatment of livestock – the herd basis
IR14/15   Construction industry tax deduction scheme

IR85	Business Expansion Scheme – private rented housing
IR86	Independent taxation – a guide to mortgage interest relief for married couples
IR87	Rooms to let – income from letting property
IR89	Personal Equity Plans (PEPs)
IR90	Independent taxation – a guide to tax allowances and reliefs
IR91	Independent taxation – a guide for widows and widowers
IR92	Income tax – a guide for one-parent families
IR93	Separation, divorce and maintenance payments
IR95	Shares for employees – profit-sharing schemes
IR97	Shares for employees – SAYE share options
IR99	Schemes for employees – executive share options
IR103	Private medical insurance
IR104	Tax and your business – simple tax accounts
IR105	How your profits are taxed
IR106	Capital allowances for vehicles and machinery
IR109	PAYE: Inspection of employers' and contractors' records – how settlements are negotiated
IR110	Can you stop paying tax on your bank and building society interest
IR111	How to claim a repayment of tax on bank and building interest
IR112	How to claim a repayment of Income Tax
IR113	Gift Aid – A guide for donors and charities
IR114	TESSA – Tax-free interest for taxpayers
IR119	Tax relief for vocational training
IR120	You and the Inland Revenue
480	Income tax – notes on expenses payments and benefits for directors and certain employees
P7	Employer's guide to PAYE
CGT4	Capital gains tax – owner-occupied houses
CGT6	Capitals gains tax – retirement relief on disposal of a business
CGT11	Capital gains tax and small businesses
CGT13	Capital gains tax – the indexation allowance for quoted shares
CGT14	Capital gains tax – an introduction
CGT15	Capital gains tax – a guide for married couples
CGT16	Capital gains tax – indexation allowance – disposals after 5 April 1988
IHT1	Inheritance tax

IHT3   An introduction to inheritance tax
SO1   Stamp duty on buying a freehold house

For **IHT1**, write to:

The Capital Taxes Office,
Minford House, Rockley Road,
London W14 0DF, *or*

16 Picardy Place, Edinburgh
EH1 3NB, *or*

Law Courts Buildings,
Chichester Street,
Belfast BT1 3NU

Inland Revenue concessions

Concessions mean that you are let off paying tax that is technically due. For example, if you are a miner and opt for payment instead of the free coal you are entitled to, you won't have to pay tax on the money you receive instead.

Below we give a brief summary of the income tax concessions in Section A of Inland Revenue leaflet *IR1* – this section deals with income tax and individuals. In some cases you'll need to look at the exact wording of the concession.

A1 Flat rate allowance for cost of tools and special clothing   You can claim an allowance if you have to pay for the tools and clothing you need for work. For most kinds of trade, a flat rate is agreed with the relevant trade union(s). If you spend more than the flat rate, you can claim back more.

A2 Meal vouchers   You won't be taxed on the first 15p per working day of meal vouchers given to you by your employer provided that the vouchers are non-transferable, and they are used for meals only.

A4 Directors' travelling expenses   If you're a director of more than one company within the same parent company, you won't be taxed on travelling expenses you receive for business travel from one company to the other(s). This includes hotel expenses, provided they are reasonable and necessary. The same applies if you're an employee of one company and director of another.

A5 **Expenses allowances and benefits in kind** There are three provisions, the most important of which is that you won't be taxed on (reasonable) expenses you receive from your employer when you move house if you are doing so because you take up new employment or you have been transferred within the same organisation. This includes relief for bridging loans provided by your employer. Where the existence of a bridging loan causes tax to be charged on other cheap or interest-free loans that your employer provides, you can claim relief against this extra tax as well.

A6 **Miners: free coal and allowances in lieu** Miners do not pay income tax on free coal or on cash they receive in lieu.

A7 **Business passing on the death of a trader** Special rules apply if a trader dies and the business passes to the trader's husband or wife who was living with him or her.

A8 **Loss relief for capital allowances unused on the cessation of a business** Applying normal rules when a business ends could mean that some capital allowances are lost. A special rule allows losses which would otherwise be lost to be set against income in the final year of the business.

A9 **Doctors' and dentists' superannuation contributions** This concession deals with tax relief on personal pension contributions paid by doctors and dentists who also are required to contribute to the NHS superannuation scheme.

A10 **Overseas provident fund balances** No liability to income tax on lump sums received from an overseas provident fund (or anything similar) when employment overseas ends.

A11 Residence in the United Kingdom: year of commencement or cessation of residence Normally, on arrival in the UK in any given tax year, your income for the *whole* of that year (whether or not it was earned in this country) will be subject to UK tax (the same applies if you leave the country). But if you intend to stay for at least three years or are coming to work for at least two years or if you leave the UK to go and live abroad (intending to live there permanently), you will be liable only for tax for the part of the tax year when you were actually here, provided that you have not been ordinarily resident in the UK prior to or after this stay. There are special rules for Ireland.

A12 Double taxation relief: alimony, etc. under United Kingdom court order or agreement: payer resident abroad If you pay alimony, even if you live abroad, the money you pay counts as income arising in the UK. But relief by way of credit is allowed provided that: you are resident abroad; the money you pay comes out of your income in the country where you are resident and is taxable there; any UK tax you deduct from the payments is accounted for; and the person who receives the money is resident in the UK and effectively bears the overseas tax.

A13 Administration of estates: deficiencies of income allowed against income of another year This concession allows relief for higher-rate tax to some beneficiaries of an estate if the income of the estate (during the administration period) is a minus figure for tax purposes.

A14 Deceased person's estate: residuary income received during the administration period Special rules may lower the tax liability of legatees who are not resident or ordinarily resident in the UK.

A16 Annual payments (other than interest) paid out of income not brought into charge to income tax If you make covenant payments, maintenance payments or other annual payments from which you deduct tax, you have to account to the Revenue for the tax you've deducted. If your taxable income is lower than the gross amount of the payments, you'll have to hand over extra tax. Concession A16 gives relief against this rule if you make payments late, but – if the payments had been made in the correct tax year – you would have had enough taxable income to cover the payments.

A17 Death of taxpayer before due date for payment of tax   If this occurs and the executors cannot release the money to pay the tax, interest on the unpaid tax is waived until 30 days from the date on which probate is granted.

A19 Arrears of tax arising through official error   Often partly or completely waived, according to your income, if you haven't been notified by the end of the tax year after the year in which the error occurred. See p. 60 for further details.

A21 Schedule A: deferred repairs: property passing from husband to wife (or vice versa) on death   You can set against rents money spent on repairs or maintenance made necessary by dilapidations which occurred while your wife (or husband) was the immediately preceding landlord.

A22 Long service awards   These are not taxable provided the employee has been working for the employer for at least 20 years and has received no other such reward within the previous 10 years, and the article doesn't cost the employer more than £20 per year of service. The award must either be a tangible article of reasonable cost or shares in the company you work for (or an affiliated company).

A24 Foreign social security benefits   You don't have to pay tax on these provided they correspond to UK social security benefits which are exempt from tax.

A25 Crown servants engaged overseas   Locally engaged unestablished staff engaged overseas as servants of the Crown won't be liable to UK income tax if they are not resident in the UK for tax purposes and if the maximum rate of pay for their grade is less than the maximum pay of an executive officer working in Inner London.

A26 Sick benefits Continuing payment received through an insurance policy because of an accident or sickness is not taxed unless you have been receiving benefit throughout at least one complete tax year. But if you receive such payment from your employer, it may count as taxable income.

A27 Relief for mortgage interest: temporary absences from mortgaged property for up to a year These are ignored when determined if a property is a 'main residence'. Absences of four years are ignored if you have to live elsewhere because of your work. If you live in the property for a minimum of three months, a further four-year concession will be granted. Similarly, people working abroad can qualify for the same four-year concession if they return and live in a property for three months.

A28 Relief for mortgage interest: residents of the Republic of Ireland They qualify for UK income tax relief for interest paid on a loan from a lender in the Republic of Ireland, providing certain conditions are met.

A29 Farming and Market Gardening: relief for fluctuating profits For the purposes of the average provisions in Section 96, ICTA 1988, 'farming' includes the intensive rearing of livestock or fish on a commercial basis for the production of food for human consumption.

A30 Interest on damages for personal injuries (foreign court awards) No liability to UK income tax provided there would have been no liability to income tax on interest in the country where the award was made.

A34 Ulster savings certificates: certificates encashed after death of registered holder Interest paid after the death of the holder is exempt from income tax if the holder lived in Northern Ireland when the certificates were purchased.

A35 Mortgage interest relief: year of marriage If a new home is not bought on marriage but the husband or wife goes to live in the other person's mortgaged

367

home and sells his or her own property, full mortgage relief is still allowable on both homes as long as the second property is sold within 12 months of its being vacated.

A37 Tax treatment of directors' fees received by partnerships and other companies In certain circumstances, directors' fees will be assessed under Schedule D, rather than Schedule E.

A39 Exemption for Hong Kong officials. Extension of ICTA 1988, Section 320 Some Hong Kong officials who work in the UK are not liable to UK income tax.

A40 Adoption allowances payable under the Adoption Allowance Regulations 1991 and Section 51 of the Adoption (Scotland) Act 1978 These are not liable to income tax.

A41 Qualifying life assurance policies: statutory conditions The Revenue may count life assurance polices as qualifying policies even though they have minor infringements which, technically, means they aren't qualifying policies.

A43 Interest relief: investment in partnerships and close companies Tax relief on loans taken out to invest in or to lend money to a partnership or close company won't be withdrawn when the partnership is incorporated or the company's shares reorganised, provided that the relief would have been allowed if the loan had been taken out to invest in the new company.

A44 Education allowances under Overseas Service Aid Scheme There won't be income tax to pay on certain education allowances payable to public servants from overseas under the Overseas Aid Scheme.

A45 Life assurance policies: variation of term assured policies A term assurance policy with a term of 10 years or less continues to be a qualifying policy even if the rate of premium is reduced to less than half, following a reduction in the sum assured or an extension of the term (but the total term must still be less than 10 years).

A46 Variable purchased life annuities: carry forward of deficit in capital element   This refers to annuities where the amount of any annuity payment doesn't depend on the length of a person's life. If the tax-free part of the income – the capital element – comes to more than the annuity payment, the difference can be carried forward as an allowance in deciding the size of the capital element in the next payment.

A47 House purchase loans made by life offices to staffs of insurance associations   A loan on a qualifying policy made by a life office to a full-time employee of certain insurance associations won't count as a surrender of rights under the policy.

A49 Widow's pension paid to widow of Singapore nationality, resident in the United Kingdom, whose husband was United Kingdom national employed as a Public Officer by the Government of Singapore. These widow's pensions are exempt from tax.

A55 Arrears of foreign pensions   If you receive a foreign pension which is granted or increased retrospectively, tax due on it can be calculated as if the arrears arose in the years to which they relate.

A56 Benefits in kind: the tax treatment of accommodation in Scotland provided for employees   The annual value of accommodation provided to employees is assessed for tax by reference to the property's rateable value. By concession, the annual value of accommodation in Scotland will not be assessed on the 1985 rates revaluation. Instead, the 1978 valuation will be used in assessing the annual value of accommodation for 1985–6 and 1986–7, and for subsequent years an annual value calculated by scaling back the 1985 rating value will be used.

A57 Suggestion schemes   Certain awards (up to a maximum of £5,000) for ideas put forward through staff suggestions schemes at work will be free of tax.

A58 Travelling and subsistence allowance when public transport disrupted   You won't be taxed on (reasonable) extra travel costs of getting to work or the cost of accommodation near work that your employer pays for or reimburses when public transport is disrupted by industrial action.

A59 Home-to-work travel of severely disabled employees Disabled people who cannot use public transport will not be taxed on the value of special travel facilities or on money provided by local authorities to enable them to get to and from work.

A60 Agricultural workers' board and lodging Agricultural employees who receive free board and lodging but are entitled to higher cash wages in lieu may not be taxed on the value of the board and lodging, provided they don't count as earning £8,500 or more. They are paid net and no deduction is made from their wages to cover board and lodgings.

A61 Clergymen's heating and lighting, etc. expenses Clergy who do not count as earning £8,500 or more, and who perform their duties from accommodation provided by their (mortal) employers, won't be taxed on heating, lighting, cleaning or gardening expenses that their employer meets for them.

A62 Pensions to disabled employees If you retire following an injury at work or because of a work-related illness or a war wound, any extra pension paid over and above the amount you would have got if retiring on grounds of ordinary ill heath is not taxed. The same applies to a pension awarded solely on one of these grounds.

A63*External training courses – expenses borne by employer The cost of books and fees your employer pays for you to attend certain external training courses won't be taxed. Provided you are not away for more than twelve months, extra travel expenses and living costs met by your employer while you are on the course may not be taxable either.

A64*External training courses – expenses borne by

*Relief under concessions A63 and A64 will not be available when you get relief at source. Since 6 April 1992, most relief for vocational training has been given at source.

employee   If your employer encourages or requires you to go on a full-time external training course of four weeks or more in the UK and gives you time off work on full pay, you can get tax relief on the cost of books and fees for the course not met by your employer (unless the course is for re-sit examinations). Extra travel expenses or costs of living away from home also qualify for tax relief, unless you're away for more than 12 months.

A65 Workers on offshore oil and gas rigs or platforms – transfers from or to mainland   Workers on offshore oil and gas rigs won't be taxed on the value of travel to and from the mainland provided free by their employer, nor on reasonable overnight expenses at the point of departure from the mainland, which their employer pays or reimburses.

A66 Employees' late-night journeys from work to home
If your employer pays for taxis to take you home after working late (i.e. 9 p.m. onwards) you won't be taxed on this benefit, provided that this does not happen regularly or frequently and provided that it would be unreasonable to expect you to travel home by public transport.

A67 Payments made to employees moved to a higher-cost-housing area   Payments made to you by your employer to cover increased accommodation costs which have been incurred due to a compulsory transfer from one area to another will not be taxed provided that the payments are regular, are for a limited period of time and taper as the years progress. The total payment must not exceed the maximum amount payable in the Civil Service.

A68 Payments out of a discretionary trust which are emoluments taxable under Schedule E   Employee trusts are established to make discretionary payments to employees or their families. They pay a high rate of tax on the income they produce. Certain payments from such trusts are also taxed as income for the beneficiary. To prevent double taxation, trustees can claim back tax paid on all trust income which has been used to make payments on which the beneficiary has subsequently paid income tax.

A69 Composite-rate tax: non-resident depositors If a building society converts to company status, certain declarations which have been made to the building society will be treated as having been made to the successor company.

A70 Small gifts to employees by third parties, and staff Christmas parties
A Gifts (i.e. goods or gift vouchers) worth less than £100 given to an employee or members of his or her family by people unconnected with his or her employer will not be taxed.
B Christmas parties, or similiar annual parties open to all staff and costing less than £50 a head, will not be taxed.

A71 Company cars for family members If a relative receives a company car from your employer you will not be taxed on it provided that the relative is an employee of the company in his or her own right and provision of a car is normal for someone in his or her position.

A72 Pension schemes and accident insurance policies
You do not pay income tax on any payments made by your employer to members of your family or household on your death or retirement.

A74 Meals provided for employees Income tax is not charged on free or subsidised meals provided to employees on work premises or in any canteen where meals are provided for staff generally (or on the use of a voucher to obtain such meals) as long as the meals are on a reasonable scale and *either* are available to all staff *or* the employer provides free or subsidised vouchers for staff who don't receive the meals.

A76 Business Expansion Scheme: subscriber shares If, when a company is first incorporated, you own one of two subscriber shares (i.e. 50 per cent of the share capital), you might still be able to apply for tax relief under the Business Expansion Scheme. This applies until the company issues further shares, and provided the company does not enter into any other transactions.

A77 Motor mileage allowances paid to volunteer drivers If you're a volunteer driver, only a quarter of the amount by which your allowances exceed the cost of running and maintaining your car for voluntary service will be taxed in 1992–3. Half the amount will be taxed in 1993–4 and three-quarters in 1994–5. (The full amount will be taxed from 1995–6.)

A78 Spouse travelling abroad Special rules regarding 'residence' and 'ordinary residence' may apply if you are accompanying your husband or wife when he or she goes abroad to work full-time. This applies when your husband or wife is regarded for the period abroad as not resident and not ordinarily resident, and provided you will not be in full-time employment abroad as well.

Claims for repayment of tax (published in IR press release 10.2.92)   The Board of the Inland Revenue will, in some circumstances, make repayments of tax relating to claims made outside statutory time limits.

INDEX

375

WHAT TO DO WHEN SOMEONE DIES

When someone dies a number of formalities have to be dealt with. This long-established *Which?* Consumer Guide is invaluable for anyone faced with having to make the practical arrangements following a death, and includes information on: registering a death; how and where to obtain the necessary death and medical certificates; arranging the burial or cremation and the funeral service; how to go about claiming any pensions or other state benefits due.

Easy-to-follow charts guide you through the necessary procedures. The book also offers advice on the arrangements you can make before your own funeral.

The book covers law and practice in England and Wales and highlights in separate sections the important differences which apply in Scotland.

Paperback   216 x 135 mm   128 pages

Available from bookshops,
including the Which? shop at
359-361 Euston Road, London NW1
and by post from
Consumers' Association, Dept MBSC,
Castlemead, Gascoyne Way, Hertford X, SG14 1LH.

Access/ Visa card holders can phone FREE on
(0800) 252100 to place their order,
quoting Dept MBSC.

THE WHICH? GUIDE TO DIVORCE

This Guide, while recognising the emotional aspects of splitting up, concentrates on the legal, practical and financial issues that need to be addressed by a couple contemplating the end of their partnership.

It takes readers step-by-step all the way through from the initial application to the final decree, explaining the paperwork and procedures and helping to make decisions about, for example, the children, the family home and the financial arrangements after divorce. It describes fully how two new laws are revolutionising aspects of divorce: the Children Act and the Child Support Act.

The Guide aims to help couples cut down on the financial costs of divorce and shows how careful planning and avoiding needless legal squabbles can make the family finances go further.

Covers divorce in Great Britain and Northern Ireland.

Paperback   216 x 135 mm   272 pages

Available from bookshops,
including the Which? shop at
359-361 Euston Road, London NW1
and by post from
Consumers' Association, Dept MBSC,
Castlemead, Gascoyne Way, Hertford X, SG14 1LH.

Access/Visa card holders can phone FREE on
(0800) 252100 to place their order,
quoting Dept MBSC.